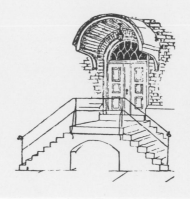

*Revising Flannery O'Connor*

Katherine Hemple Prown

# *Revising Flannery O'Connor*

## Southern Literary Culture and the
## Problem of Female Authorship

UNIVERSITY PRESS OF VIRGINIA

*Charlottesville and London*

The University Press of Virginia
© 2001 by the Rector and Visitors of the University of Virginia
All rights reserved
Printed in the United States of America
*First published 2001*

⊗The paper used in this publication meets the minimum
requirements of the American National Standard for Information
Sciences—Permanence of Paper for Printed Library Materials,
ANSI Z39.48-1984.

Library of Congress Cataloging-in-Publication Data
Prown, Katherine Hemple, 1963–
     Revising Flannery O'Connor : southern literary culture and
the problem of female authorship / Katherine Hemple Prown.
        p. cm.
     Includes bibliographical references and index.
     ISBN 0-8139-2012-4 (cloth : alk. paper)
     1. O'Connor, Flannery—Criticism and interpretation.
2. Women and literature—Southern States—History—
20th century.    3. Gordon, Caroline, 1895– —influence.
4. Southern States—Intellectual life.    5. Southern States—In
literature.    6. Authorship—Sex differences.    7. Agrarians
(Group of writers)    8. Fugitives (Group)
I. Title.

PS3565.C57 Z837 2001
813'.54—dc21                                      00-063395

*In Memory of Sam Prown*

# Contents

# *Acknowledgments*

THIS BOOK WOULD NOT have been completed without the advice and support of a number of people. Foremost among them is Susan V. Donaldson, who agreed to oversee this project when it was still in dissertation form and who in the years since has been more than generous with her time and her considerable knowledge of the subject material. She graciously shared her ideas and her work with me—both published and unpublished—and in so doing has enriched this project considerably. My research into the friendship between Flannery O'Connor and Caroline Gordon has deepened my understanding of what a "dysfunctional" mentoring relationship looks like. Working with Susan has, by contrast, provided me with a model for what it means to be a true mentor.

Other readers have also made invaluable contributions to this book. Peggy Whitman Prenshaw alerted me to inconsistencies in my argument and offered a number of important insights regarding the Fugitive/Agrarians and Christianity and the relationship between O'Connor and Gordon. The many conversations I had with Esther Lanigan opened up new lines of inquiry, particularly in regard to women writers and their relationships to region and religion. Anne Goodwyn Jones and Colleen Kennedy also brought a fresh perspective to this project and in particular forced me to look critically at its essentialist tendencies. I am grateful for the spirit of collegiality with which each of these readers has supported my efforts.

I have been fortunate as well to work with a number of talented editors. Pamela Vu, Julie Falconer, and Jane Curran helped me out of a variety of copyediting and computer formatting problems, while Boyd Zenner has acted as a steadfast and patient advocate and as an astute reader.

Various institutions have also extended their support. The National Endowment for the Humanities' offer of a dissertation grant provided me with considerable encouragement when this project was in its earliest stages. The Commonwealth Center for the Study of American Culture awarded summer research grants that made it possible for me to travel to Georgia College, while the Department of English and the American Studies Program at The College of William and Mary offered ongoing support in the form of teaching contracts and flexible scheduling.

I am also grateful to the University of North Carolina at Chapel Hill for granting me permission to publish selected quotes from the Caroline Gordon letters included in the Ward Dorrance Papers, which are housed in the Southern Historical Collection at Wilson Library. Thanks to Nancy Tate Wood for granting permission to quote from Gordon's letters and to Robert Giroux, literary executor of the estate of Flannery O'Connor, who graciously offered permission to quote from the unpublished manuscripts. Nancy Davis Bray, assistant director for Special Collections, and the staff of the Ina Dillard Russell Library at Georgia College and State University went out of their way on a number of occasions to accommodate my schedule and to answer my many questions. I am grateful for their assistance.

Numerous members of my family also assisted with this project. Margaret French and Frank E. French Jr. put their home at my disposal, making it possible for me to extend my research visits at Georgia College. I also owe my parents, Jean M. Hemple and William E. Hemple, many thanks for their endless supply of advice, support, and inspiration. They made it possible for me to undertake an additional visit to Milledgeville and, by providing extended periods of childcare, allowed me to complete the most crucial stages of my research and writing. My parents-in-law, Jules D. Prown and the late Shirley Martin (Sam) Prown, supported me in innumerable ways and never failed to offer encouragement when it was most needed. I hope the dedication to this book conveys my heartfelt gratitude to Sam for remembering this project during times when just about everyone, including myself, had forgotten it existed.

I also owe a word of thanks to my children, Henry Hemple Prown, Frederick Hemple Prown, and Edward Maloney Prown. I doubt this book is exactly what French feminists have in mind when they refer to "writing from the body," but I will say that my three pregnancies, which always seemed to coincide with crucial stages of my research and writing, have motivated me in ways that no other kind of deadline could and have altered my perceptions of O'Connor's depictions of the female body. And by asking me to ponder the eternal questions, such as "Does gum ever end?" Henry and Fred have kept my mind working during those times when raising them required me to set this project aside.

Finally, I owe my deepest thanks to Jonathan Prown, who has always been willing to take time from his own work to make certain that I could devote large and uninterrupted periods of time to mine. Without his support, his enthusiasm for my work, and his sense of humor to sustain me, I could not have finished this book.

An earlier version of chapter 2 was published as "Riding the Dixie Limited: Flannery O'Connor, Southern Literary Culture, and the Problem of Female Authorship," in *Having Our Way: Women Rewriting Tradition in Twentienth-Century America,* edited by Harriet Pollack (Lewisburg, PA: Bucknell University Press, 1995). I am grateful to Nancy Tate Wood and the University of North Carolina for permission to use selected quotations from the letters of Caroline Gordon in the Ward Dorrance Papers, #4127, in the Southern Historical Collection, Wilson Library, the University of North Carolina at Chapel Hill. Excerpts from Flannery O'Connor's unpublished manuscripts, copyright © 2000 by the Estate of Flannery O'Connor, are reprinted with the permission of the literary executor and the Estate of Flannery O'Connor.

# Abbreviations

CW     *Flannery O'Connor: Collected Works*

HB     *The Habit of Being*

LT     *The Lytle-Tate Letters*, ed. Young and Sarcone

LC     *Literary Correspondence of Donald Davidson and Allen Tate*, ed. Fain and Young

MM     *Mystery and Manners*

OMC    Flannery O'Connor Manuscript Collection

SL     *Selected Letters of John Crowe Ransom*, ed. Young and Core

SM     *The Southern Mandarins*, ed. Wood

WD     Ward Dorrance Papers

# *Introduction*

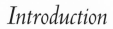

Flannery O'Connor and
the Politics of Gender:
Can a Misogynist Be a Feminist?

MY FIRST ENCOUNTER with Flannery O'Connor's fiction came in college, when a friend loaned me a copy of *Wise Blood*. I was astonished by the undercurrent of humor that runs throughout the text and, in an unsettling way, found it one of the funniest novels I had ever read. At the same time, I was thoroughly baffled, and like many first-time readers, I found myself unable to determine whether the novel represented an exercise in nihilism or in religious inspiration. Most puzzling to me was the notion that this book, which remained so preoccupied with the existential crisis of its male protagonist, was written by a woman. It displayed none of the qualities that I had come to associate with women's fiction, and I developed a secret admiration for O'Connor's ability to engage herself so adeptly, it appeared to me, with the likes of Dostoevsky, Camus, and Kafka.

In graduate school I began to read her fiction more seriously and eventually turned to it for the subject of my master's thesis. Conditioned by the blind spots of the critical literature of that period, I remained unable to read O'Connor apart from male influences and eventually settled on a comparative study examining her literary kinship to Dostoevsky. By the time I began work on my dissertation, I was convinced that O'Connor's status as a woman was irrelevant to an understanding of her writing. Instead, I became increasingly intrigued by her philosophical connections to men like John Crowe

Ransom, Allen Tate, and other prominent figures of what Eugene Genovese terms "the southern conservative tradition."[1]

When I traveled to Milledgeville to examine the O'Connor papers at Georgia College, I fully expected to find evidence linking her fiction to southern conservative thought. In a general sense, my instincts were correct. Yet the connections were manifested in ways that forced me to rethink entirely my conception of O'Connor as a latter-day southern conservative. In fact, I found surprising evidence of an internal struggle, as she worked to mold her fiction in conformity to the literary, aesthetic, and political frameworks that constitute its published forms. More surprising, I found undeniable evidence that her earliest fiction was imbued with a strong female presence entirely unlike anything that appeared in her published work. Again, I was baffled. How was it possible to account for the radical transformation her work undertook and, more specifically, for the female-sexed voice that, in her earliest fiction, spoke in *opposition* to the conservative vision of culture and society promulgated by men like Ransom and Tate?

My research eventually led me to conclude that, indeed, Ransom, Tate, and their Fugitive/Agrarian associates were a strong influence on O'Connor's literary development. But her conformity to their vision of southern literature and culture was not the simple result of her allegiance to conservative values. Instead, the evidence I uncovered points to the many ways in which her allegiances to those values were profoundly ambivalent. The ambivalence I detected in her relationships to her profession, her social role, her region, and her religion centered, finally, on the conflicts associated with her attempts to ally herself with a masculinist literary and cultural tradition. By *masculinist,* I mean any political, cultural, or literary construct that privileges male subjectivity, perpetuates an androcentric world view, endorses patriarchal social relations, and denies or obscures female subjectivity and agency.[2] O'Connor's manuscripts and their gradual silencing of a female-sexed voice revealed the extent to which the tradition she was working within demanded allegiance to masculinist values. My original understanding of her as a female author whose gender was a negligible influence gave way to a recognition of gender as the key influence around which all others revolved.

In recent years the critical literature on O'Connor has expanded to include greater consideration of gender as a factor in her literary development.

Critics such as Josephine Hendin, Martha Chew, Louise Westling, Margaret Whitt, Marshall Bruce Gentry, Sarah Gordon, and Patricia Smith Yaeger have examined the conflicts she experienced as a southern lady and professional author and have offered incisive analyses of the various strategies she used to resolve the tensions inherent in her position. The need remains for a book-length study that synthesizes this work and treats gender as a fundamental concept for analysis. At the same time, there remains a need to bridge the gap between southern literary studies and mainstream feminist criticism, which has generally neglected O'Connor's work. This study considers the reasons for such neglect and places gender at the center of its analytical framework. More generally, the study traces the cultural origins of the complicated aesthetic that informs O'Connor's fiction, both published and unpublished, and considers its relationship to the Fugitive/Agrarian and New Critical movements as well as to emerging theories concerning the nature of southern and American literary traditions.

On the most basic level, O'Connor's manuscripts offer evidence that, in an effort to fashion herself a serious writer worthy of the critical attention traditionally denied "lady writers" of the South, she radically altered her fictional landscape. Banishing female characters, silencing female voices, and redirecting her satirical gaze from men to women, O'Connor reshaped her work to appeal to a literary and critical community built on the gender-based and racial hierarchies that had traditionally characterized southern culture. O'Connor accepted the view that art rested on male prerogative, and she remained acutely uncomfortable with her own desire to usurp that privilege. True, she once admitted that women are not *necessarily* fated to "artistic sterility" since art, as she explained, "is a good deal more than a masculine drive—it is, in part, the accurate naming of the things of God" (*HB* 126). In other words, genuine art—which O'Connor somewhat paradoxically associated with a gender-neutral God at the head of a church founded on the "Patriarchal Ideal"—confers upon women the authority both to justify what is, in reality, a "masculine drive" and to overcome what amounts to a natural "artistic sterility" (99). The circular reasoning by which she sought to justify her own artistic drives suggests that, in fact, O'Connor believed women made unfit artists.

O'Connor's views on women and art did not emerge in a vacuum.

Indeed, they were the logical expression of the discourses that prevailed in southern literary culture of the mid-twentieth century. At the University of Iowa Writer's Workshop, O'Connor developed a strong identification with her native region and its literary and intellectual traditions. Her understanding of "Southern Literature" was profoundly influenced by Allen Tate, John Crowe Ransom, Andrew Lytle, and Robert Penn Warren, whose work as poets, editors, and social and literary critics in many ways defined the nature of the "Southern Literary Renaissance."[3] Though Fugitive/Agrarian theories regarding the "Southern Tradition" were neither monolithic nor consistent, certain notions regarding race and gender formed an unambiguous and cohesive pattern, resting on the assumption that African Americans and women rightfully belonged in the margins of southern culture.[4] The group's correspondence to "lady" Fugitive Laura Riding and landmark essays such as Ransom's "Criticism, Inc." and Tate's "The Man of Letters in the Modern World" offer revealing evidence of the process by which the Fugitive/Agrarians laid the groundwork for an aesthetic and critical tradition centered on opposition to the female and on the primacy of white southern manhood. Stories such as "The Artificial Nigger" and "A Late Encounter with the Enemy" suggest that O'Connor viewed blacks primarily as the signifiers through which white southern identity was constructed and embraced the Agrarians' nostalgic view of the authentic southern past. Her appropriation of dominant racial discourses allowed her to assume a position within southern literary culture that her gender would deny her. But as her manuscripts testify, O'Connor's self-consciousness with regard to her status as a woman writer was never fully resolved and in fact increased as a result of her graduate training.

Ransom, Tate, and their associates played a crucial, if indirect, role in O'Connor's growing discomfort with her role as a female artist.[5] As an undergraduate at a women's college, she had apparently felt not at all inhibited in writing about female experience. Not until she arrived at the University of Iowa did O'Connor's fiction begin to assume the masculinist tone characteristic of much of her published work. The stories she wrote as a graduate student, particularly "The Crop," bear a distinct contrast to her college stories and reflect an emerging reluctance to acknowledge herself as a woman writer. So, too, does the list of writers she would eventually claim as literary mentors. The authors O'Connor most admired were, with the exception of Caroline Gordon, all male: Joseph Conrad, Gustave Flaubert, Nathaniel Hawthorne, Henry James, and the Fugitive/Agrarians. Djuna Barnes, Dorothy Richardson, and Virginia Woolf she regarded as "nuts" (98). She described "lady journalists" as a "tribe" of which she was "deathly afraid," "while she dismissed "penwomen"—female amateurs who claimed professional status—as genteel ladies who wrote "true confession stories with one hand and Sunday school stories with the other" (*HB* 205, 231). On another occasion she admitted that she was utterly unable to "talk to" the college "girls" in the audiences to which she lectured (254).

Despite her distrust of the female intellect, O'Connor developed an extended mentoring relationship with Gordon, who played an important role in O'Connor's growing awareness of the gendered and racially inflected politics of southern literary culture. Most importantly, Gordon instructed O'Connor in the strategies she would need to cope with the contradictions created by her situation as a woman writing within a masculinist tradition. Her relationship to Gordon is integral to an understanding of O'Connor's relationship to the Fugitive/Agrarians and the southern literary establishment in general. A woman with even stronger ties, through her husband Allen Tate, to southern New Critical circles, Gordon coached the young author in the techniques necessary to maintain the high standards of "craftsmanship" and discipline she had been taught at the Writer's Workshop. Relying heavily in her own fiction on male characters and on a male point of view, Gordon had earned considerable admiration as a writer whose work remained untainted by the feminine "impurities" Andrew Lytle saw in the work of women like Elizabeth Madox Roberts or Katherine Anne Porter (*LT* 170–71). At the same time, Gordon, like O'Connor, worked hard to fulfill the superficial obligations of southern ladyhood, despite the strains that such demands placed on her work. Though Gordon was acutely aware of the double standards that informed her personal and professional lives, she continued to believe that the suppression of her female identity was crucial to her success as a writer. Both directly and indirectly Gordon made it clear to O'Connor that if she hoped to distinguish herself as a writer, then she, too, must suppress her female identity and model her work after the great "masters" of western literature. But based as it was on the underlying premise that the female intellect remained by definition inferior, the mentoring relationship between Gordon and O'Connor was deeply problematic. By insisting on the inferiority of the female intellect, Gordon established the terms by which her relationship to O'Connor would eventually disintegrate. In the end, their friendship testifies to the numerous difficulties, both personal as well as professional, facing women writers who accepted the premises by which the southern literary establishment operated and attests to the far-reaching influence of the gender-based politics that governed it.

Those politics are perhaps most clearly evidenced in the gendered landscapes of O'Connor's published and unpublished fiction, which function almost in direct opposition to one another. The landscape that characterizes much of her published fiction is overwhelmingly masculinist. Although women appear in a number of her short stories, they most often serve as comical examples of peculiarly feminine and irrational forms of behavior that invariably leave them vulnerable to attack. Rare is the adult female character who enjoys narrative respect or who survives unharmed. Among the many characters she created, for example, O'Connor admitted that she truly admired just three, Hazel Motes and the Tarwater prophets of *The Violent Bear It Away;* she preferred even the cold-blooded Misfit of "A Good Man Is Hard to Find" to the harmless and well-intentioned Grandmother he shoots (*HB* 437). Only those female characters too young to have achieved the status of ladyhood—Mary Fortune in "A View of the Woods," Sally Virginia Cope in "A Circle in the Fire," or the daughter in "A Temple of the Holy Ghost," among others—manage to escape the narrator's satirical glare. By claiming the freedom to defy the conventions of ladyhood, they manage to earn the narrator's respect. For O'Connor, ladyhood was a comical state at best, a perilous and cursed state at worse. Women who embraced it deserved their fate.

Even as O'Connor's stories endorse a misogynist politics wherein women are figured as victims of violence and humiliation, much of her short fiction is at least infused with a strong and distinct female presence. By contrast, her two novels, which she considered her most important works, are concerned almost exclusively with a few male characters. As her correspondence makes clear, O'Connor hoped that her fiction would be distinguished from that of other women by the way in which it grappled with profound theological and philosophical questions. In particular, she hoped to develop an artistic vision that could claim to express the universality of the human condition in its quest for spiritual understanding and fulfillment ("Plans for Work" OMC). Because she associated the female with the particular, the mundane, and the trivial, she refused to allow women characters, particularly those who were ladies, to represent the universal, the transcendent, or the spiritually profound. Even in short stories, such as "A Good Man Is Hard to Find" or "Good Country People," in which women seem to embody the theological questions with which O'Connor was concerned, she nevertheless managed to redirect the narrative emphasis away from the recipient of grace toward the agent, who is usually male.

O'Connor's unpublished manuscripts offer undeniable evidence of an earlier, female-sexed voice that governed her fictional landscape and that gradually disappeared as she strove to redirect the narrative emphasis of her work. The many incarnations of *Wise Blood* offer an interesting case study. The published version centers on three major characters: Hazel Motes, Enoch Emery, and Asa Hawkes. Although women like Leora Watts and Sabbath Hawkes make appearances in a number of scenes, they remain essentially minor characters who serve largely as momentary obstacles in Haze's path toward spiritual awakening. However, in manuscript versions of the novel, which O'Connor revised under Andrew Lytle's direction, the female characters, who are quite numerous, serve a different purpose. The changes she eventually made regarding these characters are revealing. In the manuscripts, for example, Haze's mother and three sisters play prominent roles as women whose out-of-control sexuality not only goes unpunished but is channeled in ways that serve God. In the published version of the novel, on the other hand, Haze takes on the role of lone existential hero, utterly bereft of family and friends, while the threat of female sexuality remains safely contained, as it does through much of O'Connor's published fiction. Similarly, in the manuscripts, Haze's girlfriend Lea actually rivals him as a protagonist, whereas in the published novel she merely serves, in the role of prostitute Leora Watts, as a temporary antidote to his uncontrollable religious impulses. Interestingly, the Lea who appears in the manuscripts is not a prostitute but an executive secretary in one series and a beautician in another; an independent woman who, unlike Leora, does not exist merely to serve men. In fact, the narrator offers a sympathetic account of her experiences of sexual abuse and describes Lea's history exclusively from her point of view. This technique represents a radical departure from the novels, which rely heavily on a male angle of vision.

Still other female characters in the *Wise Blood* manuscripts enjoy the luxury of narrative approval and interest as well. Indeed, the bulk of the manuscripts deal with Haze's sister, Ruby, who is pregnant with a child she wants to abort. The female-sexed voice that animates the manuscripts remains unable to address her experience of abortion, which is linked to the suffering of the Virgin Mary, solely within the limits of Catholic orthodoxy. The revisions that emerged in the published version, "A Stroke of Good Fortune," offer pointed evidence of O'Connor's overriding fear of the subversive implications of her manuscript treatment of female characters and their experience, which presented a strong critique of patriarchal social relations. Similarly, the revisions made on her second novel suggest that O'Connor also feared the repercussions associated with directing her satirical wit at male protagonists.

By the time she started work on *The Violent Bear It Away,* O'Connor had all but abandoned her earlier interest in female characters. However, as the manuscripts for the novel reveal, she had begun to direct at her male protagonists some of the hostility previously reserved for female characters. More specifically, she developed an extended critique of traditional masculinity and of the drive toward fraternization and domination that she identified as the impulse behind organizations such as the Ku Klux Klan and the Masonic Order. Just as she must have realized that exploring female experience and consciousness would leave her vulnerable to charges that she was not, in the end, a serious artist, O'Connor must have implicitly understood that such a blatant critique of closed male circles might be received as a feminist challenge to the literary culture in which she worked. Not surprisingly, in revision she transformed *The Violent Bear It Away* into a highly masculinist novel in which such challenges are obscured.

Foregrounding gender makes it possible to uncover other ways in which O'Connor's fiction is "sexed."[6] Her technical reliance on violence and the grotesque, for example, resulted from the need to distinguish herself from the ladylike writers who, according to the histories proposed by Tate and the Fugitive/Agrarians, dominated nineteenth-century southern letters. Traditionally critics have taken at face value claims O'Connor made in essays such as "The Fiction Writer and His Country" that she used violence and the grotesque as a means to reach a secular audience. "When you assume that your audience holds the same beliefs you do," she explained, "you can relax a little and use more normal means of talking to it; when you assume that it does not, then you have to make your vision apparent by shock" (*MM* 34). Certainly the violence that permeates her work is shocking. Yet in the fashion of early Fugitive poetry, O'Connor's published fiction is predicated on the need to shock an imagined audience of lady readers, a technique that emerged from her desire to distinguish herself as a decidedly *un*ladylike writer. O'Connor's use of the grotesque evolved from similar dynamics, reflecting her attempts to transcend female embodiment. In representing the body as ill, deformed, mutilated, subject to aberrant sexual urges, and ultimately bound to decay, O'Connor could bring into stark relief the spiritual questions with which she was preoccupied and claim literary kinship to the Christian traditions embraced by the New Critics she most admired. At the same time, her rejection of embodiment in favor of spiritual disengagement could function as yet another strategy for marking her work as transcendent of her femaleness.

To avoid associating herself with the banalities of ladyhood, O'Connor insulted the sensibilities of lady readers, subjected her adult female characters to violence and humiliation, and ignored or omitted them altogether whenever she believed they might detract from her larger purpose. Without doubt, O'Connor built her reputation on her ability to create a body of fiction that, in its attempts to transcend the particularities and banalities of female experience, conformed to the expectations of a male-dominated and androcentric literary and critical tradition. Importantly, however, O'Connor's suppression of the voice that informs her manuscripts was, despite her extensive efforts to obscure it altogether, never complete. In rejecting ladyhood, for example, the androgynous young girls of stories such as "A Temple of the Holy Ghost," "A Circle in the Fire," and "A View of the Woods" register their protest against a social order that would confine them to a narrow existence. In contrast to women like Mrs. Hopewell of "Good Country People," these characters frequently conduct themselves in a highly unladylike manner, reflecting O'Connor's ongoing, if latent, awareness of the difficulties involved in growing up female in a society that offered few creative outlets for women. And while *Wise Blood* and *The Violent Bear It Away* conform to traditionally masculinist narrative forms, namely the quest narrative and the bildungsroman, both novels manage to defy the conventions around which these forms have historically centered. Neither character achieves independence or autonomy; instead, Haze and Tarwater are both forced to conform to the will of a power greater than their own. In accepting passivity and dependence as their lot, they renounce all claims to a traditional male identity and instead become "feminized." In the end, O'Connor remained unable to suppress entirely the female-sexed voice that speaks in her manuscripts, and her male characters came to function as encoded representations of the difficulties and limitations of female experience.

Thorough attention to the gender-related dynamics at play in O'Connor's work makes it possible to uncover a range of new readings that suggest the many ways in which her fiction is, despite appearances, reflective of her identity as a woman. Indeed, it would not be unreasonable to conclude that gender influenced virtually every aspect of O'Connor's literary development. Her reliance on the grotesque, her use of violence, her treatment of male and female characters alike—all represented strategies for transcending, neutralizing, or denying her gendered self and its potential for upsetting the hierarchies on which her profession was built. And in terms of her professional development, these strategies certainly seem to have succeeded: from her earliest days as a professional writer O'Connor enjoyed a level of status rare among the literary women of her generation. She was quickly recognized as a bold and unique talent by the likes of Lytle, her instructor at the University of Iowa Writer's Workshop, and Ransom, the influential editor of the *Kenyon Review,* and she soon earned a place for herself among the "first-rate" American writers of the twentieth century (*SL* 374). Indeed, if the publication of her work in the Library of America series is any indication, then her place in the American literary canon—in the company of such luminaries as Herman Melville, Henry James, T. S. Eliot, and William Faulkner—remains secure.[7]

Curiously enough, despite O'Connor's early distinction as a female author of canonical status, much of the standard feminist criticism on American women writers has neglected her work.[8] In recent years, feminist critical theory has increasingly foregrounded the concept of "difference"—those qualities distinguishing female-authored texts from the androcentric traditions that have historically dominated western literature and criticism. Because O'Connor consciously strove to embrace, rather than transcend, androcentrism, and because she openly rejected the feminist critique of patriarchy, her work seems to resist straightforward feminist analysis. Indeed, the strain of misogyny that runs throughout her work—manifested at the most obvious level in the repeated depictions of the figurative rape of female characters—makes the identification of O'Connor as a feminist problematic, if not impossible. Yet precisely because gender was such a crucial factor in her literary development, feminist theory offers perhaps the most useful approach to understanding her work. Despite the growing attention accorded the role of gender in her fiction, the literary criticism on O'Connor has been limited by the general view that her status as a Catholic and a southerner remain exclusive to an understanding of her fiction and her career.[9] While O'Connor's allegiances to her religion and her native region were strong, her relationship both to the Catholic Church and to the South was profoundly ambivalent. This ambivalence found its roots in gender issues, in the tensions created by her latent fears regarding the subversive nature of her professional ambition and her artistic drives. Neither the standard criticism on O'Connor nor recent theory concerning women's writing has entirely accounted for the aesthetic strategies employed by her and by other writers who attempt to deny, obscure, or transcend what they view as the limitations of female experience and identity.

As a number of critics have noted, O'Connor's standing within southern literary culture might best be described as a "contradictory subject position" (Belsey 50).[10] A white southerner from a "good family," O'Connor identified strongly with the dominant culture and occupied a secure place within it. But as a woman, she simultaneously occupied the "muted" cultural space characterized by a range of female experiences that lay beyond the knowledge or interest of men (Showalter 262).[11] As both "insiders" and "outsiders" within the same culture (Du Plessis 278), women writers may find themselves possessed of what W. E. B. Du Bois referred to as "double-consciousness, this sense of always looking at one's self through the eyes of others" (45). To give voice to this muted experience through the lens of dominant discourses—many of which are rooted in misogyny—becomes a difficult, if not impossible, task. Female writers can find their attempts to resolve the tensions inherent in such a position overwhelming. "One way of responding to this situation," argues Catherine Belsey, "is to retreat from the contradictions and from discourse itself, to become 'sick.' . . . Another is to seek a resolution of the contradictions in the discourses of feminism" (50).

O'Connor's work suggests that embracing masculinist forms and conventions and, indeed, misogyny, offers another strategy. Indeed, southern women writers, as Anne Goodwyn Jones has demonstrated, have enjoyed a long history of obscuring rebellions—both in life and, for their heroines, in fiction—behind "the veil of an acceptable formula" (39). O'Connor was no exception. Her career is perhaps best distinguished by the way in which she discreetly managed to mask the subversive potential of her artistic drives, delicately occupying both dominant and muted spheres at once. While she founded her career as a writer in opposition to an explicitly "female" aesthetic, her very insistence on transcending femininity served in itself as a distinctly female strategy, one designed to obscure the muted voice that speaks so powerfully in her manuscript fiction. Her manuscripts essentially confirm theories that posit the existence of a subversive and self-consciously female-sexed voice in women's writing. But the androcentric orientation of the published versions of her two novels and the misogyny that imbues her short stories raise complicated questions regarding the nature of female aesthetics. Neither subversive nor self-consciously "female," O'Connor's published work suggests instead that women writers may respond to the conflicts and pressures that have historically been brought to bear against them by retreating into an apparently genderless state built on the denial of female subjectivity. Like the literary foremothers who are the subject of Sandra M. Gilbert and Susan Gubar's work, O'Connor developed this strategy in an effort to equalize, as much as possible, her professional status.

Gilbert and Gubar have offered one of the most comprehensive analyses of the status of women writers throughout the nineteenth and twentieth centuries and have provided an extensive history of the various strategies male writers and critics have employed as a means of excluding women from serious literary consideration solely on the basis of gender (*No Man's Land* 147–49). Though their work is concerned primarily with non-southern writers and critics, it nevertheless suggests that—viewed within the broader context of twentieth-century American and European literary cultures—Fugitive/Agrarian views on the relationship between gender and literature were hardly unique.[12] To make sense of O'Connor's particular situation as a southern writer, it is crucial to pay close attention to the more specific discourses on race and gender that were unique to Fugitive/Agrarian theory and criticism. The patterns of dominance at the root of traditional southern social relations created a regional literary culture wherein racially inflected constructions of manhood would emerge as a central preoccupation. White southern men like Ransom and Tate, argues Susan V. Donaldson, remained haunted by the specter of the black man in a "contest determining the masculinity of each," which resulted in the need to marginalize "anything remotely subordinate and feminine, including white and black women" ("Gender, Race, and Allen Tate" 511). In adopting a masculinist persona grounded specifically in the discourses of southern literary culture, O'Connor was forced into the awkward position of attempting to place herself not only above African Americans but above and against other women as well. On the one hand, her allegiance to the dominant racial values of the white South made it possible for O'Connor to deflect, in part, the subversive potential of her status as a woman writing within a male-dominated tradition. But on the other hand, her identification with and appropriation of the racial discourses on which southern literary culture was founded required her to embrace the centrality of white consciousness and experience at the expense of acknowledging her own status as the woman whose marginality was essential to the hegemony of white men.

As Jon Lance Bacon argues, O'Connor accepted the widely held theory that the region's distinctive culture was rooted in the ongoing struggle to define racial boundaries (88–89). And like Ransom, Tate, and their Fugitive/Agrarian colleagues, O'Connor embraced the underlying premise that the South was, by definition, white (Wood, "Flannery O'Connor" 6). Though she stopped short of supporting segregation, like many of her white southern contemporaries O'Connor remained unequivocal in her belief that integration should proceed slowly, without the direct interference of politicians and activists (*HB* 253, 404). Her infamous refusal to entertain James Baldwin at her Georgia home points to the care she took to remain aloof from the politics of the civil rights movement. In short, the concerns of African Americans remained peripheral to O'Connor's vision of southern culture and its literature; in her view the importance of the civil rights movement lay not so much in the potential it held for African Americans but in the changes it posed for whites and in the opportunities it offered white artists like herself to explore these changes (Bacon 109). O'Connor's allegiance to dominant southern values regarding the intersection of race and gender necessitated the subordination of her subversive female-sexed voice to the needs of a white, masculinist aesthetic. Yet in a paradoxical way, her anti-feminist silencing of the muted voice of her manuscripts and her appropriation of racist discourses functioned as a means of achieving the feminist end of earning equal consideration as an artist. While this strategy certainly helped her achieve critical success, it created a textual landscape divided against itself, wherein a female author adopts a misogynist stance founded on the need to shock lady readers, deny female subjectivity, and humiliate and wreak violence on female characters.[13] This sense of division—the dominant voice that characterizes her published fiction versus the muted voice that speaks in her manuscripts—pervaded O'Connor's personal and professional lives and remains key to an understanding of her work.

The conflicting obligations of her personal and professional lives required O'Connor to satisfy the needs of her muted, artistic self without appearing to subvert the social role expected of her, which was founded on the ideals of southern ladyhood. As a "dutiful daughter," O'Connor understood that she must try to "conform to the ways of the Southern world, at least in appearance" (Whitt 42–43; also see Westling, "Flannery O'Connor's Revelations" 15, and Hendin 14–15). Her traditional southern upbringing instilled in her a great respect for the customs of her society, which dictated that white women of middle- and upper-class origins act as "ladies," devoting themselves to husband, family, and household and cultivating such virtues as compliance, chastity, and the ability to remain politely self-effacing.[14] Throughout her life, as Margaret Whitt argues, O'Connor maintained a veneer of conventionality and appeared, at least on the surface, to conform to the social role expected of her. In this way she was able to meet the obligations of southern ladyhood without being entirely subsumed by them. Her careful attention to the more superficial requirements of her social role allowed her to violate many of the rules of conduct imposed on young women of her race and class and attend to the needs generated by her "unnatural" artistic drives.

Her status as an unmarried woman offers an interesting case in point. Certainly it would be inaccurate to suggest that the society in which she lived did not tolerate unmarried, or even unconventional, women. Indeed, it may have been quite possible for O'Connor to have openly and unapologetically pursued her professional interests and to simply have accepted whatever disapproval might have ensued. What remains particularly interesting about O'Connor is that, whenever presented with the choice, she invariably decided to create the illusion of conformity. Her published letters generally remain silent on the subject, which suggests both that she liked to encourage the impression that her refusal to marry was not the result of deliberate choice, but of her illness, and that marriage was a touchy subject she preferred, if possible, to ignore. Nevertheless, in a letter to "A" [Anonymous],[15] the correspondent with whom O'Connor shared the most personal information (Westling, "Flannery O'Connor's Revelations" 15), she admitted, "There is a great deal that has to either be given up or be taken away from you if you are going to succeed in writing a body of work. There seem to be other conditions in life that demand celibacy besides the priesthood" (*HB* 176). Like countless other female writers Adrienne Rich has termed "marriage resisters," O'Connor quietly managed to avoid marriage so that she might be able to devote herself entirely to her work (163–64). Keeping her motivations for remaining single largely to herself, she was able to maintain the illusion of social conformity, delicately balancing the needs of her muted self with the demands of her allegiance to dominant values.

Her status as an "invalid" enhanced O'Connor's ability to adhere to the more superficial aspects of her social role and simultaneously violate some of the more fundamental requirements of southern ladyhood. She often attributed her growth as an artist to her struggles with lupus erythematosus, preferring to emphasize the opportunities for spiritual growth it provided. Yet Louise Abbot recalls a far more practical benefit, namely freedom from household chores, which on a farm like Andalusia could be considerable. During their many visits together, Abbot never remembered O'Connor doing more than the dishes. And because her illness left her so fatigued, she could readily justify the strict household rules regarding her work: mornings were devoted to writing, and visitors were rarely allowed before lunch. "I'm fortunate," O'Connor told Abbot, "in that this disability relieves me of other duties" (66). Though largely dependent on her mother's care, she managed to pursue friendships with some of the leading *literati* of her day, including, among others, Robert Lowell, Elizabeth Hardwick, Gordon and Tate, Andrew Lytle, Katherine Anne Porter, Eudora Welty, Robert Penn Warren, Robert Giroux, Robert and Sally Fitzgerald, and Elizabeth Bishop. Many of these writers were able to visit her periodically, thereby bringing the world of letters to her front door. When her health permitted, she traveled extensively, visiting friends and delivering lectures at colleges and symposia. Professing to hate the lecture circuit, O'Connor, ever the dutiful daughter, cited family finances as the reason she traveled so frequently (*HB* 472). Beneath this disclaimer lies the more telling point that her travels offered her the opportunity to cultivate and nourish a wide circle of friendships that no doubt provided her with a strong sense of intellectual companionship.[16] More importantly, such friendships, nurtured by a voluminous correspondence, allowed O'Connor to remain a part of both Milledgeville and the American literary scene of the day. And as devastating as her illness was, on a certain level it too allowed her a freedom she might not otherwise have claimed. These circumstances made it possible for "Mary Flannery," by all appearances the dutiful daughter, to build a protected space for "Flannery," the bold and unladylike writer whose work threatened to upset the social order into which she had been born.[17]

O'Connor appears to have worked hard to cultivate the image of herself as a dutiful and submissive daughter, a devout Catholic who remained unmarried not out of choice but from circumstance, an invalid whose illness necessitated time alone and respite from domestic duties. However, the evidence suggests that her more rebellious self—the daughter who chafed at the notion of remaining in her mother's house, the "priest(ess)" who embraced celibacy and demanded the time and freedom to pursue her literary calling— may have in fact been O'Connor's true self. An incident that occurred early in her career, before illness had forced her return to Georgia, reveals the depth of her professional ambition and illustrates the cracks in the ladylike facade she attempted to construct. Insulted by the "Sears Roebuck Straight-shooter" criticism *Wise Blood* received in the hands of editor John Selby, O'Connor wrote to her agent complaining that his report on the novel was "addressed to a slightly dim-witted Camp Fire Girl." In a letter to Selby himself, she clarified her position, frankly explaining that "I would not like at all to work with you as do other writers on your list. I feel that whatever virtues the novel may have are very much connected with the limitations you mention." She was, she conceded, "amenable to criticism," but not if it interfered with "what I am trying to do." She would not, O'Connor concluded, "be persuaded to do otherwise" (*HB* 9–10). Hardly the conduct expected of the polite, self-effacing, and compliant southern lady, her strong language here points to the ways in which O'Connor refused to sacrifice her professional status for the sake of propriety. A similar pattern emerges in her correspondence to John Crowe Ransom regarding "The Artificial Nigger." While she took great pains to appear polite and deferential, assuring Ransom she was willing to "change the ending or anything else," beneath the surface she made it clear that, in fact, she had no intention of changing the story or its controversial title (182). O'Connor made this last point by insisting that Ransom must have mistakenly received an earlier draft of the story; otherwise he could not have found cause for dispute. To add to her case, she appealed to Caroline Gordon's authority for support. In response, Ransom assured O'Connor that he did indeed have the correct draft, but her tactic worked, and he agreed to abide by her wishes. Her original version of the story, along with the controversial title, remained intact. Although she may have employed more apparently "ladylike" tactics with fellow southerners like Ransom, O'Connor was no less shy in asserting her editorial authority when she believed the integrity of her professional self was at stake.

The published letters and reminiscences of friends and acquaintances support the conclusion that O'Connor's true self did not entirely conform to the conventional image she worked so hard to cultivate. James Tate and Father Edward J. Romagosa, neither of whom was particularly close to O'Connor, describe her as a thoroughly conventional young woman. "She was," Tate writes, "the most unobtrusive person I've ever known" (66).[18] By contrast, two of O'Connor's most intimate friends, Betty Boyd Love and Maryat Lee, recall that she was out of place in Milledgeville. Love, a college friend, attempts to emphasize O'Connor's conventionality, but her recollections suggest that O'Connor was not entirely comfortable in the social milieu in which she lived. "The Southern butterfly," Love writes, "may not have been her type of social creature, but she never exhibited any personal rebellion against the social conventions whose absurdities she portrayed so well" (70). O'Connor's "conventionality" notwithstanding, Love devotes a considerable portion of her essay to describing the various qualities that distinguished O'Connor from her neighbors. Noting that she "didn't really enjoy" the various social functions that were a part of Milledgeville's social fabric, Love concludes that O'Connor was a "genuinely unusual individual" who was also, perhaps, just a little "eccentric" (71).

Less guarded in expressing her views on O'Connor's eccentricities, Lee offers an illuminating account of their first meeting. What she had expected to find in O'Connor was simply "another local lady writer, somewhat prim in dress, stockings, and shiney [*sic*] shoes" (40; also see Sarah Gordon, "Maryat and Juliat"). At first glance O'Connor's physical appearance did not surprise Lee, but her candor about coming to terms with life in the South did. Lee was impressed by the "halting" tone of O'Connor's voice as she described the effects her illness had had on her plans. To Lee her manner implied that the return home had created a "morass of confusion, conflict, and depression" that had forced O'Connor to develop "an intricate plan so that all the personal and professional problems were resolved harmoniously" (41). Describing herself as a "rebel" who opposed the provincial ways of her native region, Lee admits that she saw in O'Connor a kindred spirit. For her part, O'Connor admitted to Lee how uncomfortable her living arrangements sometimes made her feel. "She said that being in the house [Andalusia] didn't contribute to her articulateness. . . . Her ambition was to convert the henhouse into a private office, complete with refrigerator" (42).

Lee's portrait offers insight into the difficulties O'Connor experienced in attending to the conflicting demands of her personal and professional roles. The tensions inherent in her "contradictory subject position" became particularly acute as she struggled to adopt a highly *un*ladylike aesthetic without offending the ladies in her own family. She understood that to earn a reputation as a serious writer she would have to produce fiction in stark contrast to the feminine verses long associated with the nineteenth-century literary traditions the Fugitive/Agrarians and New Critics hoped to reject. Such fiction was, according to prevailing critical standards, best distinguished by its appeal to ladies, dilettantes, and other poor judges of literary merit. The ability to write fiction that might prove not only incomprehensible but also downright shocking to an audience of ladies eventually became one of the driving forces behind O'Connor's artistic vision and a great source of personal pride as well. For example, she wrote to Paul Engle concerning the reception *Wise Blood* had received at Rinehart, where she was currently under contract. "I learned indirectly," she admitted, "that nobody at Rinehart liked the 108 pages but Raney (and whether he likes it or not I couldn't really say) [and] that the ladies there particularly had thought it unpleasant. . . . [This] pleased me" (*HB* 13). O'Connor considered it a mark of her talents as a serious writer that she was able to offend lady readers. Early in 1952 she proudly relayed evidence that this strategy was a success. "Harcourt sent my book to Evelyn Waugh," she wrote to Robert Lowell, "and his comment was: 'If this is really the unaided work of a young lady, it is a remarkable product'" (35). To claim she had produced a work of art that would have proved impossible for most young ladies was for O'Connor the supreme compliment.

Yet beneath the surface lay the lingering fear that perhaps she had gone too far in overstepping boundaries. Particularly acute were her insecurities regarding her status as a southern writer, and she frequently expressed concerns that somehow she did not deserve the literary status she had earned. William Faulkner stood as a particularly intimidating figure, reminding her that she may indeed have entered an arena in which she did not belong. In public she explained that "the presence alone of Faulkner in our midst makes a great difference in what the writer can and cannot permit himself to do. Nobody wants his mule and wagon stalled on the same track the Dixie Limited is roaring down" (*MM* 45). In private she admitted that "the real reason I don't read him is because he makes me feel that with my one-cylinder syntax I should quit writing and raise chickens altogether" (*HB* 292). Other southern writers, particularly the Fugitives and Agrarians, inspired the same feelings of inadequacy. Among the few truly "respectable" writers who actually belong to what is popularly conceived as a "Southern School" are, O'Connor admitted, the Agrarians (*MM* 28). Though she keenly admired Faulkner's talents, she felt a stronger kinship with the Fugitive/Agrarians, whose conservative vision of southern culture she shared (*HB* 148).[19] That she shared a common artistic vision with these writers—particularly in regard to the importance of the southern past and the traditions it inspired—only intensified her desire to "measure up" to the literary standards they had established throughout the 1920s and 1930s. Indeed, each of these men exerted a strong influence, both directly and indirectly, on O'Connor's development as a writer. To O'Connor, writers like Ransom, Tate, Lytle, Warren, and, to a lesser extent, Gordon embodied the standards, as far as southern literature was concerned, she should strive to meet.

Although she believed she possessed the talent necessary to meet such high standards, she frequently doubted that her work actually fulfilled its potential. Typical is the letter she wrote Lytle regarding his favorable reaction, amid the generally poor reviews, to *The Violent Bear It Away*. "I feel better about the book," she admitted, "knowing you think it works. I expect it to get trounced but that won't make any difference if it really does work. There are not many people whose opinion on this I set store by" (*HB* 373). Before she had finished the novel, she had been sure to send the drafts to Lytle for his criticism; other writers whose opinions she "set store by" and who received copies of her work included Warren, Gordon, and, frequently, Tate (353). Her nearly obsessive reliance on the criticism of others— she never published a story or novel before it had been reviewed by numerous friends and colleagues—was the result both of her training at Iowa, where revision was strongly emphasized, and of her doubts about her ability to utilize her talents to their fullest.[20] Even after publication, she frequently expressed fears that her writing had failed to do her talent justice. Of *The Violent Bear It Away*, O'Connor commented, "I wish the book were better but I am glad it is not another *Wise Blood*" (371). Her discomfort with the label *Southern* was the result of the lingering fear that perhaps her work did not merit the consideration and attention accorded *true* southern writers like Faulkner, the Fugitive/Agrarians, and their more talented associates like Gordon. O'Connor's lack of confidence was no doubt related to the latent fear that in becoming a writer she had assumed an undertaking that was not only inappropriate but presumptuous.

Embracing Christianity and, more specifically, Catholicism became one of the chief means by which O'Connor attempted to ease these anxieties and veil the subversive threats posed by her literary voice. By claiming that her writing served the needs of God, O'Connor could justify even its most shocking elements—particularly the unrelenting violence—within the context of Christianity and in so doing justify as well the needs of her artistic self. O'Connor's joking reference to Sally Fitzgerald about her mother's insistence that she write a "proper" introduction to *Wise Blood*—so as to keep Cousin Katie from being "shocked"—suggests that despite her glee in offending the ladies at Rinehart, O'Connor nevertheless remained concerned about offending the ladies in her own family. Relieved to find that the ladies in her family more often than not found her work boring, she explained to one of her correspondents the process by which she finally attempted to free herself of anxieties regarding such issues (*HB* 33). Early in her career, O'Connor admitted, she had been "worried about this thing of scandalizing people." She questioned a priest about the problem, and he reminded her that she did not "have to write for fifteen-year-old girls." Reassured, O'Connor concluded that "if your conscience is clear, then . . . you have to leave the rest in God's hands. When the book leaves your hands, it belongs to God" (142–43). Her Catholic faith did not serve merely as the mechanism by which she attempted to understand humanity's relationship to God but, more importantly, as the impetus behind her desire and, indeed, her very ability to write. "I write the way I do because and only because I am a Catholic," she explained. "I feel that if I were not a Catholic, I would have no reason to write, no reason to see, no reason ever to feel horrified or even to enjoy anything. . . . I have never had the sense that being a Catholic is a limit to the freedom of the writer, but just the reverse" (114). Her ability to write was, she concluded, "first of all a gift," and it was her responsibility to use it properly (92). In "The Nature and Aim of Fiction" she explained that there "is no excuse for anyone to write fiction for public consumption unless he has been called to do so by the presence of a gift." Such a gift is "a considerable responsibility . . . a mystery . . . something wholly undeserved, something whose real uses will probably always be hidden from us." Although she would not have presumed herself to explain exactly the hidden uses behind her own art, she would admit in the same essay that "the reason I write is to make the reader see what I see . . . writing fiction is primarily a missionary activity" (*MM* 81). By explaining her creative drives in essentially passive terms as impulses that enjoyed the approval of the highest of male authorities—God himself—O'Connor could, in part, resolve the professional dilemmas posed by her gender. Catholicism offered her a means of justifying her desire to write, allowing her to conceive of her work not as a frivolous and misguided usurpation of male privilege but as a responsibility to which she must faithfully "submit" (*HB* 126).

O'Connor's ongoing efforts to couch her rebellions in conventional terms profoundly influenced her professional and personal development, even as both were strained by the cracks in her carefully constructed facade. Yet she remained steadfast in her attempts to mend these cracks, as she struggled first to silence the voice that speaks in her manuscripts and then to adapt it to the demands of a masculinist aesthetic, all the while claiming that her subversive artistic drives remained entirely compatible with her roles as dutiful daughter and devout Catholic. Given O'Connor's use of strategies that oppose and devalue rather than celebrate female experience, her lack of confidence in her own talents, and her need to provide religious justifications for her artistic drives, it is little wonder that feminist critics have generally overlooked her work. O'Connor, in short, falls far short as a feminist role model. But precisely because she chose to rely on aesthetic strategies that involved conscious opposition to female subjectivity, her fiction particularly lends itself to feminist analysis. Studies that consider her Catholic or southern heritage apart from the tensions posed by her gender are necessarily limited. It remains impossible to account for the complexities inherent in her personal life and in her relationship to her profession, her religion, and her region without making reference to gender: the ambivalence that characterized these various relationships found its origins in her status as a woman. In the end, an analysis of the ways in which gender influenced O'Connor's artistic development not only offers deeper insight into her relationship to the South and the Catholic Church but provides a new perspective on the complexities and multiplicities of female aesthetics. As O'Connor's response to the literary culture in which she worked suggests, female aesthetic strategies do not always involve overt forms of opposition and subversion. Indeed, it is quite possible for women writers to identify against themselves as a means of undermining masculine claims to artistic privilege. At the same time, O'Connor's fiction suggests that it is also possible for women writers to use masculinist narrative forms and male characters as vehicles for encoding representations of female identity and experience. To be sure, O'Connor consciously avoided the path set by such "nuts" as Virginia Woolf and sought instead to identify herself intellectually and artistically with men. In so doing she was forced, as her manuscripts in particular testify, to alter radically her literary vision. In the process she developed an aesthetic that, while hardly feminist, was nevertheless peculiarly "female."

# 1 · *The Dixie Limited*

O'Connor and Fugitive/Agrarian
Discourse on Gender, Race, and the
Southern Literary Tradition

JOHN CROWE RANSOM, Allen Tate, and their Fugitive/Agrarian colleagues played a crucial role in the modern emergence of a self-conscious body of southern writing and criticism. Their work as poets, as novelists, and, more importantly, as critics and editors helped lay the groundwork for what would later be termed the "Southern Literary Renaissance." The aesthetic and critical principles that Flannery O'Connor adopted owed their genesis in large part to Fugitive/Agrarian ideals regarding the nature of southern writing and the influence of what Tate termed the "genteel tradition" ("Profession of Letters" 530). Critics continue to debate the influence of particularly the Agrarians, arguing, for example, that since O'Connor did not even read *I'll Take My Stand* until 1964, the influence was likely minimal.[1] Yet the Fugitive/Agrarian influence lay not so much in O'Connor's conscious adaptation of their views. Rather, their influence stemmed from the central role they played in the dissemination and, eventually, in the institutionalization of the foundational theories and discourses underpinning the modern emergence of a self-conscious body of southern writing and literary criticism and in the formulation of broader theories regarding the interpretation of literature generally. In addition to being an instrumental force behind the Fugitive and Agrarian movements, for example, Ransom developed many of the seminal theories behind the New Criticism; as founder and longtime editor of the state-of-the-art *Kenyon Review* (1939–59), he served as arbiter of taste for the latest in fiction, poetry, and criticism. Widely regarded as the most innovative of the Fugitive poets as well as among the most cosmopolitan of the Agrarians, Tate earned a national reputation as a poet and critic. Under his editorship, the *Sewanee Review* (1944–46) established itself as one of the nation's leading literary journals. Somewhat more provincial than Ransom and Tate, Lytle, particularly in his endeavors as a novelist, aligned himself more closely with the "Southern School." As an instructor at the University of Iowa Writer's Workshop, however, he played a crucial role in training a generation of American writers, including O'Connor. And though Robert Penn Warren's career was perhaps best distinguished by his contributions as a novelist and poet, he too was among the leading critics of his generation. As coeditor, with Cleanth Brooks, of the *Southern Review* (1935–42), as coauthor, also with Brooks, of the widely used anthology *Understanding Fiction* (1938, 1950, 1960)—which O'Connor frequently cited as an important influence—and, finally, as an instructor of playwriting at Yale University (1951–56), Warren also stood as a formidable presence in the world of American letters. In their roles as critics, instructors, novelists, and poets, each of these men played a prominent role in the evolution of the hegemonic discourses that prevailed within both the American and southern literary circles of the mid-twentieth century.

One of the key tenets of Fugitive/Agrarian discourse on southern writing centered on Tate's formulation of the "genteel tradition," which would figure prominently in the development of O'Connor's own aesthetics. Based on sentimental and domestic conventions, the South's genteel tradition functioned for Tate and his colleagues as a code for anything hinting of the feminine and came finally to embody the antithesis of every aesthetic principle they sought to establish (Donaldson, "Gender, Race, and Allen Tate" 492–93). Central to their mission as poets and critics was the effort to replace the idealization of the female—which they understood as one of the central features of nineteenth-century southern literature—with an assertion of the primacy of the male intellect and of white southern manhood. A look at early Fugitive poetry offers an intriguing glimpse into the emergence and eventual codification of the aesthetics that would later dominate southern letters and exert such a powerful influence on O'Connor's literary sensibilities. While

Fugitive historians have traditionally focused on the group's efforts in establishing a national audience, much of the group's early poetry suggests that the authors were as interested in shocking the genteel sensibilities of local readers as they were in establishing a national audience.[2] The group implicitly envisioned these local readers as female—an audience with tastes hopelessly mired in the sentimental, romantic traditions of the nineteenth century. With this audience in mind, the Fugitives appear to have fashioned much of their early poetry as a direct response to the "poetic principles" for which nineteenth-century critic Edgar Allan Poe—whose romantic verses, Tate once noted, had been staple volumes in the southern libraries of his youth— had long campaigned ("Our Cousin, Mr. Poe" 385).[3] As "the most elevating of all emotions," Beauty, Poe explained in "The Philosophy of Composition," should form the "sole legitimate province of the poem." Because the most highly developed forms of beauty "invariably excite . . . the sensitive soul to tears," it follows that Melancholy should comprise the "tone" of all good poetry. And since death is the most melancholy of all subjects, Poe concluded that "the death, then, of a beautiful woman is, unquestionably, the most poetical topic in the world" (1082–84). Poe had merely articulated the rationale behind an aesthetic principle that had informed much popular nineteenth-century poetry. But for Tate and the other Fugitives—men who prided themselves on their cosmopolitan sophistication, intellectualism, and, often, cynicism—melancholy verses that lovingly described in sentimental terms the death of a beautiful woman had come to epitomize the worst of Southern Literature. To reject the romantic tradition and make genuine their rebellion against Southern Literature, it would therefore be necessary to reject aesthetic principles based on beauty, melancholy, sentiment, and gentility. By linking these aesthetic principles to a female audience, the group was able to lay the foundation for a new aesthetic, one founded on rejection of the feminine.

While the death of women became a staple theme of much of the poetry that would appear in *The Fugitive,* the group conspicuously avoided characterizing such deaths in sentimental, romantic, or beautiful terms. Typical is Tate's "Elegy for Eugenesis."[4] Describing in unemotional and even flippant terms the death of a woman in childbirth, the cynical persona likens mother to protoplasmic "jellyfish" and child to mere "homunculus with bald head."

In a somewhat dismissive tone the speaker declares, "We buried you in the unremissive ground," and, lighting a cigarette with an affected air, says simply, "I went home." These deaths are, as he admits, "quite cold" or, in other words, utterly meaningless. Even the woman's husband has to feign sadness, pretending he is brokenhearted while "[w]inking at his cocktail, talking dollars carefully" (92). On one level the poem functions as a means of exposing the bankruptcy of modern values, which the speaker himself embodies. Yet at the same time, "Elegy for Eugenesis" and other Fugitive poems serve as forums for exposing and violating the "poetic principles" upon which the average reader of Southern Literature had come to rely. Here Tate and his colleagues laid the groundwork for the development of a new aesthetic, linked to the broader modernist effort to create bold new literary forms but grounded more specifically in the need to distinguish their efforts from the "formless revery" and "inflated oratory" that characterized nineteenth-century letters ("Profession of Letters" 524–26). As far as Tate and the other Fugitives were concerned, neither female beauty nor motherhood nor even the death of a child in infancy were sacrosanct; any topic that could be expected to shock the "Victorian" morality of local readers was worthy of attention. In making such topics the subject of their poetry, Tate and his associates no doubt understood that their local audience, conditioned by years of reading verses like Poe's "The Raven" and "Annabel Lee," would recognize *The Fugitive* as an affront to their aesthetic expectations and tastes. O'Connor's own fascination with the death of female bodies owes much to the dissemination of an aesthetic in which the unsentimental depiction of the death of a woman is understood as the very antithesis of the Margaret Mitchell school of southern writing that O'Connor so studiously attempted to avoid (Fitzgerald, "Master Class" 844).

Central to the Fugitive effort to shock the sensibilities of local readers was the effort to appeal to another, more discerning audience capable of appreciating genuine art. The first audience, shocked by graphic images of sexuality and death, was implicitly defined as female, while the second audience, able to recognize the truth inherent in such images, was implicitly defined as male. Ransom's "Judith of Bethulia," for example, directly addresses this second audience, reminding them that "a wandering beauty is a blade out of its scabbard," a weapon more powerful than an army of men.

Recounting Judith's defense of her city against a marauding horde of invaders, the speaker explains how she used her beauty as a "sword" and found the "destruction" of the invasion forces and their leader "easy." The aftermath of this "orgy" of violence was, as the speaker recalls, quite grim:

> The heathen are all perished, the victory was furnished,
> We smote them hiding in our vineyards, barns, annexes,
> And now their white bones clutter the holes of foxes,
> And the chieftain's head, with grinning sockets, and varnished,
> Is it hung on the sky with a hideous epitaphy?
> No the woman keeps the trophy.

Rather than commending Judith for her valiant defense of his city, the speaker instead identifies with the plight of the men she murdered. In this sense his verses emerge as a direct appeal to all men, cautioning them to remember Judith's legend and reminding them of the dangers inherent in female flesh: "You know how dangerous, gentlemen of threescore? / May you know it yet ten more." Invoking a community of men—speaker (and by extension poet), audience, the "heathen" army and its murdered leader—the poem opposes masculinity, defined through the common fear of and desire for Judith, against femininity, symbolized by Judith's treacherous sexuality. All of the men in this community, like the murdered leader of the invasion forces, were, as the persona explains "desperate to study / The invincible emanations of her white body." Yet, he sadly admits, her actions in their defense have left young and old alike simultaneously "[i]nflamed by the thought of her naked beauty" and "chilled with fear and despair" (140–41). Banishing Judith and the community of women she represents from the poetic landscape, the speaker envisions female identity, defined through sexuality, as the objectified and horrifying symbol against which male identity, defined through poetry and art, is formulated. Thus the speaker establishes a fraternity of sorts, one founded upon a common male experience that transcends the boundaries of nationality and becomes emblematic of the literary culture the Fugitive/Agrarians were themselves in the process of creating.

Much of Ransom's Fugitive poetry, like "Judith of Bethulia," works on a variety of levels, serving at once as a vehicle through which to confront, offend, and exclude female readers as well as a means through which to invoke a cohesive and united fraternity of male readers. "Piazza Piece," for example, assumes the form of a dialogue in which a "gentleman in a dust-coat" and a "lady young in beauty waiting" represent these two audiences of readers to whom much Fugitive poetry was directed. The "gentleman," who must have his "lovely young lady soon," is "trying" to make her listen, warning her of the "roses on your trellis dying" and the "spectral singing of the moon." But her "ears are soft and small / And listen to an old man not at all." Naively disregarding his warnings, she prefers instead to wait until "my truelove comes." Her "truelove," however, never arrives, and in his place appears the menacing specter of death. "Back from my trellis, sir," she pleads to no avail, "before I scream!" (21). Here the figure of death becomes the eroticized embodiment of male sexual aggression. A poetic landscape where death is associated with rape—"gentlemen" with knowledge and power, and "ladies young in beauty" with ignorance and sexual vulnerability—"Piazza Piece" offers Ransom's fraternity of male readers a voyeuristic glimpse of female innocence violated and his frivolous and superficial audience of female readers a warning about the dangers of male sexual aggression. More specifically, Ransom confronts the latter audience with the unavoidable fact of male potency and domination—through the humorous irony that is directed at the young woman in her naïveté as she awaits what is surely an inevitable fate and through the consequent affirmation of the *inevitability* of masculine superiority that this fate represents.

The Fugitives' fascination with female bodies owed its genesis both to the broader effort to define themselves in opposition to nineteenth-century southern writing as well as to their philosophical kinship to high modernism and its valorization of the Christian and the broader Western Tradition. In western philosophical and religious discourse, the body has historically been associated with the female. Western creation myths and the ways in which they are linked to cultural constructions of the female body offer useful insight into the ancient origins of the male mind/female body split upon which Fugitive/Agrarian aesthetics were built. In early texts such as the *Theogony,* notes Robbie Pfuefer Kahn, "Mother Earth holds the generative power of matter *and* of words, for she both creates matter and is the first to speak," reflecting a world view wherein the female body is the source both of the intellect and the transcendent divine (157). In later Judeo-Christian texts, however, creation is achieved through the Word alone, reflecting a world view wherein the body is no longer the source of creation. As a result, the specific female bodily processes of menstruation, gestation, birth, and lactation become increasingly associated not with creativity but with mortality and decay (167). "Rather than treat the body as a site of knowledge, a medium for thought," argues Jane Gallop, "the more classical philosophical project has tried to render it transparent and get beyond it, to dominate it by reducing it to the mind's idealizing categories" (3–4). In western religious and philosophical traditions, then, to acquire language and intellect is to transcend the body and, more specifically, to transcend the mortality and decay associated with the female body. Fetishizing the death of female bodies, depicting female sexuality in threatening terms, and, finally, transcending the female body altogether and reasserting male potency became the techniques through which Ransom and his associates could lay the foundation for a masculinist aesthetic easily distinguished from the romantic, sentimental, genteel, and, most importantly, feminine verses characteristic of earlier southern writing.

In rejecting the aesthetic principles they understood as the basis of most nineteenth-century southern literature, the Fugitives sought above all to create a thoroughly "Modern" body of poetry. Though the group engaged in heated debates over the merits of literary modernism, they generally agreed that their common goal was the creation of poetry that readers would recognize as antithetical to the "moonlight and magnolia" tradition. Idealized references to the lush bounty of the plantation would be replaced by cynical descriptions of life in industrialized cities.[5] Adoring references to ethereal feminine beauty and virtue would give way to detached and even sarcastic descriptions of decaying and corrupt female flesh. And finally, descriptions of contented, faithful black companions whose hardworking devotion made possible the flowering of a great civilization would be replaced by allusions to the ancient origins of Anglo-European civilization in the Greek, Roman, and medieval past. Despite their admitted goal of forging a new literary tradition in the South, more often than not the Fugitives employed these so-called new themes to achieve old ends. Banishing African Americans from the poetic landscape merely served as another means of reinforcing the centrality of Anglo-European culture. Replacing adoring descriptions of feminine beauty and virtue with misogynistic references to female treachery underscored both the centrality of male consciousness and the need for reclaiming masculine sovereignty and potency. Fetishizing the death of women and linking female sexuality to decay functioned as a means of easing latent anxieties regarding the feminization of southern literary culture, which, as Tate frequently noted, had for too long been dominated by women writers (Donaldson, "Gender, Race, and Allen Tate" 492–93). And though Ransom and Tate abandoned the simplistic aesthetics of the plantation landscape, as Agrarians they would later adopt the image of the antebellum South as emblematic of the glorious Anglo-European past; the Old South finally came to represent for them a direct link to the ancient Western Tradition. Thus the terms upon which the group's aesthetic vision was built did not essentially differ from the "poetic principles" that served as the basis for nineteenth-century Southern Literature. The Fugitives, no less than their literary forebears, envisioned a poetic landscape founded on hierarchies of race, gender, and region.[6] To enter this literary and critical landscape, O'Connor would have to embrace an aesthetic tradition constructed on the contradictory premise that, while she might claim subjectivity on the basis of her whiteness, she would have to deny any form of subjectivity grounded in her femaleness.

As the Fugitives moved on to other pursuits, their work continued to suggest a preoccupation with maintaining the primacy of male subjectivity and with defining the boundaries of southern and broader American literary traditions. Of particular concern to Ransom was the possibility that errant female bodies and the writers occupying them might attempt to usurp the privileged position of the "masters." In a 1937 review of Elizabeth Atkins's *Edna St. Vincent Millay and Her Times,* his anxieties on this matter were almost palpable. Admitting his fear of women artists, Ransom began the review with the declaration that the female writer "fascinates the male reviewer but at the same time horrifies him a little too." Ransom linked this fear, which characterizes much of his Fugitive poetry, to "the same attitudes perhaps as are provoked . . . by generic woman in the flesh, as well as by the literary remains of Emily Dickinson, Elizabeth Barrett, Christina Rossetti, and doubtless, if we only had enough of her, Sappho herself." Thus his view of women writers was inextricably bound to his latent fears regarding female bodies and sexuality and the need to control and contain both.[7] Poetry was one vehicle through which to reassert dominance, and literary criticism was another. Just as Ransom's Fugitive poetry is concerned with making distinctions between female embodiment and male intellect, so too is his criticism. Woman, he declared, "lives for love," whereas man has "lapsed from it," preferring intellectual detachment instead ("Poet as Woman" 784). To Ransom, Millay, like other women poets, was at her best when she abandoned any pretense to intellectuality and wrote verses that give a "straightforward" and "objective record of a natural woman's mind." Such light and inevitably "ladylike" verses are, in the final analysis, the most that can be expected from the average woman poet. "I imagine," Ransom mused, "that there are few women poets for whom this is not so, and it would be because few are strict enough and expert enough to manage forms, in their default of the intellectual disciplines" (801–2). In these assertions regarding the inferiority of the female intellect, Ransom could diffuse the challenge posed not only by writers like Millay but by female intellectuals like Atkins as well. Because art is the proper concern of the "male adult intellectual," it is, Ransom argued, his "general level of experience" by which a poem should be judged (798, 785). Thus if a woman is to evaluate literature scientifically and objectively, she must assume a male persona and consider the ways in which a particular poem or work of prose measures up to the average "male adult intellectual's" experience (798). That this task might be somewhat difficult, if not impossible, only proves that women are generally lacking in artistic and intellectual sensibility.

As much as he hoped to use his method of "scientific" criticism to prove the inferiority of the female intellect, Ransom found it difficult to maintain his objectivity and keep his critical work free of his anxieties regarding the threat posed by female writers. His review of Millay's work is peppered with lapses in his usually rigorous critical standards, as he resorts to such unsupported statements as "Miss Millay is rarely and barely very intellectual, and I think everybody knows it" and "cluck forth" is a "miscegenation, from which issue is unlikely" (786–88). By the conclusion of the review he succumbs finally to the circular logic at the heart of his theories regarding women writers and declares that Millay's inferior verses are the result of her "deficiency in masculinity" (797). His status as a "male adult intellectual" became the sole basis of his critical authority; if he pronounced a verse "weak," then it became weak. As a "male adult intellectual" disturbed by the audacity of "poetess" and critic alike, Ransom saw fit to undertake the admittedly "rather pretentious task of showing how a genuine Donne influence would have rejected or modified this sonnet." Willing to violate one of his most cherished principles as a critic—the sacred inviolability of the text— Ransom rewrote the final line of one of Millay's poems, changing "For age to invest in compromise and fear" to the apparently superior "For age to invest it, and in what but fear." Subsumed by his anxieties regarding the transgressive power of the female body and the artist occupying it, Ransom attempted, finally to erase both from the page altogether, replacing Millay's "womanlike" verses with his own, presumably more masculine, efforts (786– 88, 801–2). Erasure of the female became, finally, one of the governing forces behind Fugitive/Agrarian discourses on literature and literary criticism and functioned as perhaps the strongest influence on the development of O'Connor's aesthetic sensibilities.

As Ransom refined his theories concerning the nature of formal analysis and what would become the New Criticism, his latent anxieties regarding the female intellect and the female body continued to influence his thinking, as did his concerns about the state of southern manhood. In "Forms and Citizens" he drew an intriguing analogy between the artist's relationship to his "object" (i.e., art) and man's relationship to woman. In both instances, the mediating force in the relationship between man and object functions as what Ransom termed a "code." In art, formal structure serves as the mediating code, a function that in life is served by a highly developed system of manners. "The form actually denies [man] the privilege," Ransom explained, "of going the straight line between two points, even though this line has an axiomatic logic in its favor and is the shortest possible line. But the woman, contemplated in this manner under restraint, becomes a person and an aesthetic object; therefore a richer object." Here Ransom referred to the relationship between man and woman, but, interestingly, he made little distinction between woman and aesthetic object. Women, that is, function as objects whether the subject is man or artist; in either case, the appropriate female role is passive, inspirational. While women in primitive societies, where mediation between desire and action is virtually nonexistent, are subject to the unrestrained whims of men, women in civilized societies are, through elaborate encoding systems, elevated to the protected and venerated status of "individual objects" whose value rests on their ability to offer support to male endeavors. The parallels between women and art, Ransom assumed, will remain clear enough: the artistic "objects" found in the most advanced cultures are, under ideal conditions, the products of highly structured and complex codes ("Forms and Citizens" 62–63). Yet unlike Ransom's objectified and encoded woman, art exists as an object in itself. It is the *product,* not the vehicle, of creation; it exists in order to be interpreted, admired, and appreciated. Hence the need for a "new" criticism equipped to decipher and interpret the formal codes through which the true, or "civilized," artist mediates his vision.

Ransom's configuration of woman as art/object reveals the ways in which a metaphor he no doubt considered "natural" actually served in itself as a gendered "code." At the same time, his theory on the role of women in art reveals the ways in which his preoccupation with southern manhood inevitably seeped into his critical writing. To Ransom's understanding, societies where "manners prevail"—like his idealized version of the agrarian South—offered women and art alike a far higher status than they could enjoy in so-called primitive societies where man continues to exist in his "natural," unmediated state. In such a state, man, when desire comes upon him, is apt to "seize," "as quickly as possible," any woman who happens to appeal to him. If he "does not propose for himself the character of the savage, or of animal, but the quaint one of 'gentleman,' then he has the fixed code of his *gens* to remember, and then he is estopped from seizing [woman], he must approach her with ceremony, and pay her a fastidious courtship." Desire has not been abandoned but has instead taken a "circuitous road and become a romance." Ransom has thus placed women in so-called civilized societies on the proverbial pedestal where, "contemplated in this manner under restraint," they achieve unequaled status not as subjective beings but as "individual objects" sufficiently encoded, mythologized, and, ultimately, contained so as to inspire the art (and artist) produced only by the most advanced cultures (61–62). "Woman writer" thus became a contradiction in terms, an object claiming a subjectivity that nature denies her and from which civilization protects her.

Ransom's emerging critical theories depended upon male subjectivity and on the centrality of the male intellect. His "science" of criticism—systematic, structured, and objective—was antithetical to the intuitive and subjective forms of reasoning that have traditionally been associated with women. As Gilbert and Gubar argue, critical theories generally reinforced a trend among writers that had become common by the mid-twentieth century: the creation of literary movements that by virtue of their avant-garde elitism functioned as ad hoc men's clubs that could be dismantled and rebuilt whenever the perceived threat of female competition became too fierce (*No Man's Land* 154–56). Yet these "men's clubs," Ransom's theoretical musings suggested, had to be reestablished within the real walls of educational institutions before the "new," scientific critical endeavor would be allowed to flourish. Rather than continuing to promote "amateur" criticism, Ransom argued, "[c]riticism must become more scientific, or precise and systematic, and this means that it must be developed by the collective and sustained effort of learned persons—which means that its proper seat is in the universities" ("Criticism, Inc." 94). Thus the "men's club" Ransom and his colleagues were in the process of establishing would be protected from female encroachment by relying on an androcentric philosophical tradition (science) and by retreating to an institution where male dominance was sanctioned both by law and by tradition (the university). The institutionalization of literary criticism would eventually make possible the codification and dissemination of Fugitive/Agrarian theories regarding the nature of southern and American literary traditions and the role of women therein.

The practice of literary criticism functioned for Ransom, Tate, and their colleagues as more than the appreciation of a finely wrought poem. Criticism became, finally, the vehicle through which to assert authority within the culture at large as interpreters of the Word, which in all its forms was deified by New Critical theory. The "letter," Tate claimed, "the letter of the poem, the letter of the politician's speech, the letter of the law," remains the "one indispensable test of the actuality of our experience." Ransom's "male adult intellectual" and Tate's "man of letters" became the ideal figures for the task of interpreting the letter and its meaning in the modern world. Though the chief responsibility of the man of letters remains the "recreation and application of literary standards," he must use them in a way that is "more than literary." He must, in other words, work to "preserve the integrity, the purity, and the reality of language wherever and for whatever purpose it may be used" ("Man of Letters" 13–14).[8] Alluding to Ransom's "science of criticism"—the criticism necessary to interpret the concrete whole that fiction or poetry assumes—Tate concluded that language serves as the only vehicle through which experience can be measured. The highest calling, then, belongs to the masters of language, those able to forge mere words into the tangible, structured reality of a poem, thereby reconstituting language *as* reality. Men of letters throughout the modern world, Tate concluded, must reclaim their rightful place in society and assume a leading role in supervising the "culture of language." Though Tate's theories were somewhat ambiguous with reference to the precise relationship among literature, culture, and politics, he nevertheless assumed that power and authority would serve as the driving forces behind the man of letters' search for truth. Tate's man of letters, like Ransom's male adult intellectual, feared the emasculating potential of a changing cultural landscape, one in which the masters of language must defer to the rule of the marketplace. And Tate, no less than his modernist colleagues, identified the market, particularly the literary marketplace, with female domination (Donaldson, "Gender, Race, and Allen Tate" 492–93). In the "republic of letters" he and Ransom envisioned, the concept of a "woman of letters" would thus remain an anomaly. Instead, women—mistresses of the genteel tradition—would emerge as the figures who must be displaced in order for the man of letters to restore his lost authority. As "The Poet as Woman" made it clear, those women who intentionally stepped beyond the confines of this sphere and attempted to appropriate the claims to universality that writers like Ransom and Tate considered their birthright could expect to meet active, even hostile, opposition.

This lesson was not lost on O'Connor. As she entered graduate school and began the formal study of literary theory, she gradually came to the realization that to claim status as a woman writer was to label herself an inferior artist. Always a good student, she eventually learned that if she wished to distinguish herself as a serious artist, she must be careful to assume the persona of Ransom's "male adult intellectual": she no doubt understood that her literary reputation could only be enhanced if she adopted the masculinist aesthetic that characterized Fugitive/Agrarian poetry and criticism. Walter Elder's 1955 review of Eudora Welty's *The Bride of Innisfallen* and *A Good Man Is Hard to Find* offers an interesting example of the way in which these tactics would eventually work to enhance O'Connor's growing reputation as a bold and unique talent. Although Elder focused on each author's status as a "lady," he displayed greater admiration for O'Connor's "profane, blasphemous, and outrageous" work than for Welty's "delicate thread of reasoning" on "the trivial essence . . . of a single, sought emotion" (665, 661). And though Elder accused both "ladies" of redundancy, he admired O'Connor's "astonishing," and by implication more masculine, aesthetic, which he saw as transcendent of region (670). In his view, her clearly unladylike stories placed her securely above Welty, whose work was far too "delicate" to earn serious critical attention. Reviews such as these, along with O'Connor's experiences at Iowa—where the accolades and rewards seemed to coincide directly with the "de-feminization" of her work—must only have reinforced her awareness that her literary reputation depended upon her ability to keep her fiction free from the taint of femininity.

The Writer's Workshop, where she immersed herself in the precepts of New Critical theory and Fugitive/Agrarian aesthetics, provided O'Connor with the opportunity to study under the direction of leading figures of both movements. Not surprisingly, it was during her Iowa years that her work first began to reveal an acute self-consciousness with regard to her status as a woman writer. Aware that the stakes were high, she soon abandoned many of the subjects that had interested her in high school and college. The tone of these early manuscripts, for example, is playfully comic as she explored a wide range of female characters and experiences. Among her surviving high school drafts is a story about a woman named Mitzbeth Boldtower, who had a "phobea [*sic*]" of dancing, until she met a psychologist who told her she must dance with him. She agrees, strangles him afterward, and overcomes her phobia (File 2, OMC). Similarly, many of the female characters from O'Connor's surviving college manuscripts commit various acts of violence or fantasize that they will. The victims are men, mother figures, or children. In one story, for example, a third-grade teacher with a particularly rambunctious class decides she would like to slap her students, concluding that most theories on how to treat children are incorrect (Files 4i, 4h, 4g, OMC). Other college stories focus on women's domestic work or on the social world at the local beauty parlor (Files 4f, 4g, OMC). As incomplete as they are, these early manuscripts suggest that O'Connor enjoyed poking fun at male arrogance and that she remained sympathetic with women who rejected traditional roles and behavior. At this point in her development as a writer, O'Connor was also able to take the lives of her lady characters seriously, without the hostile and often punishing tone that pervades much of her published work.

O'Connor's first year at Iowa was spent as a student of journalism; not until her second year of graduate school did she enroll in the Writer's Workshop. It is at this point that her manuscripts took a distinct turn, offering perhaps the most convincing evidence of the ways in which her graduate training and the Fugitive/Agrarian influence shaped the gender dynamics of her fiction. By this time she had become an avid student of the southern New Critics, and *Understanding Fiction* became her graduate school bible (Fitzgerald, "Chronology" 1241). O'Connor's writing during this period began to reflect a changing orientation, as she incorporated more male characters and male-oriented plot lines into her stories. Women, too, began increasingly to assume the role of Other, represented not through their own consciousness but through the eyes of men. Her first "penwoman"—a talentless amateur who strove for professional status—makes an appearance, as does a subtle sarcasm, which her narrator began to direct at lady characters. A few of O'Connor's unconventional women nevertheless remain, including Mary Fleming, who kisses chickens, and Caulda, who fantasizes that the chicken her mother has killed is her brother. Significantly, however, Caulda assumes the role of punished upstart who populates so many of O'Connor's later stories, as her mother warns her that an approaching man is really "Death" (Files 8–11, OMC). Moving further from the enclosed female world of her college years, O'Connor was becoming increasingly aware of the masculinist ethic that pervaded the university as well as the literary theories and aesthetics to which she was drawn. At the same time, these early manuscripts, which she never incorporated into her published work, suggest that the more seriously she began to take the role of professional writer, the more reticent she became to reveal her identity as a woman. Her student manuscripts suggest a progression of sorts, as O'Connor gradually abandoned characters and plot lines she feared would brand her a penwoman and turned instead to material she hoped might earn her distinction as a serious artist.

Although these efforts may have generated a certain amount of personal conflict, on a professional level they were largely a success. Early in her tenure at Iowa, Workshop director Paul Engle took pains to bring her stories to the attention of visiting lecturers like Ransom and Warren and encouraged her to submit her work for publication. Thanks in no small part to Engle's interest and encouragement, O'Connor was able to obtain a fellowship to continue her studies at Iowa following her graduation in 1947. That same year she was also awarded the Rinehart-Iowa fiction prize, which provided a $750 stipend in addition to a provisional contract with Rinehart. Though most of her earlier stories had been rejected, in 1947 *Mademoiselle* accepted "The Turkey," while the *Sewanee Review* published "The Train," which was to be the first chapter of her novel in progress. Recognition came from other quarters as well, and in early 1948 Workshop instructor Andrew Lytle, whose own writing O'Connor much admired, agreed to supervise the rest of her work on *Wise Blood* (Fitzgerald, "Chronology," 1240–42).

During the next few years O'Connor continued to enjoy the support and patronage of influential writers, critics, and institutions. Her fellowship at Iowa was extended for an additional year, and she received two consecutive invitations from the Yaddo Foundation to live at their Saratoga Springs artists' colony (1243). Such support not only provided her with the encouragement she needed to prevail despite her frequent doubts about her first novel but, more importantly, reinforced her growing awareness of the genderless direction her fiction must take. One of her graduate-level stories, "The Crop," offers a glimpse into this process at work. At first glance, it appears as though the story's protagonist, a writer named Miss Willerton, is herself a serious artist. The narrator describes her domestic routine and the ways in which she tries to keep it from infringing upon her work, to which she seems devoted. But gradually the narrator assumes an increasingly sarcastic tone, wryly noting, for example, that Miss Willerton finds "the hardest part of writing a story" is deciding on a subject (*CW* 732). Offering a glimpse into her interior thoughts, the narrator reveals Miss Willerton's intellectual and creative bankruptcy, as it occurs to her that bakers might make an interesting topic. They are, she thinks, so "very picturesque . . . Aunt Myrtile Filmer had left her four color-tints of French bakers in mushroom-looking hats." Deciding against bakers, she settles finally on sharecroppers. "Miss Willerton," the narrator explains in a mocking tone, "had never been intimately connected with sharecroppers but, she reflected, they would make as arty a subject as any, and they would give her that air of social concern which was so valuable to have in the circles she was hoping to travel!" (732–33). Here, then, the narrator establishes Miss Willerton as something less than a serious artist. She clearly has no interest in expressing the transcendent concerns of human existence and hopes at first merely to write a quaint story set in an exotic locale. Finally, though, she commits what may be the greater artistic sin and settles on a politicized subject that will offer her the opportunity both to make a "social statement" and to travel in the more fashionable literary circles. Thus Miss Willerton has violated a number of New Critical principles, using literature to explore the trivial, the political, and the "extra literary," with only the questionable goal in mind of impressing a trendy group of critics.

Miss Willerton, in fact, bears more than a passing resemblance to the dreaded penwomen O'Connor would write so disparagingly about in later years. Once she became more established as a writer, she often complained that one of the most unpleasant aspects of her work was the never-ending round of speaking engagements at women's clubs, where she was invited to address groups of aspiring authors. In 1957, for example, she offered a number of correspondents an entertaining and revealing account of the events that transpired at the Jamboree, an Atlanta symposium for amateur writers. O'Connor described the event as a farcical gathering of "Penwomen! Nothing but penwomen." Virtually no men were in attendance, with the exception of the man who ran the symposium ("he had to be there," she noted) and Mr. Meadows, an eccentric old "poet" who, much to O'Connor's delight, had been "sent I am sure to be a plague to the penwomen." He stole the floor away from the ladies at every turn, and when they attempted to analyze novels with vapid and clichéd comments, the old man stood up and admonished them with speeches regarding what Jesus had said to the adulterous woman. "Then," O'Connor explained, "I . . . saw the point: he hoped they might all be dammed [*sic*], all penwomen. His eyes were glittering with a secret wisdom. The women were growling under their breaths for him to sit down, but he held on until the bell rang. He was worth my trip" (1039–40). As her description of the events makes clear, O'Connor identified not with the other women in the audience but with Mr. Meadows, whose hostile and misogynist attitude only added to his appeal. In keeping with the critical principles to which she adhered, the man's hostility toward these obviously inferior "scribblers" rendered him a genuine artist, a "poet."

Characters such as Miss Willerton functioned as the vehicles through which O'Connor could distinguish herself from the penwomen who attended the lectures and symposia at which she spoke. On the surface, Miss Willerton shares a great deal in common with O'Connor—both are unmarried women writers with masculine first names who hope to write shocking fiction, and Miss Willerton frequently lectures to ladies' organizations. Yet these superficial parallels functioned as a means of calling attention to the many other ways in which O'Connor was really *not* like Miss Willerton or the ladylike characters who would follow her. In this sense Miss Willerton's character became a kind of blueprint listing all of the qualities to which penwomen are prone, alongside all of the qualities O'Connor herself not only avoided but openly disparaged. In this way Miss Willerton allowed O'Connor to define "what a woman writer is by delineating what she is not or cannot be" (Sarah Gordon, "'The Crop'" 115). For instance, Miss Willerton reads scandalous novels from which, the narrator snidely implies, she learns about the sexual habits of sharecroppers. Worse, she hopes herself to write the kind of racy bestsellers that epitomized Tate's genteel tradition and settles finally on a formulaic plot involving the "type of woman" who, because of her "wantonness," drives the protagonist to murder (734–35). But as the story progresses, Miss Willerton changes direction and, blurring the lines between fantasy and reality, enters the world of her own narrative. Killing the "wanton" woman, Miss Willerton assumes her place as the protagonist's wife and weaves a romantic tale about their struggles together and the eventual birth of their daughter. As her fantasy life testifies, Miss Willerton would really prefer to be a wife and mother. Indeed, by the end of the story she finds herself thoroughly "depressed" by all of the "trifling domestic doings" of the world and in particular by the couples and children she encounters in the grocery store (739–40). At forty-four years of age Miss

Willerton is no longer able to assume the role of wife and mother, and this dim realization, the narrator implies, is no doubt the true source of her depression. Here O'Connor suggests that penwomen like Miss Willerton not only violate literary standards but, in making the pretense to intellectual creativity, violate the laws of nature. As Miss Willerton's hackneyed fiction confirms, she is far better suited to domestic than to artistic pursuits. But instead of admitting her failure, she retreats into a fantasy world where her self-delusion remains untouched, and in this way she becomes a cliché of the lonely, unmarried professional woman.

In this satirical portrait of the life of a "lady writer," O'Connor could thus demonstrate to her instructors that she was aware of the deficiencies of the female intellect. By emphasizing the narrator's awareness of Miss Willerton's delusions and by outlining the numerous pitfalls to which penwomen might be prone, O'Connor could also suggest that through this knowledge she herself was in a position to overcome the problems associated with female authorship. Miss Willerton was simply the first in a long line of female characters through whom O'Connor could distinguish her own intellectual sensibilities as transcendent of the petty concerns of penwomen.

Throughout her career O'Connor continued to create ladylike characters who became the objects of the narrator's satire and contempt and who thereby served as the vehicles through which she could distinguish herself from penwomen. From the inane Mrs. Wally Bee Hitchcock to the domineering Sarah Ruth Parker, few of O'Connor's female characters are deserving of respect or admiration. And few of O'Connor's female characters manage to escape the fate they deserve. As David Havird argues, "it is the author's strategy . . . to knock these proud female characters down a notch . . . by forcing upon them, in a sexually humiliating and often violent way, the humbling knowledge that they are after all women" (15). Havird is referring here to the figurative rapes that occur in "Greenleaf," "Revelation," and "Good Country People," and he focuses for the most part on the theological basis of O'Connor's contempt for female pride. Yet his conclusions apply to most of her female characters, even those who escape violence or sexual humiliation. "The point in all these stories," argues Louise Westling, "seems to be that daughters must be punished by fathers for any kind of assertion or claim of authority" ("Fathers and Daughters" 118). Similarly, whenever the narrative emphasis appears to lie with a female character and her spiritual plight, it frequently shifts to focus instead on the male protagonist, thereby robbing female characters of the opportunity for genuine and meaningful salvation. The Grandmother in "A Good Man Is Hard to Find," for example, appears to serve as the story's protagonist. It is she, after all, who undergoes a profound spiritual crisis and transformation as she faces death at the hands of the Misfit. Yet the Misfit may nevertheless emerge as the true protagonist; violent as he is, he escapes the satire that the narrator directs at the Grandmother. Furthermore, his unfulfilled quest for faith is ultimately more meaningful than the Grandmother's traumatic encounter with grace, which is dismissed altogether when, after wiping her blood from his glasses, the Misfit announces that she "would of been a good woman . . . if it had been somebody there to shoot her every minute of her life" (153). As O'Connor explained, he, in fact, speaks for God in pronouncing judgment on the Grandmother, whose own story nearly becomes lost under the profound weight of her killer's crisis of faith (*HB* 389).

Similarly, in "Good Country People" the power of Hulga's awakening is diminished by the banality of the circumstances in which it occurs. Whereas the Grandmother's encounter with grace is traumatic, Hulga's is merely humiliating. Whatever positive or elevating lessons she might have learned from her experience are lost in the indignity of her realization that she, who holds a Ph.D. in philosophy, has been outsmarted by a country bumpkin. To add insult to injury, the aptly named Manley Pointer—Bible-thumping, leg-stealing con man that he is—arguably emerges as the more admirable character. Hulga's belief in "nothing," like the Grandmother's belief in Christ, is little more than false bravado. But like the Misfit, Manley Pointer has, as he triumphantly explains to Hulga, "been believing in nothing ever since I was born!" (293). Able to recognize and act upon the logic of his beliefs, he becomes the victor. Stealing her leg and appropriating the sense of identity with which she has invested it, Manley leaves Hulga both literally and figuratively paralyzed, herself reduced to nothing.

Julian's mother, of "Everything That Rises Must Converge," has likewise been robbed of both of her status as protagonist and the opportunity for salvation that accompanies it. Despite her obvious banality, she has more integrity than her son, whose hypocrisy appears a greater sin that his mother's nostalgia. While she speaks fondly of her childhood memories on the family's decayed plantation, Julian refuses to admit that he too longs for those bygone days at the old place. "It occurred to him," the narrator notes, "that it was he, not she, who could have appreciated it" (488). While his mother has cheerfully adjusted to their present life in a "dingy" neighborhood, Julian remains embittered at the idea that his family's circumstances have been so reduced. And though she has happily made sacrifices so that he could have a better life, Julian continues to delude himself into the mistaken belief that he had merely "permitted her sacrifices" because "her lack of foresight had made them necessary" (491). By all appearances it is his mother, and not Julian, who seems to have greater potential for spiritual growth. But instead she merely becomes the vehicle for her son's own salvation, as she literally crumples beneath the force of the black woman's blow and the social changes it represents. By the end of the story, Julian's mother has been rendered senseless, pitifully calling for her childhood nurse, while Julian has come to a profound realization that will culminate in his "entry into the world of guilt and sorrow" (500).

Characters such as Julian's mother, Hulga, and the Grandmother represent O'Connor's own anxieties regarding her ability to conform to the standards she had learned during graduate school. Aware that she might be mistaken for a writer of Miss Willerton's caliber, O'Connor assumed the persona of Ransom's male adult intellectual and studiously avoided writing stories that could be interpreted as the "objective record of a natural woman's mind." Instead, she created as much distance as possible between herself and her female characters, mocking them for their mistaken pride, chastising them for their domineering ways, forcing them to serve as the vehicles for male characters' salvation, or redirecting the narrative emphasis away from their plight and thereby negating the power of their epiphanic revelations. And like Ransom and his Fugitive/Agrarian colleagues, O'Connor developed an aesthetic that not only depended upon shocking female readers but upon fetishizing the containment, mutilation, and death of female bodies. The deformed, hideous, and mutilated bodies that populate O'Connor's fiction have been traditionally characterized as an essential component of her use of the grotesque.[9] "To be able to recognize a freak," she explained, "you have to have some conception of the whole man," and by depicting the body and the spirit it houses as less than whole, her fiction could "lean away from the typical social patterns, toward mystery and the unexpected" (*MM* 44, 40). For O'Connor, the grotesque functioned as a means through which to reflect what she saw as an age "in which religious feeling has become, if not atrophied, at least vaporous and sentimental" (161). Violence, she claimed, functioned similarly, as a means of "returning my characters to reality and preparing them to accept their moment of grace" (112). Yet these statements belie the other purposes to which violence and the grotesque could be put, namely, to mark the body—and through it the female—as the site of physical and spiritual decay and the spirit as the site of enlightenment and salvation. And by repeatedly containing the threat posed by the errant female body, O'Connor could ally herself with the spirit, with God, and, above all, with the male intellect.

O'Connor's fictional reenactment of the containment of wayward female bodies suggests that she shared with the Fugitive/Agrarians a latent fear of the subversive power of female sexuality and embodiment. Because western philosophical and religious discourses have rendered the female body an "ailing or dead figure . . . the cause and location of inhibitions," a woman who writes of the body in an affirmative way, argues Hélène Cixous, necessarily commits a subversive act. In her view the authentically female-sexed text—powerful enough to "shatter the framework of institutions" and "blow up the law"—is grounded in both the recognition and the celebration of the body unmediated by patriarchal discourse (284, 292, 281). O'Connor appears to have implicitly understood the transgressive nature of bodies unmarked by patriarchal discourse, and her published fiction depends upon an aesthetic in which the body—implicitly associated with the female—is ever the "ailing" and "dead figure" on which violence and punishment are enacted.

Sarah Ham, the "little slut" of "The Comforts of Home" whose physical self is "the very stuff of corruption," hints at the frightening power of the female body (*CW* 580). Her "intimate leer" and "appreciative grin" are enough to render the usually articulate Thomas mute, while her impudent challenges to his authority thoroughly emasculate him. As a result, he is made unfit to obey the voice of his dead father, a man who, as the sheriff reminds Thomas, "never let anything grow under his feet. Particularly nothing a woman planted" (578, 590). Thomas's passivity in the face of her power over him suggests the potential for female agency through the unmediated body. Sarah, for example, refuses to acknowledge her own corruption and in fact glories in the discomfort it poses for Thomas, while her sexual aggression in many ways subverts patriarchal discourse regarding female submission and chastity. Yet disturbing undercurrents in the text assure that the threat of Sarah Ham's body remains safely contained. Her history contains a long series of sexual abuses, first at the hands of her stepbrother and later at the hands of "perverts and sadists so monstrous that their acts defied description." The narrator, deferring to the authority of the family lawyer, dismisses this history with the statement that Sarah Ham's tale of "repeated atrocities was *for the most part* untrue" (577, emphasis added). Her potential for agency is thus contained first in the original act of abuse—as the reader learns that her "corruption" is hardly the result of her enjoyment of unmediated sexuality but is instead the product of her victimization under patriarchy—and then throughout the text as the narrator denies the meaning behind her history of abuse. When Thomas shoots Sarah with his father's gun—the very symbol of phallic power—he assures that her body and with it her subjectivity will not simply be contained, but erased. By the end of the story any potential threats posed by Sarah Ham have been subsumed by the sheriff's final thoughts as he remakes her into the "slut" who died while plotting to kill her lover's mother. Her body, target of abuse, object of fear and contempt, thus becomes the script upon which patriarchal fantasies and fears are enacted.

In "A Stroke of Good Fortune" Ruby's body similarly functions as the site of domination and containment, as she slowly comes to an understanding of the implications behind her husband's failure to uphold his promise to "take care of" birth control (193). Her pregnant body is anything but a source of pleasure for her. The narrator tells us that Ruby is "fat and beautiful," but she likens the symptoms pregnancy brings, including pains in her chest and stomach, nausea, breathlessness, and swollen ankles, to a state of disease, and she begins to fear she will die (188). In short, pregnancy has alienated Ruby from her body, forcing her to struggle against the many discomforts it imposes. Even a simple act like climbing the steps to her apartment becomes almost impossible as she finds herself overwhelmed by assorted pains and by feelings of nausea and breathlessness, which leave her with the impression that the steps are "going up and down like a seesaw with her in the middle of it" (187). Her interior physical space has been taken over by a force outside of her control: the "little roll" that Bill Hill has planted within her lies "resting and waiting, with plenty of time" to force Ruby to relinquish ownership of her body and submit to the forces of male authority represented by her husband, by Hartley Gilfeet, and by the doctor she hopes so much to avoid (196). Hartley's "nine inches of treacherous tin," which figuratively penetrate Ruby as she sits on the pistol he leaves on the stairs, remind her of the arbitrary nature of that authority and of her own vulnerability to it. At the same time, the menacing figure of the doctor reminds her that she will no longer be permitted to maintain authority over her own body. Proud of her ability to doctor herself, with "no bad sick spells, no teeth out, no children," Ruby believes that she "would have had five children right now if she hadn't been careful" (187). To her understanding, physicians operate as figures of male authority who would subject her to the unrelenting requirements of childbearing. By avoiding the doctor—during her single visit at the age of ten she managed to run away despite the three people restraining her—she has thus managed to carve out a physical space for herself unfettered by patriarchal discourse regarding female sexuality and reproduction. Thus her body has, until now, been a source of pleasure and good health, but it becomes clear to the reader that her pregnancy will force her, like her two sisters with four children apiece, to accept the indignities of finding herself repeatedly "jabbed at with instruments." In the end, she will have to submit to the phallic power of the doctor (186).[10] As Ruby gazes back into the "dark hole" from which she emerged, the reader understands that her fate has been decided and that she, like her mother, will get "deader and deader with every one of them" (196, 186). Her body, and with it the transgressive pleasures it once offered, have been safely contained.

For most of O'Connor's characters, pregnancy, perhaps the most visible expression of female embodiment, invariably serves as punishment. Tarwater's mother, "unmarried and shameless," is described as a "whore" who died a presumably well-deserved death giving birth to him after a car accident (355), while Carramae's continuous and clearly pathological vomiting is the frequent topic of conversation in "Good Country People." Whether women attempt to enjoy their sexuality outside the bounds of patriarchy, or whether they stay within the bounds of male authority, they remain subject to the same punishing forces—forces centered ultimately on the body. Compare, for example, the experiences of Manley Pointer and Hulga. Manley Pointer enjoys the freedom to roam the countryside, indulging his fetishes and enjoying sex without the fear of pregnancy—he does, after all, practice "safer sex." [11] His body is a source of pleasure as well as of power. Hulga's experience of embodiment, on the other hand, is, like Ruby's, one of alienation. The loss of her leg has provoked a strong sense of detachment from her body; when she is kissed for the first time she finds herself "pleased to discover that it was an unexceptional experience and all a matter of the mind's control" (278). Her attempted seduction of Manley Pointer—in reality an attempt to subvert patriarchal gender relations by assuming the dominant role over a younger lover—is swiftly punished as it becomes clear that she will never experience pleasure in her body. Thus Hulga's experience becomes emblematic of the fate suffered by most of O'Connor's women. While her body is a source of pain and suffering—the site on which Manley Pointer enacts his fantasy of domination and possession—her attempts to distance herself from it are equally futile. In O'Connor's literary landscape a woman with a Ph.D. in philosophy is an anomaly. Like Ransom's encoded woman, Hulga attempts to become the impossible: an object attempting to claim an intellectual detachment and subjectivity that her embodiment has rendered impossible. Without her leg, Hulga is trapped, just as Ruby finds herself trapped by her pregnancy. For O'Connor's women, the body itself is a trap; the "nasty companion" that ever reminds them of their inability to attain the spiritual transcendence that comes with intellectual detachment (Cixous 284).

Perhaps the image that best exemplifies O'Connor's fears regarding the potential for the female body to upset patriarchal order is that of the unnamed woman in *Wise Blood* whose naked body the young Haze pays fifteen cents to see. Lying in a casket, she is described as "something white" and "squirming," and the image that she provokes in Haze is that of a skinned animal (*CW* 35). The threat posed by this body has been contained on a variety of levels. The casket, for example, marks it not as life-giving but as the site of decay and death. Likened to an animal, the woman is dehumanized, and her status as an object of torture and abuse is alluded to when she is described as appearing "skinned." Yet even this vision of a female body robbed of subjectivity and agency is so powerful that it provokes the first of Haze's many episodes of self-punishment, wherein he subjects his own body to mutilation and pain in his attempts to attain transcendence and salvation.

Haze's continually performed drama of mutilation is characteristic of the fate suffered by many of the bodies that populate O'Connor's fiction, which comprises what Patricia Smith Yaeger terms a "poetics of torture" ("Flannery O'Connor" 187). Certainly neither Haze nor Tarwater nor children like Norton or Bishop are spared. Yet female bodies overwhelmingly remain the victims of violence in O'Connor's published fiction. More to the point, the death of female bodies is fetishized, as O'Connor struggled to adopt the aesthetic that had served as the organizing principle behind much early Fugitive poetry. The Grandmother's dead body, the bodies of Julian's mother and Mrs. May, Mary Fortune's beaten and dead body, Lucynell Crater's mute body, an object of exchange whose purpose is aptly symbolized by the red cherries that line the brim of her hat—these images function on a variety of levels as the means through which O'Connor could ally herself with a modern aesthetic founded in opposition to Poe's idealized depictions of the death of a beautiful woman. In subjecting female bodies to repeated acts of violence, O'Connor could also display her allegiance to the disembodied male intellect and, perhaps, work through some of her personal ambivalence regarding the illness that so visibly compromised her own physical integrity. As Michael Kreyling argues, critics have underestimated the role O'Connor's experience of embodiment played in the dramas of violence that characterize her fiction. In a culture in which the female is defined as body and the body as female, woman, argues Simone de Beauvoir, will necessarily become "imprison[ed]" by "subjectivity" and "circumscrib[ed]" by the "limits of her own nature," which will ultimately be defined by the "peculiarities" of possessing both a uterus and ovaries (43). Lupus no doubt forced O'Connor into an acute awareness of the "peculiarities" and "limits of her own nature." Even in illness, such limits manifested themselves in ways that were linked to her female self: the medical crisis that precipitated her death, for example, involved the surgical removal of a uterine fibroid. Given O'Connor's strong desire to transcend the constraints of female embodiment, this last manifestation of her illness must have been particularly unwelcome (Fitzgerald, "Chronology" 1255). The physically disabling effects of lupus—a disease that makes a "public spectacle of its victims, turning the body into a vivid display of disease"—no doubt enhanced her experience of embodiment as a trap from which there was no escape (Kreyling, introduction to *New Essays,* 5–6). While on the one hand her fictional deaths offered O'Connor the opportunity to display allegiance to the disembodied male intellect, on the other hand they likely offered her a means of asserting symbolic control over her own errant body.

Critics have found other kinds of liberatory potential in O'Connor's use of violence, attributing it to her protests against the racial order of her society or to the sadistic pleasures involved in creating what Yaeger refers to as a "masochistic machinery that gobbles up her readers" and "produces terrifying elegies for a system that lives but does not work" ("Flannery O'Connor" 204).[12] Such readings, however, become problematic when viewed in light of the erotic undertones at work in O'Connor's use of violence. A master of New Critical techniques that called for detailed, concrete representation as the proper foundation of a discrete artistic expression, O'Connor created fictional landscapes abounding in graphic, almost technicolor, images that borrow from the aesthetics of modern cinema. Most important, O'Connor's fiction depends upon the kind of subject positions characteristic of cinema, wherein the male viewer/subject is opposed to the female spectacle/object. Film narrative, argues Kaja Silverman, is most often organized around "a demonstration and an interrogation of the female character's castrated condition," or what might more generally be termed the female character's "difference." This demonstration and interrogation of difference "have as their ultimate aim the recovery of a sense of potency and wholeness for both the male character and the male viewer" and are meant simultaneously to alleviate the "anxieties of the male viewer" and heighten "those of the female viewer" (229). The function of the plot is to "rearticulate the existing symbolic order in ideologically orthodox ways" by questioning that order only to restore it at the end. In O'Connor's fiction, as in the horror film, female bodies represent the most prominent threat to the symbolic order. This order is ultimately restored through the enactment of eroticized violence, creating a textual landscape divided against itself, wherein a female author invites the male reader/viewer to share in the voyeuristic pleasure of watching as characters await their deaths/rapes, much in the same way that Ransom permits his audience of male readers to watch as his lady "young in beauty waiting" awaits her death/rape in "Piazza Piece." The moments leading up to Mrs. May's death in "Greenleaf," for example, are described in titillating detail as the narrator pictures her staring "at the violent black streak bounding toward her as if she had no sense of distance, as if she could not decide at once what his intention was." The reader, however, knows his intention and is permitted to view the figurative rape as the bull buries "his head in her lap, like a wild tormented lover" (*CW* 523). The viewer's subject position brings with it an implied power over Mrs. May; the reader knows death is inevitable but does nothing and in this voyeuristic passivity becomes complicitous in the violence inflicted on her body. As Laura Mulvey argues, voyeurism "has associations with sadism: pleasure lies in ascertaining guilt . . . asserting control, and subjecting the guilty person through punishment or forgiveness" (205). O'Connor herself repeatedly insisted that the violence inflicted on her guilty characters was an avenue for grace and, by implication, forgiveness, but she ignored altogether the sadistic pleasures to which these dynamics could give rise. Such pleasure is predicated on the potential it offers male readers/viewers to recover the sense of potency that is threatened by characters like Mrs. May. At the same time, the sadistic pleasures offered by O'Connor's fiction depend upon the heightened anxieties of female readers, ladies in particular.

In "A View of the Woods," Mary Fortune's eroticized beatings and death depend upon a similar kind of opposition between the male reader/viewer and the female object whose body becomes the signifier of difference. The reader watches as her grandfather "pounce[s]" on her from behind, grabbing the "tail of her dress" and lifting her up to him as she goes "suddenly limp in his arms," like the heroine of a romance novel. Mary Fortune may resist her grandfather's beatings, but the narrator informs us that she respects her father because "even with no just cause, he beat her" (*CW* 543). Deferring to the rules of authority at work under patriarchy, she willingly submits her body to her father but refuses to acknowledge her grandfather's claim. While she puts up a good fight against him, it becomes clear to the reader that she will be defeated in the end, and repeating the pattern, the moments leading to her death are described in painstaking detail. Here, too, the reader is permitted the voyeuristic pleasure of watching as the death/rape scene unfolds and the old man literally mounts Mary Fortune, "looking down into the face that was his own" with his hands "tight around her neck." Privy to the knowledge that Mary Fortune's body has been claimed and that death will follow, the reader shares in the power over her, watching as the old man smashes her head against a rock not once but three times (545).

These acts of violence are not merely meant to shock female readers but to exclude them altogether. Much as early Fugitive poetry was meant to appeal to a fraternity of male readers, the narrative gaze in these stories, like the gaze at work in modern cinema, "carries with it the power of action and possession" (Kaplan 31). More to the point, it depends upon a male angle of vision wherein the domination and mutilation of a female body is displayed for the voyeuristic pleasure of the reader/viewer. In this way, perhaps, O'Connor could on a personal level address her fears regarding the dangers posed by, and the impending death of, her own body. On a rhetorical level, these deaths functioned as the means by which she could simultaneously oppose herself to the aesthetics of nineteenth-century southern writing, display her own awareness of the problematic nature of female embodiment, and, finally, ally herself with the detached and transcendent male intellect. In short, O'Connor, like the Fugitive/Agrarians and the aesthetic they adopted, figured her artistic mission in opposition to the female, and in so doing she sought, like them, to reject the "hopelessly inflated oratory" of the South's genteel tradition. Her situation, however, was obviously complicated by her status as a woman occupying a diseased female body. To participate in an effort that was founded on the misogynistic premise that the female intellect was inferior and the female body a source of danger to the social order required O'Connor to find means of identifying against herself. Her female characters and the deaths they suffer served just such a purpose.

Throughout her career, O'Connor was rewarded—earning grants, fellowships, and critical acclaim—for writing fiction that relied on the masculinist aesthetics promoted by Fugitive/Agrarian and New Critical theory. Adopting an apparently genderless literary persona founded on opposition to the female, despite the conflicts such a strategy may have generated, no doubt represented a rational tactic given the gender politics at work. By contrast, the brief Fugitive career of Laura Riding offers an instructive account of the pitfalls facing female writers who, unlike O'Connor, assumed that the literary and critical movements forged by Ransom, Tate, and their associates would welcome or appreciate the presence of women artists.[13] Since *The Fugitive* served as much as a fraternity as it did a literary club, Riding's membership in the group is somewhat remarkable in itself. That her status as the lone female member generated such controversy—which continued well into the 1980s as Fugitive historians struggled to make sense of the episode—offers perhaps the earliest and most telling example of the extent to which the group remained troubled by the intrusion of women into their professional lives and unable to relate to women as intellectuals, artists, or colleagues. Indeed, their initial interest in her came not out of respect for her work but out of paternalistic concern for her well-being, and as it became increasingly clear that Riding was not willing to accept the paternalistic terms on which her membership in the group was based, Ransom, Tate, and their colleagues grew increasingly troubled by her sexuality and by her seemingly contradictory status as both woman and artist. Their opinion of her work diminished while their anxieties regarding her sexuality increased in direct proportion to her demands to be treated as a colleague worthy of equal consideration. Ultimately the group transformed Riding from a "poor little woman" in need of care and concern to a Jezebel intent on using her feminine wiles to seduce and then divide the "Brethren": Riding-the-damsel-in-distress was deserving of assistance but Riding-the-Jezebel threatened the very foundation on which *The Fugitive* had been established. In short, her association with the group brought to the surface a number of gender-based tensions and anxieties and forced Ransom, Tate, and their associates to make explicit the rules that would subsequently govern Fugitive/Agrarian theories regarding the relationship between women and art.

The tensions that lay at the heart of the group's relationship to Riding were apparent from the start of their association with her. Despite their public claims regarding the merit of her work, the Fugitives held ongoing and frequently heated debates regarding her qualifications for membership. That she received the attention she did was due in no small part to the efforts of Tate, who prided himself on his knack for "discovering" new poets. Moreover, as his correspondence to Donald Davidson suggests, Tate was hoping to outsmart rival editor Harriet Monroe by publishing Riding's work first (*LC* 97–100). And perhaps most importantly, as Fugitive historian John L.

Stewart has noted, Tate and his colleagues sought to reward Riding for her devotion to the group. When the journal was experiencing financial difficulties in 1924, according to Stewart, Riding undertook the "pathetic, funny, and unsuccessful" project of selling subscriptions to wealthy patrons in Louisville, Kentucky. "Taking all this and her winning the Nashville Prize into account," he concludes, "the Fugitives asked her to attend a meeting" (82). Stewart—whose history is based largely on interviews with former members of the group—attributes Riding's admission to factors other than her literary talent. His and other accounts suggest that paternalistic gratitude and concern for her well-being seem to have been the most prominent motivations for sponsoring her membership.

Using much the same language he would later apply to O'Connor and her work, Ransom wrote Robert Graves to ask his assistance in getting a volume of Riding's poems published. Referring to her as a "brilliant young woman, much more so in her prose and conversation even than in her verse," he noted that due to her "foreign (perhaps Polish Jew?)" heritage, the "English tradition is not native to her." As a result she "cannot to save her life . . . achieve her customary distinction in the regular verse forms" and "tries perhaps to put more into poetry than it will bear. With these misgivings I will go as far as you or anybody in her praise." Hardly the most enthusiastic recommendation—Ransom concluded by noting that on a personal level Riding made for very "intense company." To their credit, Ransom and his associates saw in Riding a fellow poet suffering from the neglect of an ignorant reading public and from the humiliation of "doing literary hack work" (*SL* 144). But Ransom's views were colored by his paternalism, which dictated that, as a woman, she was deserving of his assistance but not necessarily of his endorsement as a critic. His concern centered as much on her well-being as it did on her reputation as a poet, a matter about which he took no pains to hide his "misgivings."

Tate shared Ransom's gentlemanly concern for Riding. "She will be thrilled over Graves' liking for her work," he wrote Davidson with excitement. "I pass on the news. I feel almost paternal!" (*LC* 98). But his initial enthusiasm seems to have been influenced as well by his sexual attraction to her. Interestingly, in Tate's absence—he remained for a brief time her most devoted patron—the group decided that they could not publish any of her latest verses. "This batch of poems was," Davidson wrote Tate, "very diffuse. If these are the poems Harriet Monroe rejected, I can't say that I blame Harriet. Don't my boy let your admirations color your aesthetics, which I thought you were constantly submitting to a regular litmus test!" (107). Davidson's comment suggests that his fellow Fugitives dismissed Tate's admiration for Riding's work as the result of nothing more than sexual attraction. The sexual tensions between Tate and Riding gradually altered the group's perception of her, as they increasingly grew unable to separate her art from her sexuality. "Undoubtedly," Ransom admitted, "we were rather absurd in the way we received Laura at Nashville—prim, formidable, and stiff." Riding, he acknowledged, was really just a "poor little woman" looking only for "human companionship." Instead she received a "rather formal welcome," which, according to Ransom, she somehow misinterpreted as the result of "suppressed libidinous desires." What Riding failed to understand, Ransom concluded, was that the group was "open to literary relationships but not to personal" (*SL* 151). Admittedly uncomfortable with Riding's presence and concerned that she would demand a "personal" relationship with the group, Ransom, Tate, and subsequent Fugitive historians have constructed a history of the episode whereby Riding's sexuality emerged as a direct threat to the group's brotherly sense of camaraderie. "They meant no discourtesy," argues Paul Conkin in his Fugitive history, "but as an established in-group were not about to capitulate to her charms" (22). According to other histories, most of which draw on the Fugitives' own version of events, Riding—a "shrewd, avant-gardist, brittle and more than a little superficial" woman—"overstayed her welcome at the hospitable Frank home" and in the process deliberately created a rift in the group (Bradbury 79–80; Stewart 82). She "misinterpreted their motives, became disillusioned, plagued the final editors with too many sloppy poems, and by gossip in 1927 almost, and perhaps deliberately, tried to fan a new fight between Tate and Ransom" (Conkin 22). Through this narrative of events, originated by Ransom and Tate and subsequently legitimized by Fugitive historians, the group managed to transform Riding from the "little woman" in need of assistance to the Jezebel whose sexuality and malicious gossip threatened to upset their carefully constructed sense of fraternity.[14]

"I think," Ransom declared, "I have a sort of formula to explain" Riding's actions. "She is," he noted in a letter to Tate, ". . . in such obvious search of a protector and master" that she decided "it would be a thrill" to have the two of them "fighting for the prize, which was none other than Laura." Unable to make up her mind, he continued, she first sided with Ransom and then with Tate and yet remained "committed like a natural woman to a profession of intrigue and coquetry all the same." As "men capable of making up our minds for ourselves," Ransom continued, it was time for Tate and him to register their protest. "I hate to abuse a small woman," he concluded, "but I won't accept the role she has thrust upon me." What he failed to note here is that he and Tate had had a long history of dispute—they had recently had an extended falling-out over the merits of Eliot's poetry—yet neither those directly involved in the controversy, nor those who have attempted histories of it, have seriously entertained the possibility that Ransom, Tate, or both had actually made the critical remarks that generated this particular rift. As Ransom himself noted, Fugitive meetings were founded upon criticism, and he and Tate frequently engaged in heated arguments that led to extended disputes. Moreover, this event is unique in Fugitive history. Other "Visitors" had been asked to join the group, including Robert Penn Warren, a young man noted for his often volatile personality, yet none had provoked such strong discomfort and controversy.[15] Clearly the real issue was Riding's gender, not her personality. Opening the pages of the journal to women was one matter, but opening the doors of the Frank home—a sanctuary of male camaraderie—was a boundary the Fugitives were not prepared to cross. By defining the situation in the language of gendered oppositions—"men capable of making up our minds for ourselves" versus a "natural woman" given to "intrigue and coquetry"—Ransom, Tate, and subsequent historians have revealed the ways in which this episode brought into stark relief the basis upon which the group had been established. Claiming the principles of mutual "respect," "uncompromising purity," "heroism," and "philosophical ideas," the Fugitives would define themselves against the treacherous "coquetry" and "intrigue" of women like Riding (*SL* 150–51).

Had Riding remained within the bounds of the paternalistic formula Ransom and Tate had laid out for her and accepted her role as a "poor little woman" in need of their assistance, she may possibly have managed to enjoy their continued approval and support. In the role of "woman poet" demanding equal status as both artist and intellectual companion, however, she was a threat. Indeed, the correspondence between Ransom and Tate suggests that as Riding's requests for critical endorsements by the group increased, so too did their impatience with her. As long as she refused to play the role of "child" to their "protector" and "master," she could remain assured that her literary reputation would suffer in their hands. Indeed, by 1927 Tate himself, always her most ardent defender, had considerably reevaluated his opinion of her work. Riding's most recent volume of poetry, Tate wrote, contains a number of "interesting specimens of her work." He continued the review in a subtly sarcastic tone:

> If the reader, already familiar with her almost innumerable poems scattered in the course of the last few years through the magazines, find his own preferences not amply represented, he must reflect that Miss Gottschalk will not be held to the narrow bounds of a "first volume." At the outset of a career that must be, in the end, a brilliant success—for Miss Gottschalk, even Miss Gottschalk, performs those emotional revelations which give poetry by women much of its charm, if not its value—at the outset of her career, she has completed a bulk of poetry which a more finical artist might envy at middle age.

As far as Tate was concerned, Riding's emotionalism, along with her literary promiscuity—her lack of loyalty to *The Fugitive* and her indiscriminate bartering of "innumerable" poems to any journal that would have them—assured that her status as genuine poet would be revoked. In sacrificing quality to quantity, he implied, Riding revealed her true nature: *"even"* she, as "ambitious" as she is, cannot transcend her gender and in the end creates verses best distinguished by the taint of her femininity and her wayward sexuality (*Poetry Reviews* 54–56). In Tate's eyes, when Riding refused to accept the paternalistic terms on which their professional relationship was founded, she renounced any claim she might have had to the title "artist" and deserved instead relegation to the rank of "woman poet"—a literary trumpet with no regard for the sanctity of the Word. The rules had been made clear: women should strive at all costs to suppress any "feminine impurities" that might taint their art, but at the same time they should be prepared to accept the inevitable truth that, in the end, their art would always be defined by those very same impurities.

Women like Riding clearly provoked anxiety among Ransom, Tate, and their associates, an anxiety that continued to echo through their subsequent literary and critical endeavors. Yet it would be misleading to deny the contributions the Fugitive/Agrarians made in advancing the careers of a number of female writers. In fact, the group used their influence as critics and as editors of major journals to promote the work of, among others, Katherine Anne Porter, Eudora Welty, Caroline Gordon, and, later, Flannery O'Connor. What might account for this apparently contradictory behavior? First, although the Fugitive/Agrarians increasingly viewed their literary endeavors as largely transcendent of region, they continued to recognize that southern writers in particular were often subject to lingering prejudices regarding the provinciality and general inferiority of the region's literature. No doubt the group understood that promoting the work of as many talented southern writers as possible, male and female alike, represented a benefit to them all. Second, the Fugitive/Agrarian circle of friends and associates was extensive and included not simply official members of both groups but a considerable number of other writers as well. Southern writers of the period formed close-knit professional ties and friendships, in part as a response to the recognition that mutual assistance was the best defense against a sometimes hostile literary establishment, and in part as the result of a shared sense of experience and identity. Ransom, Tate, Lytle, and Warren would likely have considered it a violation of simple good manners not to have lent their assistance to fellow southerners like Porter, Welty, and Gordon.

At the same time, it is important to recognize that Fugitive/Agrarian patronage of women writers was extended with specific limitations. The paternalism that characterized the group's relationship to Riding continued to prevail in their relationships with other women writers as well. That is, Ransom, Tate, and their associates for the most part preferred assuming the role of benefactor rather than colleague in their professional relationships with women, and like other male intellectuals and artists of the era, the Fugitive/Agrarians tended to view the artistic efforts of women through the lens of various gender biases. Though Ransom, for example, considered O'Connor a "first-rate" writer who deserved his support, he remained hesitant to recommend her for a *Sewanee Review* fellowship after she had been previously awarded one from the *Kenyon Review*. He explained his reasoning on the matter to Monroe K. Spears. "I think mighty well of O'Connor," he wrote, "and I'm told she needs the help." Adding the same sort of qualifications he applied in Riding's case, he admitted that he was "a little bit jealous on behalf of democratic principle of scattering our benefits." Though he felt "tempted" to make an exception, particularly if it meant O'Connor would be "looked after," Ransom felt neither "entitled," nor "obliged" to "form an opinion, which might be worrisome." In any case, he concluded, "it's really up to you" (*SL* 370).[16] As his letter suggests, Ransom preferred to view O'Connor as a young woman in need of his assistance, rather than as a junior colleague who might be deserving of extraordinary recognition. As far as her work itself was concerned, he preferred not to reveal his opinion, which was not particularly favorable (374).[17] Instead, he made his decision based on his personal concern for her well-being, which suggests that he could envision himself as her benefactor but not as her mentor or potential colleague.

Ransom's letter is not an isolated example of the ways in which gender influenced Fugitive/Agrarian relationships with women writers. A crucial step in the canonization process involves critical recognition. Writers' reputations depend not simply on publication but on the attention generated by journal essays. The mere fact of having received critical notice—whether positive or negative—confers a certain level of distinction generally denied writers whose work is deemed unworthy of attention. A review of the journals edited by the Fugitive/Agrarians reveals an interesting pattern. Willing, as editors, to publish stories by women, the group remained reluctant, as critics, to offer those writers the same attention. In their roles as editors, for example, Ransom, Tate, and Warren published relatively few critical pieces on women writers; far more numerous are short stories and other works of fiction by women. The same does not hold true for male colleagues, including the Fugitive/Agrarians themselves, southerners such as William Faulkner, and other contemporaries such as T. S. Eliot, who consistently received critical attention under the group's sponsorship.

Literary historians have for the most part overlooked these trends. Gordon Hutner, for example, argues that under Ransom's editorship the *Kenyon*

*Review* was quite progressive in its editorial slant. "Committed as Ransom was to the poets and theorists that the New Critics favored," Hutner contends, "he also brought forward proletarian writers, reviews of Latin American authors, pieces by Marshall McLuhan, Erwin Panofsky, Walter Gropius, and studies of Bertolt Brecht, Henry Miller, Frank Lloyd Wright, and Jean-Paul Sartre" (105). Yet Hutner is forced to admit that the journal's record was "as sorry as any other mainstream publication in apprehending the claims of minority cultures, especially blacks," and that Ransom exhibited a certain "blindness . . . that today we would see as class-, race-, and gender-bound" (108–9). A review of the contents of the journals Ransom and his associates edited bears out this last point. The vast majority of critical essays appearing in the *Kenyon Review,* the *Sewanee Review,* and the *Southern Review* were written by male critics about male writers. The *Kenyon Review*'s record is in many ways typical. Of the journal's regular contributors—R. P. Blackmur, F. O. Mattheissen, Lionel Trilling, Ransom, Tate, and Warren—only Warren occasionally authored a piece on a female writer. And although Ransom, as the journal's editor, did make some room for fiction by women, the overwhelming majority of the stories and poems he published were written by men. Volume 10 (1949) offers a representative illustration of these trends. During that year twenty critical essays appeared; although two were written by female critics, Vivienne Koch and Hannah Arendt, none were written about female authors. Of the twenty-four collections of poetry and short stories that appeared, only three were written by women.

This pattern is repeated in both the *Sewanee Review* and the *Southern Review.* During the three-year period of Tate's editorship at the *Sewanee Review,* for example, no work on female writers appeared at all. Instead, the majority of essays concerned a core group of writers: T. S. Eliot, F. Scott Fitzgerald, Henry James, Edgar Allan Poe, William Shakespeare, Ransom, Wallace Stevens, and Warren. Like Ransom, Tate also favored certain critics. Though he published a total of seven essays by women during his tenure at the journal, the vast majority were written by critics such as John Peale Bishop, Cleanth Brooks, Jacques Maritain, Marshall McLuhan, Lewis Mumford, Ransom, Warren, Richard Weaver, and Yvor Winters. As coeditor of the *Southern Review,* Warren provided a more hospitable forum for fiction by female writers, yet he also neglected to publish more than an occasional essay about a female author. The reasons for such neglect, to be certain, are numerous, and many were no doubt beyond the control of individual editors. Critics, male and female alike, had been trained to favor the work of male writers, and submissions on female writers were likely few and far between. Moreover, within the broader context of twentieth-century American literary culture, these trends are hardly unique. Yet these trends nevertheless offer intriguing evidence of the subtle gender biases that prevailed within southern literary culture and suggest the ways in which O'Connor's decision to fashion herself as an "unladylike" writer represented a calculated strategy dictated by a particular set of circumstances. In short, though Ransom, Tate, and Warren tolerated and may have even solicited fiction by women, they made little or no effort to promote critical consideration, and with it the canonization, of female writers.

In their own roles as critics, the group devoted the bulk of their attention to male writers. Moreover, there exists a qualitative difference in the criticism the Fugitive/Agrarians offered on male and female writers. Following a widely accepted New Critical practice, Ransom, Tate, Lytle, and Warren employed a system of "ranking"; ability was measured according to how an individual writer compared to others in the same "class." As Ransom had explained in "Criticism as Pure Speculation," "the intent of the critic may well be . . . first to read his poem sensitively and make comparative judgements about its technical practice" (129). Brooks and Warren explained the philosophies behind this principle in the preface to the second edition of their widely distributed anthology, *Understanding Fiction.* In this text, on which O'Connor had relied so heavily during her graduate studies, Brooks and Warren advocated the use of what they termed an "inductive method," by which "concrete cases" may be "investigated and interpreted and compared with each other." By "understanding the functions of the various elements which go to make up fiction and by understanding their relationships to each other in the whole construct," they concluded, "it is possible for students to understand a given piece of fiction." As teachers, critics, and editors, the Fugitive/Agrarians, following the precepts of New Critical theory, worked under the assumption that the internal "structure" of a given piece of literature could be objectively interpreted and evaluated. Thus, the authors of *Understanding Fiction* explained, they deliberately included "inferior" stories in their collection so as to provide students with the opportunity to compare "minor" writers with "major" ones and, presumably, to learn to arrive at the appropriate conclusions concerning a given writer's "rank" (xiii–xiv).

Critics of the period tended to assume that a given writer's rank was self-evident, when in fact rank was more often than not determined by the application of critical theory and the practice of interpretation. "Major" writers, for example, were compared to the likes of William Shakespeare, John Donne, or Henry James. These comparisons would, in turn, become an indication of "major" rank. By contrast, "minor" writers were faintly praised for their technical ability, dismissed for their lack of objectivity and proportion, or accused of promoting "social science" under the guise of literature. In the hands of the Fugitive/Agrarians, as essays by Robert Penn Warren and Andrew Lytle suggest, women like Katherine Anne Porter, Eudora Welty, and Caroline Gordon naturally emerged as "minor" writers whose significance rested not on any qualities they may have shared with the "masters" but on technical ability.[18] Relying on adjectives such as "sensitive," "consistent," "scrupulous," "detailed," "precise," "subtle," and "delicate," Warren and Lytle managed to brand Porter, Welty, and Gordon as talented but nevertheless minor writers whose work lacked the force and breadth of truly "great" literature. Since such adjectives denote traditionally feminine, generally passive qualities, they served at the same time to allude to a fundamental inadequacy that in itself implicitly justified the relegation of women writers to the rank of "minor."

As Warren elaborated in a 1969 interview, the quality that perhaps best distinguished writers like Porter, Welty, Gordon, and O'Connor was a lack of power and breadth, points he illustrated by emphasizing the size of their work. Repeating a commonly held critical view that he and his colleagues were, in part, responsible for perpetuating, Warren concluded that women were generally at their best writing "novelettes" and short fiction. For instance, Porter's *Ship of Fools* is, he explained, "a big important book, but . . . its powers are powers of a series of novelettes imbedded in it. . . . It is faulty, but I was expecting it; the end is not the end of a novel. You've had some wonderful novelettes on the way, I think." Realizing the implications of such comments—that the small and feminine diminutive, "novelette," referred

by definition to a form inferior to the larger and, presumably, more masculine "novel"—Warren attempted to qualify his views by admitting that Porter "might probably" have two of the "top twenty novelettes." The same
holds true, he continued, for Welty, Gordon, and O'Connor. "I think Eudora's best stories are at the top level," he remarked, concluding that she is
among the few "natural short fiction writers." Similarly, "Caroline Gordon
has two beautiful stories," while O'Connor also deserves to be ranked "in
that group of the best short-fiction writers. She's written some beauties.
Much better than her novels" ("Interview in New Haven" 133–35). Relying
again on gendered adjectives to describe their work, marking it diminutive,
feminine, and thereby inferior, Warren both summarized and reified the
critical views on Porter, Welty, Gordon, and O'Connor. As far as he and his
colleagues were concerned, femininity in itself signified a certain "lack" that
by definition prevented women writers from assuming "major" status. Porter, for one, was aware of the pejorative meaning behind these terms. She
asked readers of her collected stories to "please" refrain from calling "my
short novels *Novelettes,* or even worse, *Novellas.* Novelette is classical usage
for a trivial, dime-novel sort of thing; Novella is a slack, boneless, affected
word that we do not need to describe anything. Please call my works by their
right names . . . short stories, long stories, short novels, novels" (*Collected
Stories* vi).

In sum, though the Fugitive/Agrarians were generous in their support
of certain female writers, the group's patronage was extended without significantly violating the hierarchies that characterized prevailing discourses,
both southern and nonsouthern, on literature and critical theory. Southern
women writers, like their colleagues in modernist circles, were thus caught in
a double bind, earning critical praise only when their fiction displayed the
"masculine" qualities that the Fugitive/Agrarians admired. When they failed
to meet these standards, women were, as Jones and Donaldson have argued,
relegated to minor status.[19] Not all writers necessarily recognized gender discrimination as such, but the logic at the heart of the gender issues of the
period essentially left O'Connor and other women writers with two choices:
remain content with second-rate status or work to create an apparently genderless fictional landscape in the hopes of earning more serious critical
attention.

But gender was not the only factor that influenced O'Connor's aesthetic development. As a southerner she was forced to confront the issue of race as well. Here, too, she looked to the conservative vision of southern culture that had been promulgated by Ransom, Tate, and their associates. Though she may not have read the volume until the final year of her life, she did admire *I'll Take My Stand* as the product of "real minds" who genuinely understood the South (*HB* 566). The text itself was not as much of an influence as were the underlying premises on which it was based, which were themselves central to defining white southern intellectuals' conceptualization of the racial issues and questions of the day.

During their early Fugitive period, Ransom, Tate, and their colleagues had simply hoped to transcend racial issues altogether. As the scarcity of references to African Americans and the lack of *Fugitive* poems by blacks suggest, the group considered blackness too uncomfortably linked to the nineteenth-century plantation tradition.[20] Yet in choosing to focus instead on Anglo-European culture, they helped codify the long-standing view— central to the work of white southern historians such as Ulrich B. Phillips— that white consciousness and experience were dependent upon the marginalization and oppression of blacks. African Americans, Tate argued in "The Profession of Letters in the South," were, in fact, responsible for the deplorable state of the arts in the antebellum South. An "alien" peasantry, African Americans acted as "a barrier between the ruling class and the soil" and thereby as an impediment to the rise of an artistic tradition (525). Moreover, slavery and the burdens it imposed on white southerners utterly drained the region of its artistic impulses. The only choice, Tate acknowledged, had been for whites to close ranks and exclude African Americans from definitions of southern identity altogether. "When one is under attack," he wrote, "it is inevitable that one should put not only one's best foot forward but both feet, even if one of them rests upon the neck of a Negro slave" ("Southern Mode" 589). Just as Ransom's New Criticism would influence a generation of literary critics, Tate's theories on the role of slavery in the development of (white) southern identity influenced a generation of literary historians. Louis P. Simpson, for example, argues that "in its politicization the antebellum Southern literary mind did not undergo an experience of alienation from its own—the Southern—society; and lacking this experience failed to experience the reaction to modernity—the deep discontent with modern civilization—which informs and gives power to the modern writer" (38). Because of its reliance on a slave economy, the antebellum South, in other words, had not yet adopted the premises of bourgeois individualism and therefore had not yet experienced the "alienation" from the past that serves as the driving force behind modern literature. In a similar vein, Louis D. Rubin argues that white southerners' persistence in defending an institution they instinctively knew to be evil required an effort of the will that left neither the time nor the inspiration required to produce a healthy artistic tradition. While Simpson and Rubin identify different reasons behind the centrality of slavery—and the political effort expended in defending it—both nevertheless followed Tate's lead in viewing the white, male, and largely upper class southern experience with slavery as central to an understanding of the culture and its artistic traditions. Implicit in Tate's history and those that would follow is the understanding that the South is, by definition, white.[21]

Tate's conceptualization of southern racial relations owed its genesis in large part to the collaborative effort that would culminate in *I'll Take My Stand*. The controversies that emerged as Tate and his colleagues developed the series of essays offer a number of insights into the early development of Fugitive/Agrarian discourse on race. Just as the Fugitives had hoped to transcend race, Tate's first proposal for the Agrarian manifesto included every conceivable aspect of southern culture but made no mention whatsoever of the "negro question" (*LC* 232).[22] It was Davidson himself, the most openly racist member of the group, who first proposed including the topic. His reasons were centered on his hope that an essay on race could help forge a sense of common cause among white southerners and thereby further the Agrarian agenda. "The Southern people," he noted, "are not actually united on anything these days—except the Negro question, and they do not know each other as well as they used to. . . . Too bad that the second Ku Klux Klan came along when it did. We shall have to be careful not to fall into that slough" (237). Echoing Phillips's theories regarding the link between white southern identity and the oppression of blacks, Davidson hoped to use the proposed volume to restore what he nostalgically saw as a lost unity. When Warren produced an essay that did not conform to his hard-line views,

Davidson was absolutely "shocked" and eventually attempted to prevent its publication. He wrote Tate that he believed it was "not very closely related to the main theme of the book," nor did "The Briar Patch" do justice to "our ideas as I understand them." Davidson concluded with the statement that he was "inclined to doubt whether RED ACTUALLY WROTE THIS ESSAY!" (251). Fellow contributor Frank Owsley, he added, agreed with his assessment. When Tate replied that he supported Warren, Davidson became somewhat exasperated, as he explained in an emotional letter to Tate. "I must beseech you, good friend Allen, for God's sake to stick your head under the pump; or take calomel and castor oil and go to bed to ponder on your immortal soul; or do something else to revive your practical sense, which seems to be getting clogged up with foreign vapors" (253).

The controversy regarding Warren's essay was eventually subsumed by the more divisive controversy regarding the book's title and its allusions to white southern nationalism.[23] Concerned that the book's publication would be delayed by these disputes, Davidson, the general editor, refused to change the title but reluctantly allowed Warren's essay to appear.[24] The irony at the heart of these various controversies lay in the fact that, in reality, the Agrarians were in agreement regarding the book's fundamental philosophical orientation. That is, they shared the common, though implicit, understanding that blacks, whether or not segregation remained intact, served as the signifier through which white southern identity was constituted. Explained Warren, "If the Southern white man feels that the agrarian life has a certain irreplaceable value in his society, and if he hopes to maintain its integrity in the face of industrialism or its dignity in the face of agricultural depression, he must find a place for the negro in his scheme." The importance of the "negro question," in other words, lies in its relationship to the "problems" facing the white South. Whereas Davidson maintained that white southern culture was best measured by the extent to which it was capable of effacing the presence of blacks altogether, Warren argued instead that if the "white man" intended to preserve the agrarian basis of southern culture, then he in turn must let "the negro sit beneath his own vine and fig tree" ("Briar Patch" 263–64). Though Warren's proposal was more realistic and more humane, both arguments incorporated the same fundamental precepts: the South's identity was to be found in white culture, which could only maintain its boundaries by defining blacks, whether as mute and invisible inhabitants of the landscape or as fellow agrarians with a "separate but equal" vine and fig tree, as Other.[25]

As far as the Agrarians were concerned, if white southern culture was to maintain its integrity in the face of rapid change, African Americans must remain in the margins. Yet they were not the only figures in the Agrarian landscape who served in the role of Other. Conforming to the logic long employed by defenders of the "old order," who had linked the fate of blacks to the subordination of white women, the group held that southern identity could be established only by defining itself against not only African Americans but against women as well. Implicit in this configuration of southern culture was the centrality of white consciousness and male subjectivity. Although the Agrarians avoided falling into the "slough" characteristic of groups like the Klan—they did not, in other words, propose violence against African Americans as a method of protecting white womanhood—their logic nevertheless followed the same path. In the Agrarian version of the South, neither blacks nor women could lay claim to subjectivity. Confined to the margins, they existed instead as signifiers whose identity was subject to the needs of the true culture, the boundaries of which remained closely defended.[26]

Just as Tate's original outline of *I'll Take My Stand* made no mention of the "negro question," neither did it contain any references to the "woman question." That organized feminism had not made the impact in the South that it had in the Northeast no doubt accounts, in part, for the almost total absence of references to women and issues involving them. Yet, at the same time, it appears as though the contributors made a conscious effort to keep the volume free of the taint of femininity. Indeed, Tate wrote Davidson that he would like to include novelist Stark Young as a contributor, but he was concerned that his essay on "The Southern Way of Life" would consist of nothing but "anecdotes of his grandmother" (*LC* 237). Instead, Andrew Lytle was asked to write on agrarian life, while Young contributed an analysis of New South progressivism. Tate and his colleagues, as the essay Lytle eventually produced testifies, preferred women as the supporting players in the Agrarian drama, not as leading ladies (see "Hind Tit").[27] Rather, women served best as the self-effacing, silent helpmates of men; when the essayists did refer to women, it was to chastise them for their complicity, as agents of socialization, in encouraging the most crass and destructive tendencies of American culture. As Ransom explained, the "feminine form [of complicity] is . . . hallowed among us under the name of Service." Although this word "has many meanings," its most significant refers to Eve and "the seducing of laggard men into fresh struggles with nature." The ideal of Service applies most directly to the "apparently stagnant sections of mankind . . . with the heathen Chinee [*sic*], with the Roman Catholic Mexican, with the 'lower' classes in our own society." The impulse behind Service is "missionary," and its "watchwords" include "Protestantism, Individualism, Democracy" ("Reconstructed but Unregenerate" 10–11). Propelling men on their quest to subjugate the natural world and its less cultivated inhabitants, women, as the descendants of Eve, are thus responsible for the destructive cultural tendencies Ransom and the other essayists claimed to resist. Ransom did not condemn this "missionary" activity as a form of cultural imperialism but instead criticized the meddlesome interference of women as misdirected. In the hierarchy the Agrarians envisioned, women, along with the less civilized nations, the lower classes, and African Americans, posed a threat to "stability" and "harmony" when they attempted to step beyond the bounds of their natural and dependent role. The "Southern way of life," and with it the highest ideals of western civilization, could be saved only through the efforts of men like the Agrarians themselves—educated men who recognized that, if order was to be restored, *all* Others, including women, would have to be forced back into silence and subordination.[28] The assumption that authentic southern culture was white, like the concomitant assumption that it was male, would emerge as one of the central aesthetic tenets upon which the Southern Literary Renaissance and the literary theories supporting it would be constructed.

The critical literature on O'Connor's racial stance generally overlooks its origins in the assumptions that prevailed within southern literary culture and that governed Fugitive/Agrarian discourses on race. Though critics have paid increasing attention to O'Connor's views on race, they have for the most part remained preoccupied with determining whether she was, in fact, a racist. Ralph Wood and Sarah Gordon have addressed the issues raised by O'Connor's unpublished correspondence with Maryat Lee, letters Wood admits will only "worsen . . . fears" that O'Connor was a "closet racist" ("Where Is the Voice" 90). While Gordon dismisses the letters as "a parody of racist vernacular," Wood defends O'Connor's "ready and easy recourse to the word *nigger*," her propensity for repeating racist jokes, and her admitted "distaste for Negroes" as the product of a "cultural conservatism that made her rightly skeptical of self-righteous social reformers." (Gordon, "Maryat and Juliat" 31; Wood, "Where Is the Voice" 94, 90). Other critics have similarly defended O'Connor's racism as simply part of her broader effort to, as Rob Johnson explains it, "practice one's own version of equality by condemning equally" (16). In the rush to defend O'Connor against charges of racism, critics have generally overlooked both the origins and the function of her racial attitudes. While Johnson, for example, concludes that O'Connor's "use of the topical attempts to render the timely timeless," he ignores the larger question of why she felt such pressure to avoid the "topical" in the first place (7). As Wood concludes, O'Connor shared the views of such figures as Tate, Lytle, and Davidson, that "for all its many faults, the South preserved a sense of place and tradition that the rest of the nation was abandoning at its peril" ("Where Is the Voice" 98). But what critics have failed to note is that this view, as articulated both in Ransom's and Tate's central work and in the literary and cultural histories it spawned, is itself founded on the racist premise that blacks, whether or not they assume equal status with whites, remain outside the South's real tradition, and that this tradition, in fact, depends upon the subordination of both African Americans and women. The subsequent rise of New Critical apoliticism was more than coincidentally linked to Fugitive/Agrarian discourse on race. By claiming that the "topical," or political, is somehow irrelevant to more "timeless" concerns—and thereby dismissing any challenges to white hegemony—critics like Ransom and Tate could ensure the centrality of white consciousness and at the same time lay claim to a dispassionate objectivity that in itself justified the transformation of blacks into Other. O'Connor's strict adherence to New Critical standards similarly enabled her to ignore the broader implications of racial questions, creating narratives in which "the issue of race," as Johnson argues, "remains of secondary importance to a dehistoricized, context-less narrative of redemption" (2). By using blacks as a "metaphor of redemptive humility" and "universalizing their victimhood," O'Connor, concludes

Claire Kahane, "defuses the potentially explosive social consequences of black rage and white guilt" and "fictively destroys the political rationale for rebellion" (184). To achieve this end, O'Connor followed the Fugitive/ Agrarian lead and rested her racial narratives on the notion that white experience remains central to southern identity, which may only be defined, finally, in opposition to blacks.

"The Artificial Nigger" reveals some of the ways in which O'Connor incorporated these strategies into her work. Published in 1955, the story was written before the civil rights movement had become an unavoidable fact of life for most white southerners. Thus it displays none of the hostility toward liberal reformers and African Americans that characterizes "Everything That Rises Must Converge" or "The Enduring Chill." In fact, the black characters in "The Artificial Nigger" are rendered in a sympathetic and dignified manner. The man who passes Nelson and Mr. Head on the train is a case in point. Described as a well-dressed "coffee-colored" man adorned with a ruby pin, a sapphire ring, and a "stomach which rode majestically under his buttoned coat," the narrator notes that he walks with "a deliberate outward motion," refusing to meet the gaze of the white passengers as he slowly makes his way to the car reserved for blacks. Indeed, Nelson, never having before seen a black person, does not even recognize the man on the train as a "nigger." Here O'Connor concedes the point that race is not a biological but a social construction and that racism is the product of a "fierce raw fresh hate" that must be learned (*CW* 215–16). Yet this point serves merely as an aside to the story's broader implications regarding what O'Connor termed the "redemptive quality of the Negro's suffering for us all" (*HB* 78). Mr. Head expects their trip to Atlanta will teach Nelson a lesson about pride and respect, one the old man hopes will convince his impudent grandson that "only with years does a man enter into that calm understanding of life that makes him a suitable guide for the young" (210). Nelson's encounter with "his first nigger" ignites the initial spark of this awareness, as he begins to understand "why his grandfather disliked them." The boy's growing racism allies him with Mr. Head in other ways as well, as the older man conducts a tour of the train, pointing to African Americans and explaining how "They rope them off." Gradually it dawns on the boy that his grandfather does indeed know a great deal more about the world, and it occurs to him that "the old man would be his only support in the strange place they were approaching. . . . A terrible excitement shook him and he wanted to take hold of Mr. Head's coat and hold on like a child" (216–18). Black "suffering" and the racist response it inspires does not in itself become a theme in the story but functions instead as a means of uniting the pair and propelling them on the journey that will ultimately culminate in redemption.

This journey is not without its interruptions. The boy's growing confidence as they tour the city and his renewed insistence that it is really his second trip infuriate his grandfather, and the pair again become alienated from one another. Their pride and alienation blind them, and they become both literally and figuratively lost as they descend deeper into what the narrator ironically describes as a Dantean hell. Only when they find themselves in an African American neighborhood do they begin to remember the bond that unites them. Again, their mutual fear and hatred of blacks become the ground they share in common. Nelson's encounter with the woman O'Connor described as a "black mountain of maternity" dramatically reinforces this connection, as he finds himself mesmerized by her mysterious presence (*HB* 78): "He stood drinking in every detail of her. His eyes traveled up from her great knees to her forehead and then made a triangular path from the glistening sweat on her neck down and across her tremendous bosom. . . . He suddenly wanted her to reach down and pick him up and draw him against her and then he wanted to feel her breath on his face. . . . He felt as if he were reeling down through a pitchblack tunnel." Here the woman's sexual and maternal natures are fused, as her "glistening" bosom elicits contradictory responses in Nelson: both revulsion and attraction and, more significantly, realization of his unfulfilled longing for his absent mother. Assuming the role black women have traditionally played in relation to white southern men, the woman serves at once as an object of sexual desire and as a mammy figure whose body offers comfort and sustenance. Awed by her image, Nelson temporarily reunites with his grandfather and takes hold of his hand, offering a "sign of dependence that he seldom showed" (223).

But no live black person is able to offer the comfort and sustenance provided by the "artificial nigger" the pair encounter on a white suburban lawn. By this point in their journey, in the aftermath of Mr. Head's denial of the boy, grandfather and grandson have become completely estranged from one another. Nelson even refuses to drink from the same water fountain as his grandfather, who when he "realized this . . . lost all hope. His face in the wandering afternoon light looked ravaged and abandoned" (228). Lost in a "black strange place" inhabited by "black mysterious form[s]," grandfather and grandson alike long to return home, where there "hasn't been a nigger" in twelve years (228, 212). Mr. Head sarcastically terms the city where Nelson was born a "nigger heaven," but the frightening blackness that surrounds them and draws them deeper into spiritual crisis suggests that the city is really a "nigger hell" (222). Only when they reach a suburban haven of whiteness and Mr. Head acknowledges that he truly is lost does it appear as though the pair will be saved. "I'm lost," he wails, "and can't find my way. . . . Oh Gawd I'm lost! Oh hep me Gawd I'm lost!" Though this plea is finally answered, Nelson refuses to accept Mr. Head's offer of reconciliation. But the sight of the lawn figure, which suddenly catches his attention "like a cry out of the gathering dust," offers renewed hope: "It was not possible to tell if the artificial Negro were meant to be young or old; he looked too miserable to be either. He was meant to look happy because his mouth was stretched up at the corners but the chipped eye and the angle he was cocked at gave him a wild look of misery instead." The two can only stare in awe of the statue "as if they were faced with some great mystery, some monument to another's victory that brought them together in their common defeat." This ageless, "miserable" figure represents the timeless "suffering" African Americans have endured in a culture dominated by whites. Yet in the context of the story the statue serves not as a symbol of black oppression but as a "monument to another's victory." Like the man on the train and the woman in the window, the "artificial nigger" serves in the role of Other: at once a fearful symbol that provokes spiritual crisis and alienation, and a redemptive figure whose misery becomes the means by which Nelson and Mr. Head are reunited and by which their identity is subsequently reaffirmed.[29] Mr. Head is indeed perceptive when he explains to the boy that white suburbanites must import "artificial niggers" because they "ain't got enough real ones here" (229–30). Without blacks to serve as the objects on which to project fear, distrust, and contempt, whites remain, according to the logic of the story, "lost," bereft of an organizing "tradition." Representing as it does the signifier against which white identity is defined, the "artificial nigger" becomes the very embodiment of Fugitive/Agrarian discourse on race.[30] Adopting this discourse became, for O'Connor, another means by which she could address some of the problems posed by her status as a woman writer. Although her gender may have prevented her from achieving full membership in Ransom's and Tate's republic of letters, her status as a white southerner and her use of Fugitive/Agrarian racial discourses could themselves be used to enhance her position within southern literary culture.

This strategy emerges more fully in "A Late Encounter with the Enemy" where, in her superficial and mindless worship of "Dignity! Honor! Courage!" Sally Poker Sash embodies the inauthentic version of southern history the Fugitive/Agrarians hoped to reject: a version readily exploited by the Hollywood organizers of the movie "preemy" (253). The premier itself is nothing more than a tawdry spectacle where the southern belle is transformed into an "usherette in a Confederate cap and a short little skirt" and put on display for anyone willing to pay ten dollars (255). This gilded version of southern history, like Sally's corsage of "gladiola petals taken off and painted gold and put back together to look like a rose," is based on artifice and as such is clearly intended for exploitation. General Sash, for one, is a willing pawn in the rush to profit from this false rendering of southern history and will gladly don his fake uniform for virtually any occasion (254). While Sally worships this popular, inauthentic version of southern history, the old man has no memory of nor use for history at all. "What happened then wasn't anything to a man living now and he was living now" (259). The words "Chickamauga, Shiloh, Johnston, Lee"—codes for watershed moments in white southern history and the figures who embody its ideals— mean nothing to him as he allows himself to be passively wheeled to and fro by John Wesley, the fat, sloppy, and lazy young man whose neglect of his duty in itself represents the poor state in which the modern white South exists. All around the old man people speak nonsensically of the past, reminding the audience at Sally's graduation that if "we forget our past . . . we won't remember our future" (260). Were it not for the "little hole beginning to widen" in his head, which allows the words to penetrate, the General would remain as blind as the rest of his contemporaries (259). Yet this hole proves his salvation, for when the "regular volley" of words finally enters, in their violence they bring with them the power to conjure the authentic past to life. There the old man sees one of his "bald-headed sons" and his wife wearing "round gold-rimmed glasses," where previously he could not even recall if either had ever existed. In the epiphanic moment just before his death, the words "Chickamauga, Shiloh, Marthasville" suddenly assume meaning for him, and their power is real, even deadly, as he realizes that "the past is the only future now and he had to endure it" (261). This glimpse of the real southern past, while deadly, is in typical O'Connor fashion simultaneously redemptive, as the General's death and the revelation it brings are contrasted with the figure of John Wesley, whose overriding concern during this crisis is his quest for a Coca-Cola—an ironic grail, symbol of the modern South's capitulation to the cheap allure of mass culture. The old man may be dead, but Sally will have to endure the double humiliation of John Wesley's public disrespect for the General's body and the realization that her grandfather's corpse must endure the indignities of display before the very "upstarts" she hoped to upstage at her graduation (253). In thus defining the authentic southern past as embodied in the glorious battles and figures of the Civil War and contrasting that past with the cheap and tawdry present, the story draws from Fugitive/Agrarian discourse on the primacy of white southern manhood and affirms, finally, the central importance of white experience to the formulation of southern identity.

Although Ransom, Tate, and their associates may not have been a direct or even conscious influence on O'Connor, the critical theories they promoted and the aesthetics they developed played a crucial role in the formulation of her literary identity. Fugitive/Agrarian discourse on southern and broader American literary traditions was founded on opposition to the South's genteel tradition and haunted by fears concerning the state of white southern manhood. O'Connor's preoccupation with violence and with the grotesque owed its genesis as much to Fugitive/Agrarian discourse on the "inflated oratory" of nineteenth-century southern literature as it did to her concern with religious and spiritual themes. Similarly, her fear of and fascination with the transgressive power of the female body found its origins in an aesthetic that the Fugitives had explored in their early poetry and that would continue to inform Ransom's formulation of New Critical theory. Likewise, O'Connor's gradual banishment of and increasingly punitive attitude toward female characters began in a graduate school environment governed by the literary gender biases that characterized Fugitive/Agrarian discourse and New Critical theory. Though the Fugitive/Agrarians were never united in their aesthetic and critical views, as a whole their work nevertheless rested on the racial, sexual, and class-based hierarchies that southern defenders of the "old order" had long sought to maintain. Just as the Southern Tradition centered on the experience of educated white men, so too did the larger "republic of letters" rest on the opposition between white and black, male and female. As stories such as "The Artificial Nigger" and "A Late Encounter with the Enemy" suggest, O'Connor's conception of the South's racial landscape owed much to Fugitive/Agrarian influence and its representation of the South and its literature as the rightful domain of white men, their history, and their experience.

## 2 · To Cultivate the Masculine Virtues

Caroline Gordon as Writer,
Critic, and Mentor

FUGITIVE/AGRARIAN IDEALS were central both to southern literary culture and to more broadly American literary culture, permeating the teaching and practice of literary theory and playing an important role in the emergence of a modern American canon. O'Connor's training at the Writer's Workshop, as well as her careful study of the critical principles underpinning texts such as *Understanding Fiction,* played an important role in introducing her to the rules governing postwar American literary cultures. Yet perhaps the most important influence in this regard was Caroline Gordon. As O'Connor's mentor, Gordon played a significant role in helping the young writer develop the strategies she would use to cope with her situation as a woman writer attempting to negotiate the rocky terrain of a male-dominated profession. Through Gordon's instruction, O'Connor learned to translate the gendered codes that lay at the heart of Fugitive/Agrarian discourse and to find the means of addressing the problematics of female authorship. In short, Gordon taught O'Connor that to claim status as a genuine artist a woman must remember first and foremost to follow the example set by the "masters" and learn, as Gordon explained in a letter to Ward Dorrance, to "write like a man" ([1954?] WD papers).

Gordon's own relationship to the Fugitive/Agrarians is well worth examining, for her response to the hegemonic discourses that characterized southern literary culture functions in many ways as a blueprint for O'Connor's own literary development. Personally and professionally, the two women shared much in common. Neither challenged the exclusionary basis of southern literary culture but were instead co-opted by it, accepting both the racial and sexual hierarchies upon which that culture was based. Further, Gordon, like O'Connor, cultivated a veneer of conventionality that she strategically used to mask a professional ambition very much at odds with prescribed social roles. Both women also shared a strong sense of southern and Catholic identity coupled with a pronounced ambivalence to the South and to the Catholic Church. At the heart of this ambivalence lay profound insecurities regarding their talents as writers and their status within the southern literary establishment, insecurities that were ultimately related to gender. To negotiate the conflicting demands of their professional and social roles, Gordon and O'Connor attempted to appropriate masculine authority in a number of different ways: by aligning themselves with influential male mentors, by using Catholicism to legitimate their literary endeavors, and, finally, by effacing their femaleness and identifying with the male intellect. Yet because each adhered so strongly to the notion that the male intellect was superior, their relationship was bound to suffer. That it did testifies to the difficulties facing women who accepted the premises upon which southern literary culture was built. If they embraced the masculinist politics and aesthetics on which that culture was based, then they might achieve greater critical success and patronage, but only with strict limitations and only at the expense of the realization that, as women, they could never fully attain status as "masters." In the end, their mutual acceptance of these principles made it impossible for Gordon and O'Connor to cultivate a genuinely constructive mentoring relationship.

Gordon developed mentoring relationships—some more successful than others—with a number of aspiring authors, and in this way she played an important, if largely unacknowledged, role in disseminating Fugitive/Agrarian ideas concerning literary theory and the American and southern literary traditions. Unlike Allen Tate, her husband of over thirty years, Gordon never served as the editor of a major journal, nor did she produce a large body of critical or theoretical work. She was, however, primary author of the widely distributed anthology *The House of Fiction: An Anthology of the Short*

*Story,* which was followed by *How to Read a Novel.* Through volumes like these and, more importantly, through her extensive teaching, Gordon became one of the leading voices of the New Critical movement. Like Tate, she took considerable interest in assisting the efforts of other writers. But while Tate and his associates generally offered assistance in the form of patronage—publishing stories, writing or soliciting critical works on certain writers, and recommending the deserving for fellowships and grants—Gordon's assistance most often came in the form of teaching. She first taught creative writing in 1938 at the Women's College of the University of North Carolina at Greensboro (Makowsky 145). From the 1930s onward, though she continued to work at various universities, she devoted a remarkable amount of her time outside the classroom to help nurture and give shape to the work of younger writers, including O'Connor, Ward Dorrance, and Walker Percy.

It had taken Gordon a number of years to cultivate such confidence in her critical voice. From an early age she recognized that power rested with men and that when it came to intellectual pursuits, women were rarely respected as equals. In a chapter from her unpublished biography, *The Narrow Heart: Portrait of a Woman,* she explained, "As I recall, I came to the conclusion when I was around four years of age that the world had been created as a plaything by a group of men, who, tired of sporting with it, had gone on to other pleasures, leaving it to roll on the way it would" ("Cock Crow" 557). According to biographer Veronica Makowsky, Gordon's attitude toward male and female roles developed in response to her family situation. Though she often described her mother as a "bluestocking" of considerable learning, as a child Gordon felt a stronger intellectual kinship to her father, whom she later credited for nurturing her interest in writing (Makowsky, 30–34). Throughout her life Gordon would continue to rely on male mentors and to identify with the male intellect (37). Disassociating herself from her mother and from femininity in general, she maintained a strong identification with her father and continued to describe her mother as the very embodiment of everything to which she herself was intellectually opposed, including, at least initially, religion (*SM* 27). Gordon's identity depended on her belief that she was more similar to her father, the distinguished scholar, than her mother, a woman Gordon dismissed as a superstitious religious fanatic, a vindictive "bluestocking" who made father and daughter alike "suffer for any disappointment that comes to her" (29–30). Like O'Connor, Gordon maintained a lifelong distance from what she understood as the constraints and limitations of southern ladyhood.

The strong identification Gordon felt with her father and with men in general was no doubt the result not simply of her family situation but of the same cultural forces that made O'Connor so uncomfortable with her gender role. As Gordon recalled in *The Narrow Heart,* she could not remember a time in her life when she did not want to be a writer, "when the telling of . . . stories did not seem an obligation that had been laid upon me and one which it would be dangerous to evade" ("Cock Crow" 11). Though she recalled having been surrounded by a number of strong female personalities as a child, Gordon made no mention of any professional or literary women with whom she was acquainted. Her mother may have been classically educated, but only her father had actually been able to use his education to become a scholar. When she arrived in New York as a young woman, Gordon met a number of other female writers and journalists, including Katherine Anne Porter, Josephine Herbst, and Dorothy Day (Makowsky 75). But as Malcolm Cowley recalled, women, with very few exceptions, were not considered worthy of admission to the highly exclusive group of poets and intellectuals who gathered there. Gordon, he explained, "'wasn't' one of 'us.' . . . 'We' were mostly poets and intellectuals and men," while she was a "newspaperwoman" working on "unpublished novels that 'we' didn't read." With the benefit of hindsight, Cowley admitted that Gordon was "in part . . . the victim of sexual discrimination," and it was no doubt this unpleasant realization that contributed to Gordon's tendency to identify with the male intellect (quoted in Waldron, *Close Connections* 39). In fact, it remains just as likely that Gordon's identification with her father and her estrangement from her mother was in itself a response to her early realization that when it came to intellectual matters, women were rarely respected as the equals of men.

Rather than challenging the exclusionary premises of southern literary culture, Gordon, like O'Connor, allied herself with powerful male mentors in the hopes that she could become an exception to the rule. Integral to Gordon's identification with masculine intellectuality was her acceptance of the racial and sexual hierarchies that prevailed in the literary circles with which she was associated. It is hardly unusual, given her age and her background, that racist themes should appear in both her fiction and her letters. What remains instructive about Gordon's use of racial discourses is the way in which they so closely intersected with prevailing ideology concerning gender. Like her Fugitive/Agrarian associates, she regarded the subordination of blacks to whites and women to men as crucial to the maintenance of southern identity. As a white woman, Gordon viewed her individual identity as dependent, at least in part, not simply upon her husband but upon her relationship to the servants she employed as well. Of Lucy, a woman she hired as housekeeper and cook, Gordon exclaimed, "She is a gem, young and strong and good natured and old fashioned. I find myself thinking I own her. She is more like slavery time niggers than any of the modern variety" (*SM* 156). The sarcasm aside, Gordon's description of Lucy reveals a great deal about her use of southern racial discourses. On a practical level, domestics like Lucy helped to alleviate the strains involved in attempting to satisfy the conflicting demands of her roles as wife, mother, hostess, and writer. On a symbolic level, the employment of servants functioned as a means of invoking the figure of plantation mistress who must assume responsibility for "her niggers." In this way Gordon's relationship to Lucy and other domestics became an avenue through which she might appropriate, however indirectly, the dominant subject position otherwise denied her as a woman. Thus, like O'Connor, Gordon could employ prevailing discourses on race to emphasize her status as a white southerner and attempt, perhaps, to enhance her standing in the professional circles with which she was associated.

Gordon viewed racial, sexual, and class-based hierarchies as mutually dependent and as the foundation upon which white southern identity was built. Yet, like O'Connor, Gordon remained somewhat ambivalent about her own place within this scheme. On the one hand, as her letters and short stories suggest, she fully accepted prevailing ideas concerning race, gender, and class. But on the other hand, Gordon was possessed of a strong creative drive whose fulfillment necessitated the violation of the social role to which she hoped to conform. To bridge the gap created by the conflicting demands of her social role and her professional ambition, Gordon, like O'Connor, chose to create the illusion of conformity whenever possible and even refused to vote, on the grounds that the franchise fell outside the bounds of female responsibility. Yet as biographers Makowsky and Ann Waldron both argue, Gordon, despite appearances, hardly acted the role of the southern lady. Describing her as an "avowed advocate of a patriarchal society," Waldron concludes, "Everything in her life indicates that she was a strong, independent woman—who wanted to be something else. She kept her maiden name, worked all her life, was anything but a stay-at-home housewife. She acted like a feminist, talked like a Southern ninny" (*Close Connections* 357).

Gordon's marriage to Tate offers perhaps the most interesting evidence of the extent of her attempts to conform to the role of southern lady and of the professional difficulties such conformity posed. In a letter to Dorrance she reflected on the various pressures to which her role had subjected her. "One thing that kept me on the rack than I'd otherwise have been," she wrote, "was my determination not to let my family cushion me the way some women writers are cushioned. Nancy has never hesitated to interrupt me at a crucial moment. Nobody ever thought of not having people staying in the house when I was at a crucial stage in a book. And that was the way I wanted it." Unwilling to challenge prevailing ideas concerning the relationship of a wife to her husband, Gordon did her utmost to fulfill the standards expected of her. "But," she could admit with the benefit of hindsight, "it didn't work. John Bishop told me years ago that I was trying to do something impossible" ([1946?] WD papers). The impossible task she had attempted to undertake was to maintain a professional career while attending at the same time to a gender role that required her to put Tate's professional needs first. Throughout her correspondence to Sally Wood, for example, Gordon refers to being forced to "drop" her work for a month in order to help Tate meet a deadline or "having" to lend him her typewriter because his was broken (*SM* 46, 113). When the situation was reversed, Gordon rarely demanded equal support. In 1932, for example, she wrote a children's story to earn some extra money, but as she explained to Wood, she did not insist on Tate's editorial assistance after he decided he could not bring himself to read the story. "Allen's tried to read it twice," she wrote, "and each time breaks down and says he simply can't" (112). When he did offer his advice, Gordon often feared the result and nearly abandoned work on her first published novel after hearing his verdict. As she stated to Wood, she "went to pieces pretty badly" and "got frightened when Allen told me plainly that the last chapter" was inadequate. She told him to write it and only managed to work "out of the fit" when "she got interested in trying to fix up what he had written" (78). Like O'Connor, Gordon suffered from professional insecurities aggravated by her awareness that as a woman her talents were likely inferior. At the same time, her insecurity was aggravated by Tate's apparent confidence in the superiority of his own literary judgment and talents and by Gordon's acceptance of his superior intellect. Years later Gordon analyzed Tate's method and concluded in a letter to Dorrance, "I do not think he has ever sat down and patiently tried to show me something. He has taught me most of what I know—by looks of acute boredom or disgust or by cutting inflections" ([1955?] WD papers). Here a pattern emerges. Both Tate and Gordon operated by the contradictory premise that Gordon could work as a writer and play the role of southern lady. But their adherence to the rules governing southern literary culture, which held that the lady should properly put her husband's needs first, saddled Gordon with an "impossible" task and ultimately undermined her professional development.

In paying such meticulous attention to the requirements of her roles as wife and hostess, Gordon in many ways achieved a level of conformity that O'Connor never matched. Yet as Gordon's relationship to her daughter suggests, neither was she willing to succumb entirely to the demands of traditional southern ladyhood. The 1925 birth of her daughter, Nancy, brought to the surface many of the tensions that characterized Gordon's personal and professional lives, as it became clear that she could not be both a full-time mother and a full-time writer. After much indecision, she arranged for Nancy to live with her parents. But rather than admitting that Nancy's absence would allow her to continue work on her novel, Gordon instead felt compelled to emphasize the more conventional reasons why such an arrangement would be beneficial, hoping to convey the impression that she had not strayed from the role of the self-sacrificing mother.[1] In reality, Gordon was reluctant to allow her traditional obligations as a mother to interfere with her work as a writer, and she continued throughout her career to take advantage of the opportunity to free herself from full-time childcare duties whenever possible.[2] Yet to the end, she refused to admit that her commitment to her work was more important than her commitment to assume full-time the traditional responsibilities of motherhood. Like O'Connor, she preferred to obscure her underlying motivations and drives beneath a veneer of conventional respectability.

Following her conversion to Catholicism and her second divorce from Tate, Gordon's unconventional nature found greater room for expansion. She never remarried and, as Tate's financial contributions diminished over time, gradually became self-supporting. Indeed, Gordon continued writing, teaching, lecturing, and traveling until her health began to fail in the late 1970s. By the time of her death in 1981 she had, despite her claims to the contrary, become an independent woman. Rarely one to concede a point, though, she directed that her gravestone should read, "Wife of Allen Tate." [3] Her independence notwithstanding, Gordon hoped to be remembered as a woman whose primary identity had been established through her relationship with her former husband.

Like O'Connor, Gordon never fully resolved the tensions created by the contradictory requirements of her roles as lady and writer. And like O'Connor, Gordon strove to conform whenever possible, both as a means of negotiating the conflicting demands of her personal and professional lives and as a means of neutralizing the subversive potential posed by female authorship. In this way she could ensure that her professional endeavor did not threaten to upset the order of the society into which she was born or the literary circles in which she worked. Gordon recognized that this order was built specifically on two premises: that women should remain subordinate to men and that the creation of art and literature are by definition masculine endeavors expressive of male experience. Determined to follow the rules, at least in appearance, she cultivated a self-effacing demeanor both personally and professionally and vicariously appropriated male intellectual authority by aligning herself with influential men. Tate was, of course, her primary mentor. As her correspondence suggests, she placed considerable faith in his critical opinions, often trusting his judgment over hers. And according to Makowsky, Gordon frequently relied on Tate to intervene on her behalf with publishers (108). Similarly, early in her career Gordon relied strongly for advice and encouragement on Ford Madox Ford, who employed her as his secretary. According to Gordon, it was Ford's insistence that she sit down each day to work on her novel—he "forced" her to dictate it to him—that finally gave her the confidence to finish. As she explained to Wood, he also found a publisher willing to provide her with an advance (*SM* 51). Ford's support of her work and his paternal interest in its progress offered Gordon the sort of male approval she needed to overcome her doubts about the role she had undertaken as a woman artist.

Without doubt, Gordon's relationship to men like Ford and Tate provided her with the encouragement and practical support she needed to begin her career in earnest and to maintain a basic level of productivity. Given the politics that prevailed within southern literary circles and given Gordon's uneasy alliance to the modernist writers with whom the couple associated during their early years in Europe, she was left with little choice but to rely on the patronage of male writers and critics.[4] Moreover, Gordon had already established strong intellectual bonds to her father and to men in general and simply preferred to rely on male mentors. Paradoxically, however, while these relationships made it possible for Gordon to find her literary voice, they also worked to undermine her confidence in her critical judgments and literary abilities (Makowsky 88). Finding no fault with the sometimes explosive pedagogical methods that men like Ford and Tate employed, Gordon accepted their authority without question. Their patronage was thus not offered without a price. To be certain, she had much to gain from her relationship to male mentors, but only so long as she respected the boundaries upon which their authority as critics was based. Perhaps aware of the difficulties facing women like Riding, who refused to play the role of woman-in-need, Gordon willingly accepted the premises upon which these mentoring relationships were based.

Not only did Gordon accept the authority of men like her father, Tate, and Ford as natural and inevitable, but, like O'Connor, she frequently sought to distinguish herself from other women. From an early age her mother became for Gordon the representation of all that she was not—her Other—and she continued to rely on such oppositions in her professional life as well. Insecure about her own standing, as a woman, within southern literary circles, she viewed other women writers, particularly Katherine Anne Porter, as competition and not as colleagues (166–68). Typical is a letter Gordon wrote Dorrance regarding a student attending the 1948 University of Kansas writer's conference, which is reminiscent of O'Connor's glee in the treatment her penwomen received at the hands of Mr. Meadows. "There is always," Gordon explained, "a leading old battle axe among the students at these gatherings." The young woman who became the target of Gordon's anger "started off at Allen's session yesterday with her 'Well, if thaaaat's poetry . . .'" Everyone "held their breath for a second," waiting for Tate to reply. "It was a pleasure to watch him demolish her," Gordon concluded with some satisfaction. "She thanked him when he got through with her ([1948?] WD papers). That Gordon should, under the circumstances, defend her husband is not remarkable. What remains interesting about Gordon's response to the situation is her hostility toward the young woman in question. Clearly, she resented the woman's presumption that she was qualified to challenge Tate. Yet rather than dismissing her actions as a simple case of youthful arrogance, Gordon took active pleasure in seeing the young "battle axe" publicly "demolished" and all but forced to retract her original statement. Highly respectful of masculine authority, Gordon had, at this point in her career, willingly renounced her own claim to an independent critical voice. Like O'Connor, she viewed as misplaced the efforts of other women to assert themselves intellectually, and she resented those who did not necessarily accept the premises upon which the authority of critics like Tate were built.

Only after the couple's second divorce did Gordon begin to seek other avenues for laying claim to the authority she believed necessary to legitimate her endeavor as a writer. Ironically, she followed her mother's footsteps and turned to religion. After her conversion Gordon began to assert herself to a greater extent and to rely less on accommodating Tate's needs. In a pattern that would characterize O'Connor's relationship to Catholicism, Gordon discovered that her newfound faith could function as a means of appropriating vicarious authority to justify her creative drives. She became gradually less deferential to Tate and eventually embarked on a long and ultimately successful campaign to bring about his conversion, an effort that was no doubt intended, in part, as a strategy for reestablishing the balance of power in the relationship (Makowsky 182–91).[5] Interestingly, such efforts were not restricted to Tate. "More directly than any other Catholic I had met," Walter Sullivan remembered, "she set out to convert me." She took him to mass, sought the assistance of nuns, prayed for him, and lectured him (6). Gordon employed similar tactics with Ward Dorrance. In a 1949 letter she admonished him, "You are a man, made to the image of God, and therein, I feel certain lies all your trouble. For you are not living the way you ought to live, that is your relation to God is not what it ought to be" (28 October 1949, WD papers). Such efforts, which represented a clear violation of the gender-based hierarchies Gordon had for so long respected, suggest that for the first time in her life she could claim for herself a level of authority that superseded the power of men like Tate, Sullivan, or Dorrance. Catholicism, it appears, provided her with a means of empowerment.[6] "I really would like to tell you what being in the Church is like, but can't," she explained to Dorrance. "It's like suddenly being given authority to believe all the things you've surmised" ([1950?] WD papers).

For Gordon, empowerment involved finding a literary and critical voice that was not subject to the approval of the male mentors on whom she had learned to rely. During the period leading to and following her conversion, she became noticeably more forthright and confident in her literary opinions, openly criticizing the work of respected colleagues like Andrew Lytle.[7] More-over, it was during this period that she began to take her teaching skills be-yond the classroom, acting as mentor to young writers like Dorrance, Walker Percy, and O'Connor. At the same time, she began to express her critical views with an assurance that did not characterize her earlier remarks on the subject. Signing many of her letters "La Belle Dame Sans Merci," Gordon wrote Dorrance hundreds of pages criticizing his work and explaining to him her ideas about literature. Gordon's emerging critical theories were based to a large extent on her admiration for the methods of writers like Flaubert and James, as well as on her adherence to the strictures of New Critical theory and Catholic doctrine. Quoting Jacques Maritain, for example, she wrote Dorrance that she would "risk saying that there is no art where there is no religion. (The origins of Greek tragedy, etc. will bear me out on that.) But I have a contemporary and damn good authority, too [Maritain]." She then concluded by explaining that Maritain, in turn, "has backers in Aristotle and St. Thomas." This appropriated authority offered her the confidence to sug-gest, much as Ransom might have, ways that Dorrance should rewrite his sentences. "'She was striding through patches of light and shade' etc.," Gor-don offered in reference to one of his short stories, should be rewritten, "'Her fistss [*sic*] swirled in her skirts as she strode through patches of light and shade and stopped at the end of the walk, in an odour of acrid sweet-box and whiskey" (n.d. WD papers). Armed with the vicarious authority of the "masterly" writers, critics, philosophers, and theologians, Gordon no longer needed to question her own judgment. Just as O'Connor could justify the violence in her work as Godly, Gordon could justify her critical work as a "missionary activity" meant to spread the word of God, Flaubert, James, and Maritain.

Yet Gordon, like O'Connor, was caught in a bind. On the one hand, knowing she could cite Maritain to support her opinions allowed her to state her views forthrightly and unapologetically. On the other hand, she never could lose sight of the fact that it was her identity as a woman that forced her to rely on the authority of others. Her later correspondence to Dorrance offers intriguing evidence of her fears that, in the final analysis, she had inappropriately usurped male authority. Try as she might, Gordon never could remain comfortable in her role as Dorrance's mentor: his age and, more importantly, his gender allowed him to command equal status as her colleague. As a result, the boundaries between mentor and protégé, teacher and student, remained blurred, and Gordon's authority over Dorrance was consequently undermined. By contrast, both O'Connor's youth and her gender made it possible for Gordon to remain entirely comfortable with the hierarchical terms of their relationship and permitted her to express her opinion of O'Connor's work without fear or intimidation. But because Gordon remained so bound by her reverence for the male intellect, her letters to Dorrance grew increasingly apologetic as she began to fear that her critique of his work, coming from a woman, would offend his sense of masculine superiority. Fearing that her role as his mentor had violated a sacred principle, she made more frequent attempts to compliment his work and assure him that it was "masterly" and full of "nuances" ([late 1940s?] WD papers). When these methods apparently failed to ease Dorrance's insecurities, Gordon began offering him explanations and apologies for her behavior. "There seems to be no doubt," she admitted, "that I have abused the privilege of friendship where you are concerned—speaking and writing to you far too freely, or rather carelessly." She was only trying, she explained, to use the same pedagogical methods Tate had used with her.[8] "But I am a woman. It is hard for a man to take that kind of thing from a woman. It takes an extraordinary amount of disinterestedness and artistic humility. I do not wonder that your patience has worn thin" ([late 1940s?] WD papers). While it was acceptable for Tate to apply strict methods in reviewing her work, it was unacceptable for her, as a woman, to apply those same methods to Dorrance's work. Again, Gordon was willing to accept a secondary place for herself in the hierarchy that characterized the literary circle in which she worked. Though she could recognize the inequities of such double standards, she refused to take the final step and reject altogether the premises upon which they had been constructed. Instead, she blamed herself for her inability to overcome the conflicting pressures of her roles as self-effacing southern lady and literary critic. "Just give me another chance," she finally asked Dorrance, "and I'll try to show more humility from now on. No doubt about it. It *is* the groundwork of all the virtues and the virtue I most lack!" (n.d. fragment, WD papers).

In sum, Gordon never could reject the idea that art was a male preserve wherein women must, if they are to be admitted, seek at all costs to maintain a self-effacing demeanor. In particular, she believed, women artists must reject any claims to a literary identity founded upon female selfhood. While Gordon worked hard to fulfill, at least in appearance, the traditional requirements of her role as a lady, she worked equally hard, in her fiction, to erase every trace of her female identity. As she explained to Dorrance: "I, for instance, have put in the last three days trying to get a passage written so that it will be hard enough and firm enough to hang my whole book on. This takes, if I may say so, a kind of masculine virtue. (George Eliot is almost the only woman writer who has it. God knows Jane Austen didn't.) But in a few minutes I have got to go stop writing and dress myself up and go to dinner at a dean's house and spend the evening persuading the man who sits next to me to talk about himself and if I don't do it with a fair degree of skill he will be telling people that Mrs. Tate is up-stage and conceited" (n.d. fragment, WD papers). Combining traditional female qualities in her personal life with the "hard" and "firm" qualities necessary to succeed as a writer was, Gordon recognized, exceedingly difficult. Nevertheless, she could see no way out of the dilemma and devoted much of her life as a writer to pursuing the "masculine virtues" of art. Gordon, as Sally Wood recalled, firmly "believed that with serious fiction one should not be able to tell whether the writer was a man or a woman." Since, as she understood, such "objectivity" was implicitly defined as masculine, Gordon worked hard to write "from the man's point of view" (Wood 120). In striving for a gender-neutral literary persona, she was forced to reject her feminine, "subjective" identity. In short, Gordon rarely envisioned a literary landscape, whether it centered on Agrarianism or Catholicism, outside the perimeters of a male-defined, male-oriented paradigm.[9] Co-opted first by a literary culture and later by a religious culture in which women were subordinate to men, she accepted the inevitability of male primacy even as she used her fiction as a means of undermining masculine claims to artistic privilege. These contradictions and the assumptions on which they rested were among the central literary values Gordon would pass on to O'Connor, and they profoundly shaped the direction their mentoring relationship would take.

Like O'Connor, Gordon found herself in an awkward position—an ambitious woman writer forced to rely on the patronage of a literary establishment that had been constructed on the premise that serious literature was necessarily a male creation. Gordon was instrumental in helping the young writer learn to cope with the unwritten rules by which the southern literary establishment operated and cultivate strategies for attempting to work out of the bind in which it would place them. Embracing an apparently genderless persona built on effacement of the female emerged as a logical, and for both women, largely successful—albeit conflict-wrought—strategy: just as O'Connor would receive positive reviews for her unladylike prose, so too did Gordon earn early critical praise for her ability to "write like a man." Andrew Lytle, for one, praised Gordon as a disciplined and objective writer. "If she did not sign her name, it would be at first hard to know her sex," he wrote in 1949. "This is a way of pointing out the strictness of her objectivity, and I suppose it to be the last refinement of it" ("Caroline Gordon" 562). His view did not change with time. "Caroline Gordon," he recalled in the 1984 introduction to her published correspondence, "worked for the discipline that would surmount the particular signs of sex. Nobody would mistake the sex of a writer like Katherine Anne Porter; with Caroline one could not tell whether her work was written by a man or a woman. This is evidence of the pure elevation of her style" (Introduction 1). Lytle was not alone in such views; throughout her life critics characterized Gordon as a highly skilled technician whose most remarkable talent was her ability to efface her gender.

Typical is Willard Thorp's assessment. Comparing her favorably to Elizabeth Madox Roberts, a good writer limited by her inability to create "convincing" male characters, Thorp wrote of Gordon, "In two of her novels, *Alec Maury, Sportsman* and *Green Centuries,* the leading characters are men and in *Penhally, None Shall Look Back,* and *The Garden of Adonis* the story belongs as much to the men as to the women. That she can 'do' her men as completely as her women is of the utmost importance in her art" (3). Sacrificing her claim to an explicit female identity, Gordon was able to distinguish herself as a skilled woman writer whose work did not suffer from the "impurities" that, as Lytle had commented to Tate, characterized the fiction of women like Katherine Anne Porter or Elizabeth Madox Roberts.

Given the political atmosphere of the literary culture in which she worked, it remains little wonder that Gordon chose to identify so strongly with the male intellect, despite the internal conflicts such identification generated. The example she provided no doubt proved the strongest influence on O'Connor, but one that remains difficult to quantify. More difficult is determining the specific extent to which Gordon's editorial advice directly influenced O'Connor's literary development. Unfortunately, the majority of the correspondence between the two women has been lost. What little remains has appeared in *The Habit of Being,* the *Collected Works,* and in "A Master Class: From the Correspondence of Caroline Gordon and Flannery O'Connor," all of which have been edited by Sally Fitzgerald, who deleted a considerable amount of material pertaining to Gordon. Further compounding the problem is the question of chronology. O'Connor did not actually begin to seek Gordon's advice until 1951, well after she had already completed at least two revisions of her first novel. And of the hundreds of O'Connor manuscripts housed at Georgia College, only a few have been definitively dated. The collection is therefore arranged not by date but thematically, according to the chapter-by-chapter, scene-by-scene format of the final published versions of each novel and story. Add to these difficulties the fact that O'Connor produced at least three extensive revisions of *Wise Blood* alone and the problem of establishing direct influence becomes a complicated one indeed. Many editorial decisions O'Connor made were likely prompted by her internal critical voice, a voice that had undergone exhaustive training in New Critical theory at the University of Iowa Writer's Workshop. The evidence points to the conclusion that her decision to suppress the female-sexed voice that appears throughout the manuscripts was not made in direct response to Gordon's advice but largely in response to the training she had received at the workshop. Nevertheless, Gordon's exhaustive critique of O'Connor's work did much to help the young writer to unravel the gendered codes by which the New Critical and southern literary establishments operated. Perhaps more importantly, Gordon's editorial guidance provided O'Connor with the reassurance that, in fashioning herself a serious writer whose work transcended gender, she had chosen the right path. Encouraged by Gordon's example and buoyed by her advice concerning the proper foundation of art, O'Connor learned to trust the critical instincts dictating that she purge her fiction of any feminine "impurities."

Yet the relationship between the two writers was far from simple. Although Gordon greeted O'Connor's early efforts with enthusiastic support, she gradually became convinced that her protégé's talents were limited. Having discovered O'Connor's work not long after she had embraced Catholicism, Gordon initially saw in the young writer the fulfillment of her hopes regarding the establishment of a "masterly" Catholic literary tradition. In the end, she concluded that O'Connor could not match the achievements of truly great writers like Flaubert and James. For her part, O'Connor was at first very grateful for the support and advice that Gordon so generously offered, and for the most part she readily acted on her suggestions. However, O'Connor soon grew impatient with her mentor's pedagogical methods and began increasingly to ignore her advice. Just as Gordon eventually concluded that O'Connor's work was limited by its lack of range and scope, O'Connor eventually concluded that Gordon's own methods were limited by her persistent emphasis on structure and grammar. The two women remained friendly until O'Connor's death, and the tensions that characterized their relationship remained, for the most part, beneath the surface. Nevertheless, these tensions are well worth examining, for they speak to the double bind facing women who embraced the gender biases upon which southern literary culture was based. Gordon, in effect, taught O'Connor that the female intellect was by definition lacking. In so doing, she established the premises upon which their relationship would necessarily deconstruct itself. That is, Gordon made it implicitly clear both that O'Connor's abilities as a writer must be somehow deficient and that her own authority as a critic could not be entirely trusted. In becoming O'Connor's mentor and reinforcing her ideas regarding the primacy of the male intellect, Gordon not only influenced the direction her protégé's fiction would take but, more significantly, revealed to O'Connor the limits involved in relying on the professional support and advice of another woman. Unlike Katherine Anne Porter and Eudora Welty, who managed to build a mutually supportive relationship,[10] Gordon and O'Connor were never able to sustain the kind of "nonhierarchical, multi-faceted, communal, and conversational" mentoring process that, according to Mary Wyer, characterizes the professional friendships of many women writers (562–63; also see Porter, Introduction to *A Curtain of Green,* and Welty).

It took a number of years before the tensions between the two writers would become apparent. Gordon's immediate response to her first reading of *Wise Blood* was in fact one of unmitigated enthusiasm. Knowing that she took a strong interest in Catholic literature, Robert Giroux, O'Connor's editor at Harcourt, had sent the manuscript to Gordon in early 1951. "I'm quite excited about it," she wrote him. "This girl is a real novelist. (I wish that I had had as firm a grasp on my subject matter when I was her age!) At any rate, she is already a rare phenomenon: a Catholic novelist with a real dramatic sense, one who relies more on her technique than her piety." With just a few minor changes, she concluded, the novel would be first-rate. No copy of this first set of suggestions survives, but O'Connor's correspondence to her literary agent confirms that she quickly acted upon them (Fitzgerald, editorial notes in "A Master Class," 829). In fact, O'Connor was so pleased with her advice that she asked Gordon to provide additional comments on the revisions. Gordon happily accepted and wrote a response in which she outlined the reasons why she found O'Connor's work so promising. "There are so few Catholic novelists who seem possessed of a literary conscience—not to mention skill—that I feel that your novel is very important." Gordon finished by offering her support in the way of a review as well, explaining that she would "like to do anything I can to help" ("Master Class" 830). That fall, O'Connor wrote to Sally and Robert Fitzgerald thanking them for sending her second manuscript to Gordon. Noting that she was "much obliged to her," O'Connor concluded that Gordon had "certainly increased my education thereby" (*HB* 27–28). Though Gordon saw in O'Connor's fiction certain imperfections, at this stage in their relationship she believed that she could teach O'Connor to overcome any limitations that might hamper her work. And though O'Connor was somewhat intimidated by the nine pages of comments Gordon had produced, she readily deferred to the older writer's judgment.

Above all, O'Connor was grateful for the encouragement Gordon provided. Through her, O'Connor found affirmation that *Wise Blood* held great potential for establishing her reputation as a serious artist. Expressing a tremendous admiration for the novel, Gordon had congratulated O'Connor for having achieved a level of distinction that few of her peers could match. Comparing her favorably to Franz Kafka and E. M. Forster, Gordon wrote that what impressed her the most about *Wise Blood* was the way in which it provided a "firm Naturalistic ground-work for your symbolism." Noting the similarities to Truman Capote's fiction, she was, Gordon wrote, "astonished" and "pleased" to find O'Connor putting her own talents to such "a different use." Specifically, she admired O'Connor's ability to provide a moral basis for her artistic vision. This basis was, she recognized, specifically Catholic in nature. "[H]omosexuality, childishness, freakishness—in the end, I think it comes to *fatherlessness*—is rampant in the world today. And you are giving us a terrifying picture of the modern world." Few modern writers, Gordon continued, had been able to achieve such an effect. "Genet," she explained, "achieves remarkable effects but for me they are all marred, finally, by his sentimentality. You are never sentimental." *Wise Blood* was, Gordon concluded, a "powerful" book with a "hard core of dramatic action" that should not, in any way, be "softened up" ("Master Class" 831–32). Commending O'Connor for conveying her moral vision, comparing her favorably to a number of well-regarded male writers, and complimenting her on her lack of "softness" or sentimentality, Gordon was able to confirm O'Connor's hope that the aesthetic she had developed—free of feminine impurities—would indeed enable her to achieve distinction as a serious writer.

*Wise Blood,* Gordon noted, nevertheless displayed a number of shortcomings that O'Connor would be wise to address. "What I am trying to say," Gordon explained, "is that there are one or two devices used by many novelists which I think you would find helpful." For instance, O'Connor could use a device that had been perfected by Flaubert. That is, she could make many of her scenes "more vivid by deliberately going outside" them, just as Flaubert had done throughout *Madame Bovary*. Similarly, Gordon suggested, O'Connor could employ one of Anton Chekhov's techniques by incorporating the landscape into the action of the story. *Wise Blood*, Gordon noted, was somewhat "monotonous" in its use of landscape; moreover, O'Connor had "hurried" over too many important scenes. Instead, Gordon suggested, she should try to incorporate a method perfected by Stephen Crane and W. B. Yeats. "The old Negro preacher's formula for a perfect sermon," Gordon explained, "applies here: 'First I tells 'em I'm going to tell 'em then I tells 'em, then I tell 'em I done told them.'" By way of illustration she referred to the scene in the novel where the police officer throws Haze's car over the embankment. Again citing Flaubert, she explained that the scene was too hurried and that the reader needed at least "three strokes, three activated sensuous details" to make the action appear real (833–35). At the same time, Gordon suggested, O'Connor should consider providing what James referred to as a "stout stake" by preparing readers well in advance for the title and its meaning in the context of the book. A good example of such a technique is found, according to Gordon, in *A Farewell to Arms*, near the start of the novel when the narrator comments, "The leaves fell early that year," in reference to the death that is to come. O'Connor, Gordon's comments implied, had made an ambitious start, producing a novel that not only bettered the work of many of her contemporaries but was worthy of comparison to the work of masters like Flaubert, Chekov, Crane, Yeats, James, and Hemingway (838). Her work could only improve, Gordon concluded, by incorporating the techniques these writers had perfected. At the same time, however, these comments point to the underlying tensions that plagued their relationship from the start. By using such writers as the standard and by emphasizing the ways in which *Wise Blood* was, by comparison, lacking, Gordon made it implicitly clear that the task O'Connor had assumed was not only difficult, but perhaps impossible.

The reason O'Connor remained unlikely to become a true master, Gordon's comments suggested, were ultimately related to her status as a woman. That is, the standards to which Gordon held O'Connor's work were by definition masculine in origin—"hard," "firm," and "powerful." While

O'Connor had succeeded, Gordon agreed, in coating her novel in a "hard" veneer, her gender nevertheless presented her with certain obstacles that the masters had never faced. Chief among these were the problems associated with narrative voice. The narrator, according to Gordon, is always male. "You or I," she explained, "might say that a man had a 'yellow rock head,' but the omniscient narrator . . . can't say that. He speaks and writes Johnsonian English" (838). By contrast, O'Connor's narrator, according to Gordon, frequently resorts to the use of colloquial expressions and has considerable difficulty maintaining objectivity, habits whose only effect is to "lower . . . the tone of the whole scene" (841). Gordon also pointed to a number of passages where O'Connor's narrator had failed to maintain a consistent point of view. Regarding the opening scene with Haze on the train, Gordon wrote, "I think you slip up a little on your viewpoint here. You haven't established the fact that we are seeing things through Haze's eyes, and yet you use words he would have used. . . . I think it would be better to stick to the viewpoint of the omniscient narrator here" (838). O'Connor's narrator, Gordon's comments suggested, tends to a quaint subjectivity that has no place within the "hard" and "powerful" novel she was attempting to write. If O'Connor is to achieve her ambition, Gordon made clear, then she must learn to curb her tendency to reveal, through her inappropriate use of narrative voice, her own identity not as a scrupulously objective man who speaks Johnsonian English, but as a carelessly subjective woman who speaks with a southern accent.

O'Connor, for her part, largely agreed with Gordon's assessment of the novel. Admitting that *Wise Blood* needed "all the help it can get," she expressed her gratitude in a letter to Gordon. "There is no one around here," she confided, "who knows anything at all about fiction (every story is 'your article,' or 'your cute piece') or much about any kind of writing for that matter." As far as her local audience is concerned, "Sidney Lanier and Daniel Whitehead Hickery are the Poets and Margaret Mitchell is the Writer." Given her circumstances, O'Connor concluded, "it means a great deal to me to get these comments." As her letter suggests, O'Connor saw in Gordon a critic who understood the kind of novel she was attempting to write, and she believed that Gordon recognized and appreciated her interest in becoming a serious writer of "Catholic" literature (844–45). As such, O'Connor knew she must learn to rid her work of any qualities that might suggest a kinship to writers such as Lanier, Hickery, or Mitchell. Like her mentors at Iowa, she recognized that she must define herself in opposition to the South's popular, genteel, and implicitly feminine literary tradition. Though at this stage in her career she had given little thought to her status as a "Southern" writer *per se,* she nevertheless understood that she wanted to become a member of Ransom's and Tate's broader republic of letters. In Gordon, she saw a mentor whose advice and training would help her achieve that goal.

Throughout the 1950s O'Connor continued to rely on Gordon's editorial advice. "I have," she wrote Sally and Robert Fitzgerald in late 1953, "been sending poor Caroline stories by the dozen it seems to me." Gordon, she continued, "writes me wherein they do not meet the mark." (*HB* 64–65). Indeed, O'Connor often incorporated the principles Gordon had taught her in her criticisms of other writers. Noting that Nelson Algren's work was marred by "sentimentalism and an overindulgence in the writing," she referred to Gordon's critical theories in explaining the reasons behind these faults. The narrator, she explained, must not use "the same language as the characters" or "there is a loss of tension and a lowering of tone." This lesson, O'Connor admitted, has been a difficult one for her to learn, but Gordon has served as her "mentor in matters of this kind and she has drummed it into me on every occasion so I am very conscious of it" (95). Another lesson she had learned from Gordon, O'Connor wrote, concerned the use of a "central intelligence," which, she explained, had originated with Henry James. Gordon herself "follows a kind of modified use of the central intelligence and the omniscient narrator, but she never gets in anybody else's mind but Claiborn's [of *The Malefactors*], and that's quite something to do." It is, she added, a worthwhile technique since it creates a sense of "dramatic unity that's hard to get otherwise. . . . If you violate the point of view," O'Connor concluded, "you destroy the sense of reality and louse yourself up generally" (157). Her early admiration for Gordon was, in short, unmistakable. Not only did O'Connor gratefully incorporate many of Gordon's suggestions into her work, but she developed considerable respect for Gordon's talents as a critic and writer. "When I am around her," O'Connor jokingly admitted, "I feel like her illiterate grandmother" (149).

O'Connor's respect for Gordon's authority as a critic kept the boundaries between them distinct and made it possible for the two, initially, to develop a relationship free of the discord that characterized Gordon's relationship to male protégés such as Ward Dorrance or to female colleagues such as Katherine Anne Porter. Gordon, in other words, could remain assured that O'Connor, unlike Dorrance, would accept her suggestions gratefully and without complaint or question. O'Connor's age—she was young enough to be one of Gordon's students—coupled with her pronounced sense of humility neither aggravated Gordon's insecurities nor offered the potential for the kind of competition that characterized her relationship to Porter. Ironically, however, the very same qualities that made O'Connor the ideal protégé also provided the ground in which the seeds of friction would begin to grow. Both O'Connor's age and her gender reinforced her status as Gordon's protégé rather than her colleague and prevented O'Connor from commanding the sort of respect that Gordon readily offered men like Dorrance. Consequently, it became easier for Gordon to find fault with O'Connor's efforts and to communicate her disapproval without fear of the reprisals she received from Dorrance. Established on these clearly hierarchical premises, their mentoring relationship, at least in its initial stages, appeared mutually satisfying.

Soon, however, the tensions that lay beneath the surface began increasingly to emerge. While Gordon's positive reading of *Wise Blood* undoubtedly boosted O'Connor's confidence, many of the comments only confirmed her latent fears regarding her ability to convey the artistic distinction she hoped to achieve. "I had felt," she admitted to Gordon, "that the title wasn't anchored in the story but I hadn't known how to anchor it. I am about that now. It won't be a stout stake but it'll be something." O'Connor also admitted that she had "felt there were places that went too fast" and that her tendency to "hurry" was a problem she needed to correct. "I've been reading a lot of Conrad lately because he goes so slow and I had thought reading him might help that fault. There is not much danger of my imitating *him*" ("Master Class" 845–46). Despite the encouragement that Gordon offered, her comments had reinforced O'Connor's anxieties that she was not in the same class as writers like James, Conrad, and the other masters to whom Gordon had referred. Though O'Connor continued to aspire to membership in the republic of letters, she was never able to overcome the lingering fear that she was perhaps incapable of producing great literature. As her frustrations with Gordon's advice mounted, O'Connor gradually concluded that her mentor only contributed to the problems from which her work suffered. Though O'Connor remained steadfastly polite and deferential in her letters to Gordon, she gradually became resentful of her mentor's attitude. As O'Connor's resentment grew, so too did her reluctance to accept Gordon's advice on face value.

The subtle shift in their relationship emerged more directly in the critical reviews on O'Connor's work that Gordon published from the late 1950s onward, as the eager enthusiasm with which she initially greeted the young writer's work gradually gave way to a reserved admiration. And her admiration was increasingly offered only with significant qualifications, chief among them the constant reminder that, in the final analysis, O'Connor was not a master. Gordon's 1955 review of "A Good Man Is Hard to Find" is typical of her early opinion of O'Connor's work. "This first collection of short stories by Flannery O'Connor," she began, "exhibits what Henry James, in 'a partial portrait' of Guy de Maupassant, called 'the artful brevity of a master.'" Likening O'Connor to a "lioness," Gordon concluded that her work was nothing short of "revolutionary." The integrity of O'Connor's fiction, she argued, lay in the fact that O'Connor is "fiercely concerned with moral, even theological, problems" and that in approaching these problems her talent is matched only by her orthodoxy. As Gordon's final remarks concerning the stories suggest, at this point in her career, not long after her conversion, she viewed orthodoxy as one of the most important elements in fiction. Of "The Displaced Person," she wrote that it displayed a "profounder symbolism" in the figure of the judge, who "may also—for the orthodox—symbolize the 'Old' South, his study, 'a dark, closet-like space as dark and quiet as a chapel,' the scanty provision which the 'Old' South was able to make for the spiritual needs of her children" ("With a Glitter"). Gordon certainly admired O'Connor's ability to use the southern idiom to suit her purposes. As these remarks suggest, however, she considered O'Connor's purpose—her "orthodox," or Catholic, vision—as ultimately more meaningful than the idiom through which she expressed herself.[11] Her long-standing identification with the South strained by the pressures of her uncertain marriage to Tate and by her newfound enthusiasm for the Catholic Church, Gordon initially saw in O'Connor's moral vision everything she could want in a writer.

By 1958, when she published an essay on *Wise Blood* for *Critique,* Gordon's enthusiasm had begun to wane. No longer willing to suggest that O'Connor belonged in the company of the masters, Gordon instead compared her to contemporaries like Truman Capote, Carson McCullers, and Tennessee Williams. To be sure, Gordon argued that O'Connor was "one of the most important writers of our age." Yet by comparing O'Connor to writers of her own age, the majority of whom Gordon considered inferior, she was, in effect, revising her original view of O'Connor's work. Offering an extended comparison between *Wise Blood* and *Other Voices, Other Rooms,* Gordon admitted that O'Connor and Capote did indeed have much in common. "Their characters have what we might almost call a 'family likeness.' They often behave in the same way, talk the same way" (3). Both novels are also populated almost exclusively by freaks. "Miss O'Connor writes lean, stripped, at times almost too flat-footed a prose, and her characters, as I have said, move always in the harsh glare of every day . . . [T]hey, too, are warped and misshapen by life—in short, freaks. The difference between her work and that of her gifted contemporaries," Gordon concluded, "lies in the nature and causes of their freakishness" (5). While most of Capote's work reads like a "case history," O'Connor's fiction is grounded in a moral vision that, Gordon argued, should properly form the basis of art (10). Similarly, in noting the parallels between *Wise Blood* and *A Fable,* Gordon compared not the quality of each writer's prose, but the soundness of their theology. The priest of *A Fable* serves as evidence that Faulkner's theology, "what there is of it," most likely dates from "his grandfather's time, derived, perhaps, from a reading of Renan." Haze, on the other hand, is "fully as heretical but his logical processes are more exact. And he speaks—terrifyingly—for our own time" (9).[12]

As she had demonstrated in essays such as "Some Readings and Misreadings," Gordon believed that all great literature was founded in Christian myth; as a writer whose work so soundly incorporates Christian orthodoxy, O'Connor should, according to Gordon's logic, justifiably deserve status as a master. Gordon had, after all, initially admired the skill with which O'Connor conveyed her moral vision. It therefore remains significant that Gordon now compared O'Connor's theological knowledge—her greatest literary asset—to a writer like Capote rather than to writers like Flaubert and James, whom Gordon considered greatly superior. At the same time, it is also significant that, despite her obvious admiration for O'Connor's work, Gordon became somewhat circumspect with regard to the question of the quality of her prose. O'Connor may have been "one of the most important writers of our age," Gordon admitted, but when it came to the actual expression of this vision, her prose was, at best, somewhat "flat-footed." The standards that Gordon applied to O'Connor's work were, in the final analysis, highly contradictory. While she increasingly viewed the use of Christian myth as a crucial component in all great literature, in O'Connor's case, Gordon decided to emphasize technique over moral vision. Her refusal to accord O'Connor the same status as writers like Flaubert and James, despite her Christian vision, suggests that although her reasons may ostensibly have been different, Gordon nevertheless shared with Ransom and Tate a fundamental discomfort in considering female writers worthy of admission to the republic of letters.

Though early in their relationship O'Connor wrote that she was pleased that Gordon, a fellow Catholic, had been able to recognize the moral basis of her artistic vision, by the time *The Violent Bear It Away* was published in 1960, O'Connor had begun to develop misgivings concerning her reputation as a "Christian" writer. Of *Wise Blood,* she had written in the early 1950s, "I never have, fortunately, expected to make any money out of it, but one thing that has concerned me is that it might be recognized by Catholics as an effort proper to a Catholic" ("Master Class" 844). When *The Violent Bear It Away* appeared, however, she expressed disappointment that the sole comments on the back cover came from Gordon, who, following her usual custom, emphasized the strength of O'Connor's religious convictions. The comments, she noted, "had really been written about *Wise Blood* and the stories" and not about *The Violent Bear It Away.* "In the piece," she continued, ". . . she went on to quote Blake's thing about oft in midnight streets I hear, about the harlot's curse blighting with plagues the marriage hearse, etc.; so I suppose what she had in mind was Blake's vision of evil." Admitting that she wished they "had used a variety of quotes on the back, some from other points of view," O'Connor complained that she no longer cared to be labeled a Catholic writer "in the popular sense of it, as it is then assumed that you have some religious axe to grind" (*HB* 391). Just as Gordon had begun to realize that perhaps O'Connor was not the master she had originally presumed her to be, O'Connor had in turn become somewhat disillusioned with Gordon's critical faculties. As these comments suggest, she did not think that Gordon's use of the quotation from Blake necessarily made sense. Moreover, she noted on more than one occasion that Gordon had neglected to comment publicly on *The Violent Bear It Away* (390).[13] In fact, Gordon would not publish any additional essays or reviews on her protégé's work until after O'Connor's death in 1964. O'Connor seems to have been annoyed by this somewhat sudden lack of attention, as she was by the fact that the comments that did appear on the book served only to confirm her status as a Catholic writer with "some religious axe to grind." No longer willing to take Gordon's assessment of her work at face value, O'Connor had begun to grow restless under the constraints that she believed her mentor had placed upon her.

Even as early as the mid-1950s, O'Connor had noted with some impatience that Gordon is a "disciple of James" and "a great student of Flaubert" who "is always telling me that the endings are too flat and that at the end I must gain some altitude and get a larger view" (157, 187, 78). Gordon's own fiction, she had begun to conclude, suffered from many of the same limitations. "I am still reading Caroline's stories," O'Connor remarked. "I see where Mr. Maury is a mite irritating, a mite cute at times. Too much of Mr. Maury" (*CW* 1016). O'Connor's disapproval of Gordon's personal life only contributed to her growing disillusionment. O'Connor believed, for instance, that the problem with Gordon's marriage to Tate was not so much, as their mutual friend Brainard Cheney had suggested, Tate's "spoiled" nature; instead the true "culprit" was alcohol. In O'Connor's view, excessive drinking was not an illness but a moral offense against God, one for which she held Gordon and Tate personally responsible (1012). As the years wore on O'Connor made a number of barbed remarks concerning other aspects of Gordon's behavior. Referring to an upcoming visit from Gordon as an "ordeal," O'Connor joked that she hoped the Carmelite order in Princeton had decided to reject Gordon's plans to end "her days in their establishment. I don't imagine they took too eagerly to the idea," she continued. "I guess if they've survived since the time of Elias she's no real threat, but still, they must have a sense of self-preservation" (1186, 1201). O'Connor's growing annoyance with what she considered Gordon's moral lassitude and her increasing impatience with what she somewhat sarcastically termed her excessive "Vitality" only contributed to her doubts concerning Gordon's critical abilities (1197).

By the time Gordon's essay on *Wise Blood* appeared in *Critique,* O'Connor had all but lost her initial enthusiasm for her mentor's critical orientation. Noting that the special issue of the journal, devoted to O'Connor and to J. F. Powers, was "a well-meant but not highly successful effort to do me a favor," O'Connor concluded that "Powers came out better in the people he had to write about his stuff" and that Gordon's essay was "wildly mixed up" (1082). Though she refused to elaborate, she was likely annoyed by the circumspect manner in which Gordon compared her to other writers and by Gordon's insistence that O'Connor's talent lay in her moral vision. By the early 1960s, O'Connor had become somewhat more explicit in expressing her views on Gordon's critical abilities. Of the second edition of Gordon's *House of Fiction,* she wrote, "I have looked at some of the comentaries [*sic*] in the H of F and while some are good, some seem rather poor excuses" (1130). When *Critique* devoted a special issue to Gordon, O'Connor was pleased to see that Andrew Lytle had written "a fine essay" on her work. Nevertheless, O'Connor's remarks suggest that she did not necessarily agree with his assessment. "She is death on technique," O'Connor concluded, "too death on it to my way of thinking, but as I have learned a great deal from her, I preserve more or less a respectful silence" (1146). O'Connor's remarks referred not simply to her views on Gordon's fiction but to her views on Gordon's critical orientation, which she now considered unnecessarily rigid. Though she continued to send her stories to Gordon and continued to write that she found Gordon's suggestions helpful, a note of complaint increasingly found its way into O'Connor's remarks. "I sent [Gordon] a story before Christmas," O'Connor remarked of "Revelation" in a 1964 letter, "a real good one too, better than I have pulled off in a long time, and she wrote me another six page letter about that, or rather, all about grammar which I ain't got the principles of besides not being able to spell anything" (1197). While she acknowledged that Gordon's suggestions had improved the story, O'Connor continued to refer somewhat sarcastically to the "six pages of grammar" in her letters to other correspondents (1199). Later that same year, exhausted by the series of operations and blood transfusions that preceded her death, O'Connor expressed her frustrations more openly. Referring to "Parker's Back," her final story, she wrote, "Caroline gave me a lot of advice about the story but most of it I'm ignoring. She thinks every story must be built according to the pattern of the Roman arch and she would enlarge the beginning and the end, but I'm letting it lay. I did well to write it at all" (1218).

Indeed, "Parker's Back" offers intriguing evidence of Gordon's waning influence on O'Connor. Though it shares many elements in common with her earlier fiction, it differs in significant ways. Sarah Ruth Parker, like Mrs. Turpin and many of O'Connor's female protagonists, is clearly an unnaturally domineering wife. Parker himself cannot "understand why he stayed with her . . . He was puzzled and ashamed of himself" (*CW* 655). Her pregnancy, he concludes, has no bearing on the matter; in fact, it makes him all the more determined to leave her. Nevertheless, Sarah Ruth manages to maintain a mysterious hold on Parker, "as if she had him conjured." He stays with her despite her professed distaste for his tattoos, his cursing, and his lack of faith and despite her frequent use of physical violence and his own growing sense of gloom. "Not knowing for certain why he continued to stay with a woman who was both ugly and pregnant and no cook made him generally nervous and irritable," comments the narrator, "and he developed a little tic in the side of his face" (664). Unable to make Sarah Ruth "heel," Parker has, like Claud, been robbed of the power traditionally owed him as a man.

His power is only further undermined as he seeks ever more drastic measures to win his wife's love and approval. He decides, finally, that he must get another tattoo, a religiously inspired one "that Sarah Ruth would not be able to resist" (664). The Christ figure tattooed on his back brings about a religious awakening in Parker, as it gradually dawns on him that "the eyes on his back were eyes to be obeyed." He recognizes this "instinct" as part of a pattern that has governed his life, inspiring him to cover his body in tattoos, to join the navy, and, most importantly, to marry Sarah Ruth. O'Connor's typical format would have ended the story here at this epiphanic moment of "rapture" in which Parker, like so many of her protagonists, suddenly finds himself "examining his soul" and thereby (according to the readings she hoped to encourage) entering a state of grace. Instead, however, readers are given a glimpse of Parker's post-epiphanic moments, ones dominated not by the presence of grace but by Sarah Ruth. Rising "slowly to his feet," Parker realizes that his wife will be an integral part of his new life. He thinks to himself that she will "know what he had to do" and that he will be able to rely on her to "clear up the rest of it." His desire to "please her" has resulted in his own conversion, and he looks now to his wife to guide him further on his journey (672). In this way Sarah Ruth, like Julian's mother and a number of other female characters, becomes an unwitting vehicle for the male protagonist's salvation. But in an uncharacteristic break with this pattern, Sarah Ruth channels this power to inspire religious passion as a means to serve her *own* ends. Beating Parker with her broom, she "nearly knock[s] him senseless" and leaves readers with a final image of him "crying like a baby," utterly devoid of the feelings that had inspired his awakening. Having symbolically castrated her husband, Sarah Ruth has used her own power to thwart Parker's attempts at achieving salvation.

Herein lies the difference between Sarah Ruth and O'Connor's earlier female characters. In the end, Sarah Ruth prevails over both her husband and God, pronouncing judgment on Parker, enacting punishment on him, and thereby negating the power of a religious epiphany she understands as misdirected. Refusing to accept his tattoos, his intermittent wanderings away from home, and now his vague religious yearnings, she insists on her own interpretation of events. The tattoos, she claims, are pure "Idolatry!" God, according to her view, is "a spirit. No man shall see his face" (674). Sarah Ruth adheres to a fundamentalist interpretation of Christianity, one that considers anything but the "Straight Gospel" her father preaches to be heresy (662). By O'Connor's own perspective, then, Sarah Ruth's fundamentalism, in focusing so closely on the literal, is itself misdirected. O'Connor admired Old Tarwater of *The Violent Bear It Away* because he was a "prophet in the true sense . . . inspired by the Holy Ghost, not necessarily by the dominant religion of his region." Moreover, she characterized the fundamentalist sects to which a character such as Tarwater might have belonged as "strange," composed mostly of "swindlers, the mad, and sometimes the genuinely inspired" (*HB* 407). Not being the heirs to a Catholic tradition, southerners were, in O'Connor's view, in a difficult position. "Wise blood," she explained, "has to be these people's means of grace—they have no sacraments. The religion of the South is a do-it-yourself religion . . . It's full of unconscious pride that lands them in all sorts of ridiculous religious predicaments" (350). According to this logic, Parker's tattoos represent a "do-it-yourself" attempt to develop a sacramental relationship with God, while Sarah Ruth's rigid adherence to her father's "Straight Gospel" preaching allies her with the South's "strange sects." Rejecting the fundamentalism his wife embraces and "inspired" instead "by the Holy Ghost," Parker has, by O'Connor's calculation, become a "true prophet." Nevertheless, Sarah Ruth prevails, and her husband never does achieve salvation. Ignoring Gordon's advice to "enlarge the ending," O'Connor managed to break with her established pattern, creating a story that neither ends in epiphany nor relies on the subjugation of a female character. On the contrary, "Parker's Back" depicts a pregnant female character who manages to escape punishment and who is possessed of a religious authority and physical strength powerful enough to defy God and deny the male protagonist his claim to salvation.

O'Connor's relationship to Gordon had, by the time she wrote "Parker's Back," unquestionably changed. Gordon's insistence on emphasizing O'Connor's moral vision and on restricting her to a specific grammatical and technical structure for each story now represented a limitation O'Connor found confining. Her respect for Gordon's critical abilities was, no doubt, only further undermined by Gordon's long-standing habit of privileging male critics and writers and encouraging O'Connor to purge her work of any feminine qualities. More significantly, O'Connor's relationship to Gordon had done little to improve her self-confidence. As she explained in a letter to Father J. H. McCown, she felt that her writing had become formulaic. "I've been writing for sixteen years and I have the sense of having exhausted my original potentiality and being now in need of the kind of grace that deepens perception, a new shot of life or something" (468). The following year she continued to complain about the difficulties of keeping her work fresh, and she wrote Sister Mariella Gable asking for her prayers. "I've been writing eighteen years," O'Connor explained, "and I've reached the point where I can't do again what I know I can do well, and that larger things that I need to do now, I doubt my capacity for doing" (518).[14] Believing that many of Gordon's suggestions would only add to these problems and seeing in Gordon's work many of the problems to which she herself was prone, O'Connor gradually lost confidence in her mentor's abilities as well. By teaching O'Connor that she must emulate the masters while simultaneously emphasizing the ways in which her work fell short, by encouraging her to conform to a rigid structure O'Connor believed could only stifle her creativity, and by stressing the ways in which the female intellect was inferior, Gordon virtually assured that her relationship to O'Connor would fail to meet their mutual expectations.

Gordon, for her part, never fully understood the extent to which O'Connor found the relationship unsatisfactory. Yet the reminiscences she offered in a 1968 essay suggest that on some level she understood that O'Connor had become frustrated with her emphasis on structure. At the same time, Gordon had apparently arrived at the realization that her pedagogical methods had eroded O'Connor's self-confidence. Recalling the events that transpired after she had received the manuscript for "Parker's Back," Gordon wrote that on "this occasion I followed my usual crabbed custom and sent her, by mail, along with my praise for her story, a few criticisms, for the most part minor technical matters," unaware or possibly "unwilling to admit" that O'Connor was dying. Soon after she had sent these comments, Gordon "felt impelled to send her a telegram" congratulating her "on having succeeded where the great Flaubert failed!" Gordon admitted that over the years she felt it might have been better if she had not written O'Connor about that final story. "What I said in my telegram," Gordon concluded, "better represents my wholehearted reaction to the body of her work" ("Heresy in Dixie" 266). Though this passage is somewhat vague, the implications are that the telegram had been sent out of guilt when Gordon became aware that O'Connor was dying, and that it arrived too late.[15] Viewing O'Connor's work in hindsight and clearly troubled by her lingering fears that perhaps she never conveyed to her protégé the full extent of her admiration, Gordon once again offered a revised opinion of O'Connor's fiction. She was, Gordon concluded four years after O'Connor's death, a strong and original talent whose work does in fact merit comparison to that of "one of the greatest literary craftsmen of all time and the creator of more than one masterpiece," Flaubert (289).

Even in her attempts to revise her earlier views on O'Connor's work and, perhaps, to ease her guilt regarding the comments on O'Connor's final story, Gordon remained unable, despite her claims to the contrary, to consider her protégé on equal terms with a writer like Flaubert. Indeed, by 1968 her list of reservations concerning O'Connor's work had grown along with the extent of her praise. For example, Gordon noted, a "superficial reading" of O'Connor's fiction "gives the impression that her range is limited." Her "cast of characters is small and the same characters, or characters who resemble them, appear over and over and over in what seems almost the same situation." Nevertheless, Gordon continued in an effort to make her admiration more clear, it is "the *depth* of her explorations, not their surface scope," that sets O'Connor's fiction apart. And though she falls short of the standards set by a writer such as Faulkner, she surpasses him on one count: her "ear for the vernacular is subtler than his." At the same time, Gordon noted in conclusion, "no one can deny that her stories are soundly constructed" (267–68). Despite her complimentary tone, Gordon's remarks imply that her views on O'Connor's work had not really changed. A writer of limited range, O'Connor displays her talents through her use of structure and dialogue, abilities that would hardly qualify her as a "master craftsman." Gordon's reasons for likening O'Connor to Flaubert centered, once again, on her respect for O'Connor's moral vision. While O'Connor may not compare to Flaubert or to Faulkner as a writer, as a theologian, "though by no means as learned as Flaubert," she belongs in the company of the West's great religious thinkers (291).

Despite her conclusion that O'Connor, at least in her capacity as a theologian, deserved comparison with Flaubert, Gordon devoted the vast majority of the essay not to O'Connor but to Flaubert: of the thirty-five pages ostensibly reserved for an analysis of O'Connor's fiction, over twenty concern Flaubert. A similar pattern characterizes Gordon's final essay on O'Connor, which was published in 1974.[16] Again, Gordon concluded that although O'Connor may be a master in her "proportionate" use of structure and her subtle ear for dialogue, her range is limited and her work frequently suffers "flaws of execution." The value of her fiction, argued Gordon, following her now-familiar script, can be found instead in O'Connor's moral vision: "Her originality and, I suspect, her importance in the history of American literature lie in the fact that she was the first American author, possessed of a first-rate talent, to look at the rural South through the eyes of Roman Catholic orthodoxy" ("Rebels and Revolutionaries" 50–51). Even these somewhat dubious efforts to elevate O'Connor's standing become lost under the weight of Gordon's comments concerning James, which constitute nearly half of her essay. Her admiration for James and Flaubert obscures the real purpose of both essays, effectively undermining any attempts Gordon made to promote O'Connor's literary reputation.

As much as she admired O'Connor, Gordon was simply incapable of viewing her as a writer wholly deserving of admission to the republic of letters. Even as she increasingly justified her admiration for certain writers by citing their qualifications as "Christian" artists, Gordon continued to emphasize the literary qualities that prevented O'Connor from achieving the range that distinguishes the work of a true master. At the same time, she persisted in characterizing O'Connor as a writer whose greatest contribution to the American and southern literary tradition was in fact her uniquely orthodox vision. In short, whatever criteria Gordon applied to O'Connor's work, the result was the same. Though O'Connor herself may not have fully recognized the dynamics at play, she nevertheless understood that Gordon's persistent emphasis on her religious vision, coupled with her frequent reminders that O'Connor fell short of the standards set by the masters, only served to diminish her literary standing and to undermine her self-confidence. Gordon's insistence that she should emulate masters like Flaubert and James, her habit of citing male critical and theological authorities, and her persistent emphasis on O'Connor's difficulties in establishing an "objective" narrative voice only served to confirm O'Connor's original convictions concerning the superiority of the male intellect. As a consequence, she increasingly lost confidence in Gordon's own abilities as a writer, critic, and mentor.

The resulting effects on O'Connor's work are unmistakable. Although it is safe to conclude that O'Connor, at least early in her career, often made many of the changes her mentor suggested, Gordon's influence extended beyond the formal or the technical. To be certain, Gordon (if the published correspondence is accurate) never explicitly encouraged O'Connor to "write like a man." Nevertheless, she managed to convey her message quite forcefully. Both by word and by example Gordon made it clear to O'Connor that the authorities who held the keys to her professional success scorned the feminine and valued above all the work of the "masters." Gordon's influence thus lay not so much in the changes she made on individual stories and novels but in her role as O'Connor's mentor; the woman who provided her initiation into the mysteries of Ransom's and Tate's republic of letters. Through Gordon, O'Connor learned to trust the instincts cultivated by her instructors at Iowa, and through her, ironically, O'Connor learned to distrust Gordon's own instruction. Though founded on mutual admiration, their relationship, based as it was on the hierarchies that characterized the literary culture in which they worked, was bound to unravel. That it eventually did attests not simply to Gordon's influence but, more importantly, to the force with which the politics of gender influenced O'Connor's literary development.

# 3 · *Flannery O'Connor and the Problem of Female Authorship*

The Manuscripts as Evidence

WHILE CAROLINE GORDON served as her chief mentor, O'Connor's literary development was nourished in a variety of ways, through a series of mentors both at Iowa and elsewhere. The manuscripts for her first novel, *Wise Blood,* offer intriguing evidence of O'Connor's struggle to find a voice that could express her artistic vision in terms that would be appreciated by the critical community that had nourished her work and to which she hoped to appeal. Though it remains difficult to draw definitive conclusions concerning *Wise Blood*'s development, certain facts about the novel's history have nevertheless come to light. Stephen J. Driggers, who prepared a catalog of the manuscript collection at Georgia College, has concluded that O'Connor undertook the *Wise Blood* revisions in three basic stages. By the time she applied for the Rinehart-Iowa fiction prize in 1947, she had completed early versions of five chapters, including "The Train," "The Peeler," and the untitled chapters pertaining to Haze's sister Ruby. The prize was awarded on the basis of these chapters, and O'Connor continued to work on the remaining seven until September of the following year, when editor John Selby informed her that he would need to see six chapters before he could provide an advance. By early 1949, she had completed revisions on nine of the chapters and was able to include an outline for the remainder of the book. That year she learned that Selby had not been impressed with her work, and she decided to obtain a release from her contract with Rinehart. Between January 1949 and March 1951, when she submitted the novel to Robert Giroux at Harcourt, O'Connor rewrote the novel from the beginning. Though Gordon was to make suggestions for fine-tuning certain scenes, *Wise Blood* was essentially completed by 1951 (Driggers xii–xiii).[1]

Because surviving manuscripts for the novel are not organized into separate versions or chronological order, it remains difficult to reach definitive conclusions regarding the evolution of either *Wise Blood* or *The Violent Bear It Away*.[2] Despite the difficulties, however, it is possible to draw certain conclusions regarding the revision process. Perhaps the most significant factor that emerges is the contribution Andrew Lytle made to *Wise Blood*'s development. He began to oversee O'Connor's work in 1948, the same year in which she revised the first five chapters and completed an additional four. Included among those early chapters was the long section concerning Haze's sister Ruby, which by 1949 had been omitted from the novel altogether. Published in abbreviated form first as "The Woman on the Stairs" and later as "A Stroke of Good Fortune," O'Connor throughout the remainder of her career viewed the story as her weakest. As her advisor, Lytle no doubt played a crucial role in encouraging, or at the very least supporting, her decision to omit material that was written from a female point of view and that dealt explicitly with female experience and with such subjects as pregnancy and abortion. If, as she had claimed in her 1948 Guggenheim application, her "ultimate purpose as an artist" was to "produce work which will have a human meaning and be of high literary caliber," then such female-sexed material would, according to the New Critical standards taught at Iowa, cast doubts both upon her objectivity and her seriousness as an artist (File 23, OMC). Clearly, her affiliation with Lytle and the literary establishment with which he was associated exerted a strong influence on O'Connor's literary development.

Yet the manuscripts for both *Wise Blood* and *The Violent Bear It Away* reveal that, despite her efforts to please mentors like Lytle and the critical establishment he represented, O'Connor continued to explore, often quite sympathetically, female consciousness and experience in a way that differs markedly from the treatment accorded female characters in most of her published fiction. Moreover, she frequently subjected her male characters to the satire that in her published fiction is most often reserved for women like the Grandmother, Mrs. May, Mrs. Turpin, and Julian's mother. At the same time, the manuscripts for her two longest works offer evidence of the struggle O'Connor faced in adapting her writing to conform to masculinist conventions. When read in light of the manuscripts, the published versions of *Wise Blood* and *The Violent Bear It Away* take on new meaning, as do stories such as "A Circle in the Fire" and "A View of the Woods." The "feminization" that both Haze and Tarwater undergo appears as evidence not so much of O'Connor's interest in the redemptive possibilities of androgyny, as Marshall Bruce Gentry argues, but of the lingering presence of the female characters and female-oriented plot lines that appear throughout her manuscripts.[3] Similarly, the decidedly *un*ladylike young female characters of "A Circle in the Fire" and "A View in the Woods" suggest that O'Connor never entirely suppressed the female-sexed voice that informs her manuscripts, but she managed instead to find ways to give it expression within the confines of the masculinist stance she had embraced.

In preparing an early synopsis of *Wise Blood,* O'Connor wrote of her protagonist, Hazel Motes: "His search for a physical home mirrors his search for a spiritual one, and although he finds neither, it is the latter search which saves him from becoming a member of the Wasteland and makes him worth 75,000 words" (File 22a). One of the more outstanding features of both the published and unpublished versions of *Wise Blood,* as Sally Fitzgerald has argued, is their obvious resemblance to *The Wasteland.* The characters of Ruby, Haze's sister who seeks an abortion of an unwanted child, and Laverne, an early version of Leora Watts, bear a distinct resemblance to Lil and May of Part II of *The Wasteland.* Similarly, Madame Zoleeda, the clairvoyant who predicts Ruby's pregnancy, is, according to Fitzgerald, based on Madame Sosostris ("The Owl and the Nightingale" 53). Other allusions to Eliot— Enoch's comment that the mummified "new jesus" "was once as tall as you or me," for example—are more obvious and quite possibly intentional (*CW* 56). In any case, Fitzgerald's purpose in bringing them to attention centers on her desire to prove Eliot a stronger influence than writers such as Edgar Allan Poe and Nathaniel West ("Owl and Nightingale" 55). What she fails to consider is the possibility that the most intriguing feature of these characters is not their allusion to Eliot but their allusion to female experience and their status as women in a fictional landscape populated almost exclusively by men. More significantly, Fitzgerald fails to note exactly how much of O'Connor's attention characters like Ruby and Laverne commanded; nearly half of the *Wise Blood* manuscripts are devoted to Ruby, Leora Watts, and Haze's relationship to his mother and sisters. Nor does Fitzgerald consider other reasons—besides her obvious admiration for Eliot—why O'Connor originally focused so closely on female characters.

In fact, references to female consciousness and experience abound throughout the *Wise Blood* manuscripts and support Gentry's conclusion that O'Connor's use of the female name "Hazel" was the result of an unconscious de-masculinization of her protagonist. In marked contrast to the surly character of the published novel, the earliest manuscript incarnation of Haze is almost overbearingly polite and touchingly solicitous of the ladies he meets on the train; in this way he reveals an emotional vulnerability not in keeping with his later, more stoic and "manly" incarnation. Offering to stow the luggage of almost every woman who crosses his path, he eagerly strikes up a conversation with his seatmate, Mrs. Hitchcock. "Yes mam," he remarks, "I'm a private in the army. I got me a furlough." Reminded of his mother, he adds, "My mother was a Jackson. Annie Lou Jackson," noting fondly that she "always sat on the left side going in to Chattanooga." Clearly homesick, Haze searches the train for ladies to assist and to chat with and becomes disappointed to discover that the train is mostly full of soldiers like himself. His desire for female companionship provokes in him long-forgotten memories of his aunt, his sisters, and his mother (File 19a, OMC). Unlike the Haze of the published novel, the Haze of the early manuscripts remembers his family with fondness and a sense of longing. Conspicuously missing is the hostility toward women that leads to his confrontation with Mrs. Hitchcock in the opening pages of the final version.

O'Connor completed these early manuscripts while she was still at Iowa, and it was not long before they began to take on the hostile tone characteristic of her later work, in which the female characters in particular are subject to ridicule and humiliation at the hands of both the male characters and the narrator. At the same time, Haze's evolution from the polite young man who loves his mother to the surly young man who hates and fears his mother suggests that O'Connor worked hard to purge her work of the sentimental.

Apparently, neither O'Connor nor her instructors were particularly impressed by the polite and unmistakably feminized Haze of the early manuscripts. Even as early as 1948, when "The Train" was published in the *Sewanee Review,* Haze had begun to exhibit the anti-social traits that were to distinguish him in his final incarnation. The protagonist of "The Train" is, in a sense, a composite of both versions; though outwardly polite, he secretly views the women passengers with disdain. No longer interested in striking up conversations and troubled by unpleasant memories of his mother and sisters, in the final version Haze attempts to "escape" from Mrs. Hitchcock (*CW* 755). The remainder of the story is concerned not with his relationship to his family but with his mistaken notion that one of the porters is from his hometown. Thus the published version of "The Train" shares with *Wise Blood* two important characteristics: a thinly veiled misogyny that the narrator as well as Haze direct at female characters and a diminished role for the female characters within the scope of the story. By the time she had submitted "The Train" for publication, O'Connor had decided that even minor characters like Cash, the porter, would play a more important role in Haze's spiritual awakening than his mother and sisters.

By contrast, in the various manuscript versions of these early scenes, it is the female characters who serve as the catalysts in Haze's growing realization that he cannot escape his calling. After she had completed the first four chapters, O'Connor submitted a synopsis wherein she outlined her plan for the remainder of the novel. Though this version had begun to display the belligerent tone characteristic of the published novel, it nevertheless centered, like the earliest versions, on Haze's relationship to his mother, sisters, and Lea— the precursor of Leora Watts. Summarizing the latter half of the novel, O'Connor wrote that Haze "wants Lea and he can have her without the formality of marriage, but he is afraid." Finally succumbing to his desire, he finds himself "overwhelmed with a sense of guilt," since this encounter occurs the same night his sister Ruby dies giving birth. Haze's affair with Lea becomes symbolic of his "acclimation to the city," which "now seems cheap and terrible to him. He is ready to accept God in any form" (File 22a, OMC). As this summary suggests, O'Connor intended the plot of her novel to center largely on Haze's relationship to Ruby and Lea; his spiritual awakening was to unfold in response to Ruby's doomed pregnancy and to his thwarted affair with Lea. In the manuscripts, then, God essentially uses the female characters as the medium through which to reach Haze. It is Ruby, in fact, who first introduces him to the very idea of Godlessness, the concept that in the novel eventually emerges as the Church Without Christ. By contrast, in the published version Ruby has been eliminated altogether, while Lea, as prostitute Leora Watts, plays a comparatively minor role. Hardly a catalyst for spiritual awakening, Leora serves instead as a temporary and quickly forgotten diversion in Haze's path toward the final acceptance of his calling.

Haze's mother is another character whose importance declined as the novel emerged in its published form. In the manuscripts, even as O'Connor transformed her character from the fondly remembered lady of the earliest chapters to the overbearing religious fanatic of the later versions, Haze's mother played a prominent role. Indeed, unlike the Haze of the published novel, who occasionally recalls his mother with a combination of dread and respect, the manuscript Haze is virtually obsessed with memories, both pleasant and unpleasant, of his mother, as he recalls her numerous pregnancies and their often tragic results. In fact, it is Haze's mother who originally claims the tragic reproductive history that functioned as such a menacing specter for Ruby in "A Stroke of Good Fortune." Whereas in the published story these pregnancies become emblematic of women's justly deserved fate under patriarchy, in the manuscripts they assume an entirely different meaning. In a painful litany, Haze recalls the tragic circumstance of each birth and death and maintains sympathy for his mother throughout. Haze was, he recalls, his mother's eighth child, and her last. "Her first two were twin girls." Although they survived, "the next three were buried in Sparta county at the Harmony Springs Church." He can recall each child, those who were "born dead," those who "died the first year," and those who, like his brother Davis Crater, were involved in fatal accidents. Haze's recollections of his mother's early history are similarly sympathetic. Born in Tennessee, she was raised in "a one story yellow house that was torn down ten years ago to make room for an automobile factory." Her father had "always been dead," while her mother "had had false yellow hair and wore paint on her face." Like Ruby, she was "stupid and not consciously sinful" (File 25b). More than the root cause of Haze's fanaticism, his mother serves as the link to his family and its past.

Family history, its trials and difficulties, comes alive, significantly, through her experience of female embodiment. Her parents, her childhood, her unsuccessful pregnancies, and the sense of frustrated hope that each represents become for him symbols of his own sense of dislocation. With his father mysteriously absent, his mother's embodied history functions as a metaphor for his own situation as a lost individual.

Even as Haze's memories of his mother become increasingly troubling to him, his obsession with her remains a central driving force in his spiritual quest. In the later manuscripts, he begins to confuse Ruby, Lea, and his mother. Their identities gradually merge as Haze plays over in his mind various memories and fantasies in which each woman figures prominently. Together, the three emerge as the catalyst for his spiritual dislocation as well as the agents behind his growing awareness of the need to return to God, and in this way they serve as the nucleus around which all of the action revolves. For instance, Haze remembers a number of episodes during their childhood when Ruby abandoned him or beat him for following her into town. He recalls one day in particular, when Haze's mother beat them both after they arrived home from Melsey. He never does accompany Ruby into town again, and these early memories, which figure prominently in the manuscripts, become emblematic of Haze's later estrangement from society and of the central role both Ruby and his mother played in provoking it (File 25b). Similarly, Haze's relationship with Lea, soon to be renamed Leora, becomes the defining event in his decision to abandon God. After their first sexual encounter together, Haze realizes that, without God, his attempts at finding a connection with other human beings is futile. "He had never been so utterly cold," the narrator explains, and the existential crisis provoked by his relationship with Leora lays the foundation for his final epiphany—his realization that he can no longer deny God (File 118a).

Significantly, it is through their transgressive sexuality that Ruby, Leora, and Haze's mother become the catalysts for his estrangement from and return to God. A cynical atheist who rejoices when she succeeds in aborting the baby that Haze views in part as his own, Ruby unapologetically claims the right to enjoy sex without the burden of reproduction and without concern for the proprietary claims of her male kin. While in a later version she dies as a result, in other versions her act goes unpunished and in fact becomes another in the long series of events that lead Haze back to God. Similarly, Haze's childhood memories suggest that his mother was, like Ruby, the very antithesis of the nurturing, all-giving archetype characteristic of patriarchal constructions of motherhood. Nor does she in any way conform to patriarchal ideals regarding female sexual chastity and passivity. She is, instead, a monstrous figure whose aggressive sexual appetite threatens to consume him, as he recalls the childhood episodes when he "would be . . . in bed with his mother when she would let him get in . . . and through the flannel of her nightgown she would be up against him hot through it." Readers conditioned by O'Connor's published fiction would rightly expect punishment at this point in the narrative, as it becomes clear that his mother has made a mockery of patriarchy's most cherished ideals regarding maternal nurturing and female sexuality. On the contrary, what appears is an unprecedented image suggesting orgasm as he remembers the expression on her face during these encounters, "always peculiar like it was naked and she was having a pain that gave her pleasure." Here the transgressive power of the unmediated expression of female sexuality finds its fullest, most horrifying expression, as Haze's mother initiates him into the ways of sex, teaching him "how you did it with women" (File 91a).

Leora's sexuality is likewise a dangerous and powerful force. Just as Haze's mother is the antithesis of the nurturing caregiver, so too is Leora the antithesis of the meek and submissive female. Her body, which appears "big and terrible" to Haze, "like something that was going to suck him in," hints at the threats posed by her sexual appetite. In an attempt to assume his rightful role as the aggressor, Haze grabs Leora "suddenly around the legs and pull[s] her over on him, holding his face tight against her stomach." But just as suddenly, their roles are reversed, and she becomes the aggressor and, in an encounter reminiscent of his relations with his mother, exercises total domination of him. "He felt her tearing on top of him, flinging his clothes across the room. He began to fight trying to stop her, trying to hold her hands." Yet he remains powerless in the face of her sexual aggression, which functions as a figurative rape. "You ain't gonna get me this far," Leora warns. Claiming the sexualized power that patriarchy traditionally confers upon men, Leora demands satisfaction at the cost of Haze's manhood. More to the point, her satisfaction *requires* his emasculation. Not only does this transgressive act—which reverses gendered power relations—go unpunished, but it is in fact rewarded, as Leora assumes the central role in Haze's return to the ways of God. In this way, the potential threat of female sexuality operating outside the bounds of patriarchy is channeled to serve the ways of God.

To be certain, both Leora and Haze's mother are depicted in misogynist terms as monstrous figures whose sexuality is figured as a threatening force. But here lies the fundamental difference between the women of the manuscripts and the women of O'Connor's published fiction. In the published novel, characters like Mrs. Hitchcock, Leora, and Sabbath, though banal, shallow, and spiritually misguided, remain essentially harmless. That they are spared the extreme violence so often directed at female characters in O'Connor's published fiction points to their relative unimportance to the narrative as a whole. The narrator remains preoccupied not with their transgressions—which are minor and ultimately of little relevance apart from the ways in which they help propel Haze toward his inevitable fate—but with the state of Haze's relationship with God. In the manuscripts, by contrast, the women function as central and essential characters, and their transgressions, which pose a radical threat to patriarchal order, go unpunished, not because they are relatively inconsequential, but because they remain such a crucial component of Haze's spiritual development. Collectively, Leora, Ruby, and Haze's mother mirror Haze's own situation as a lost individual, serve as the agents of his estrangement, propel him on his unsuccessful pursuit of sin, and, through the terrifying force of their sexuality, lead him finally back to God. O'Connor's transformation of female sexuality—from a powerful force that can simultaneously operate outside the bounds of patriarchy *and* be used in the service of God, to a threatening force that must be contained and punished—speaks to her latent recognition that representations of the female body held subversive potential. Her decision to rob female characters of their sexual power and of their larger importance within the narrative suggests, finally, that O'Connor understood that it would be to her advantage to contain this subversive threat at all costs.

Interestingly, not all of the female characters in the manuscripts are portrayed in misogynist terms. Indeed, perhaps the most outstanding feature of the unpublished versions of the novel is the sensitive and sympathetic manner in which the narrator often depicts characters like Leora and Ruby, who assumed a number of different personae as the story progressed. Moreover, in various passages the narrator actually assumes a female point of view, a technique that rarely appears in O'Connor's published work. In her earliest incarnations, for instance, Leora Watts is not a prostitute, but another tenant who lives in Ruby's building. In these versions Haze is introduced to readers through her eyes, as she evaluates him sexually and considers his suitability as a potential lover. Remarking to herself that Haze is "cute except for the ears," she wonders "where you get what comes in your mind." Perhaps she only wants "something new and he was something new." Looking him up and down she considers his "trunk and legs" and stops, finally, at his "hand, which was hanging over his hip as if it were being displayed." Haze's hand looks innocent to Ruby, "like it had never gone slyeyed through the placket of a woman's dress or hadn't slapped anything easier than a mule's end." The total sight of him arouses her, and the narrator offers another orgasmic image as she feels "a quick sharp thrill" that "jerked [her] like she was having a chill" (File 81). The passage here makes an interesting contrast with the narrator's depiction of Sarah Ham in "The Comforts of Home." In the published story, the narrator—violating Gordon's instruction regarding tone—refers to Sarah Ham as a "slut," as if the word referred to a clinical definition of female sexual pathology. By contrast, in this manuscript Leora's sexuality is not a terrifying or even threatening force that the reader experiences through male consciousness nor is it in any way bound to patriarchal strictures regarding female submission and modesty. Moreover, rather than acting in opposition to female consciousness and experience, the narrator embraces female subjectivity. Ignoring, for the moment, Haze's various spiritual dilemmas and obsessions, the narrator delves into Leora's psyche as the young woman considers her situation at work and as she recalls her first encounter with life in the city. Her experiences, now as an executive secretary and earlier as a naive teenager exploited by a slick con artist, stand in bold contrast to the episodes that have shaped Haze's development, which, as the manuscript progresses, unfolds largely in opposition to women.

The sequences regarding Leora's history strongly suggest that O'Connor struggled with the need to adopt an aesthetic defined in opposition to the female. Indeed, Leora begins to rival Haze as the protagonist, and her development as a character is in many ways figured in opposition to the *male;* in this way the manuscripts come dangerously close to offering a direct critique of gendered power relations under patriarchy. Leora's history, like Sarah Ham's, is one of exploitation at the hands of a series of men, but rather than dismiss these events, the narrator takes them seriously and uses them to illustrate with sympathy the sexual vulnerability of women. At the same time, the narrator remains sympathetic to Leora's distrust of and defiant lack of respect for men. As the story progresses, Haze exhibits increasing hostility toward women like Mrs. Hitchcock, yet in the early versions the narrator emphasizes instead Leora's hostility toward the men for whom she works. "She didn't have to take that guff," she thinks to herself the morning she first meets Haze, "she hadn't been with them ten years for nothing. Ten years. . . . If they wanted to find out why she wasn't there, they could call her. They knew where they'd be sitting if she quit." Leora frequently recalls her earlier naive trust in men and remembers with bitterness her relegation to the pink-collar world of the beauty parlor. "Boy had she been green," explains the narrator. "It hurt her to think about it." She remembers too how vulnerable she had been when she first made her decision to leave home at age seventeen "knowing everything" and hoping to find a job. Here the narrator radically departs from the pattern of O'Connor's published fiction and recalls the words of Pete Smith, who finds Leora a job but only in exchange for sex. "[Y]ou got to have friends," he reminds her, "nomatter how independent you are nomatter if you walked out on your folks [crossed out] and don't know where you're gonna land or even where you gonna sleep the coming night hell kid, you're lucky" (File 82). This passage is distinguished by the experimental, not to mention Faulknerian, nature of the prose, as well as by its allusion to explicit sexual exploitation that remains unrelated to homosexuality. O'Connor's published work, on the other hand, is characterized by a relatively traditional use of language; she scrupulously avoided prose that in any way suggested experimentation with form. Moreover, throughout her published work and even in many of the later manuscripts for both novels, explicit examples of rape and sexual exploitation nearly always occur between men.[4] As Louise Westling has observed, there often exists the potential for heterosexual rape in O'Connor's stories, but most often the exploitation of women by men takes other forms ("Flannery O'Connor's Revelations" 17).[5] Ben Griffith, in fact, had remarked in a letter to O'Connor that in her fiction there was often "a strong kind of sex potential that was always turned aside." She readily admitted that this was "a very perceptive comment," but she declined to explore the reasons behind this tendency (*HB* 118–19; also quoted in Westling, "Flannery O'Connor's Revelations" 18). Clearly, O'Connor was more comfortable treating sexual exploitation as a homosexual matter. To characterize the power struggle at the heart of such forms of violence as rape as a matter between men both reinforced popular stereotypes concerning homosexuality and conformed quite comfortably to one of the fundamental premises of patriarchy. That is, the sexual dynamics in O'Connor's published work evade entirely the issue of the male abuse of power over women. By suggesting that such abuse was more often directed at other men, O'Connor could serve two ends at once: she could create a fictional universe that in its exploration of controversial subjects like homosexuality remained, as she had so proudly explained to John Selby, far from conventional, but that nevertheless left safely unchallenged the premises of patriarchal social relations.

Viewed in the light of O'Connor's general reluctance to question the premises upon which male power rested, her manuscript treatment of Leora Watts's experience becomes all the more significant. Not only does Leora's story testify to the limited options available to women in a patriarchal culture where they are largely dependent on the paternal kindness—or cruelty—of men, but her experiences pointedly illustrate the potential for abuse that is inherent when relationships between men and women remain fundamentally unequal. In these early sequences, Leora is far from the predatory character who emerges later; instead she is wary of Haze, who reminds her of Pete Smith, the man who first opened her eyes to the unpleasant truth that under patriarchy male "friendship" rarely comes without strings attached. Studying Haze's face, she thinks to herself that "something about the look of him" reminds her of Pete Smith. She then recalls "the look in the hotel room, that in a second had told her all there was to know about everything." This mocking look on Pete Smith's face assumed a menacing cast, admonishing her, "kid, you hadn't ought to have run off if you didn't want this to happen." Then it gradually dawned on her what was about to occur and in that "instant the look . . . shot clear through her like a high wire" (File 89a, OMC). Though Leora had slowly come to the understanding that by accompanying him to the hotel room she was, as far as Pete Smith was concerned, consenting to sexual relations with him, her recollections nevertheless make it clear that the episode—which she likens to electrocution—amounted to rape. Seeing in Haze the same predatory look, she realizes that as a woman, she is vulnerable to exploitation at the hands of virtually any man, whether it be Pete Smith, Haze, or her boss. In marked contrast to the sexual dynamics that exist in most of O'Connor's published fiction, Leora's experiences, filtered through her consciousness and related sympathetically, suggest that relationships between men and women are fraught with inequities. By exploring the potential for abuse that accompanies male domination, O'Connor indirectly challenged the assertion that patriarchy offers women protection in return for dependence.

O'Connor's early treatment of Ruby similarly challenges the foundation upon which male domination rests. Though the passages concerning Ruby center on her attempts to abort her baby, the manuscripts relating her experience undermine O'Connor's admitted intention to create a story about the "rejection of life at its source" (*HB* 85). Instead, the passages concerning Ruby's abortion sympathetically explore the tragic consequences of unwanted pregnancy and offer a pointed critique of the male treachery that functions as a mere subtext in the published version of Ruby's story (Westling, *Sacred Groves* 149).[6] Like the Ruby of the published version, the manuscript Ruby is terrified of enduring the same hardships, largely related to childbearing, that ended her mother's life prematurely. But the two stories figure her situation in different ways—in the published version, as the inevitable destiny to which embodiment assigns women, and in the original version, as the problematic result of male treachery and exploitation. This last point emerges in the manuscripts through the sinister character of Dr. Grantland Fisher, the man who performs Ruby's abortion. Introducing himself, he explains that his philosophy of how "you get on in this word [*sic*] depends on how smart you are and who you know." Reassuring the "little lady" that her "troubles are over," he promises Ruby that "little ladies need no longer suffer." She, for one, is impressed by his manner and appreciates the fact that he "didn't stand out in the open over the counter and jaw like an ass," but "took it up with you personal in the back." As she soon learns, however, Dr. Fisher's words are merely empty promises; her womb, "where she had put the paste," begins to feel like a "nasty little bird in a cup" that "sort of ruffled itself." With vague hope that perhaps the procedure really is working, she applies the paste again and concludes with grim satisfaction that it is indeed "enough to make it ruffle itself" (File 107a, OMC). Unlike the nameless physician of "A Stroke of Good Fortune," who symbolizes the appropriate use of medical authority in enforcing patriarchal codes concerning the relationship between sexuality and reproduction, Dr. Fisher exercises clearly inappropriate authority over Ruby and her body. Echoing the empty words of Pete Smith, Dr. Fisher has similarly exploited Ruby's vulnerability, using the privilege conferred on him by his position as a doctor to profit from her unfolding tragedy. In the context of the manuscripts, then, Ruby's death emerges not as punishment for her wayward sexuality but as the tragic result of the misuse of male authority. Her experience thereby functions as yet another example of the manuscripts' sympathetic reliance on female subjectivity to explore both the power and the vulnerability of the female body in its sexual and reproductive capacities.

Despite the sympathetic treatment of abortion, the manuscripts relating to Ruby's history nevertheless attempt to remain within the bounds of Catholic orthodoxy. Interestingly, the narrator introduces religious themes through the figure of the Virgin Mary, a woman who, as Westling notes, is conspicuously absent from O'Connor's published work ("Flannery O'Connor's Revelations" 19). Wandering the streets after Ruby tells him she has taken something to make the "nasty little sparrow" inside her "shrivel up," Haze passes a church where he hears the congregation singing in Latin. Then, in English, he hears familiar words. "It said, 'Mother dearest, Mother fairest, Help of all who call on thee,' and some other. 'She's dead,' he muttered, going on. 'She cant help nothing.' She was dead, Ruby was dead. Or going to be. She was going to kill herself and it too. She was going to kill it and herself" (File 102, OMC). Ruby's situation, linked to the experiences of her own mother and of the Mother of Christ, is thus tied to the timeless suffering of all mothers, which even the most powerful among them, the Virgin Mary, is unable to alleviate. Mary's experience of embodiment and the tragic losses it entails is in turn linked to the experiences of Ruby's mother and her childbearing losses, as well as to Ruby herself and the multiple losses that accompany her abortion. Here the manuscripts frame Ruby's story entirely apart from the moral questions posed by Catholic orthodoxy on abortion and its preoccupation with the status of the fetus. Instead, the mother's experience of abortion becomes central, and the questions posed by it are not concerned with whether Ruby has committed murder but with the redemptive possibilities that her abortion offers. At the same time, by appealing to Mary as the moral authority over abortion, the manuscripts revise Catholicism itself to include female subjectivity. It thus remains little wonder that O'Connor always hated the published version of Ruby's story, which originated as a radical revision of the Catholic stance on abortion and functions as yet another example of the female-sexed voice she strove so hard to eliminate. For O'Connor, "A Stroke of Good Fortune" must have stood, in the end, as a pointed reminder of the subversive potential of her manuscripts.

Abortion, pregnancy, the rape and sexual exploitation of women, and the limited job opportunities open to them; the redemptive power of female sexuality unleashed—these are the themes around which the *Wise Blood* manuscripts revolve. That these themes were eventually revised to serve different ends or in some cases eliminated altogether suggests that O'Connor was acutely aware of the need to define her fictional landscape in opposition to, rather than in celebration of, female subjectivity. The narrator's sympathetic treatment of the female characters of the manuscripts stands in stark contrast to the hostility and satire directed at most of the female characters who appear in O'Connor's published fiction. On some level, O'Connor no doubt understood that to treat sympathetically characters who challenged the very premises of patriarchy was to challenge the politics by which southern and American literary culture operated. Though she hoped to create an unconventional novel that would set her apart from lady writers of the South's genteel tradition, at the same time she feared creating a novel that appeared to question the hierarchies that prevailed within her profession. She would, in other words, have to rid her novel of all references to female experience or consciousness and create a fictional universe in which the power of the female body was contained and male primacy was restored. To follow the path laid out in the manuscripts would have meant leaving herself open to charges that her novel lacked the objectivity that, according to the standards she had been taught at Iowa, could only be conveyed through male characters and measured according to the experiences of Ransom's male adult intellectual.

By the time she had begun work on *The Violent Bear It Away* in 1955,

O'Connor no doubt understood all too well that if she wished to be taken seriously as a writer, then she would have to veil the female-sexed voice that speaks in her early manuscripts. Indeed, perhaps the most striking difference between the manuscripts for her two novels is the marked disparity in the number of female characters. While the *Wise Blood* manuscripts center equally on male and female characters and in many ways remain focused on the experiences of women, the manuscripts for *The Violent Bear It Away* make reference to just a single female character, Mrs. Rayber, who quietly disappeared as the story progressed. Even so, her presence, however understated, represents a significant difference from the published version of the novel, where the most minor female characters have been almost entirely eliminated and where the core action is figured almost exclusively in male terms. Despite the absence of female characters, the manuscripts for *The Violent Bear It Away* equal the *Wise Blood* manuscripts in their critique of male power and egotism.

The manuscript version of *The Violent Bear It Away* shares elements with both the published novel and the short story "The Lame Shall Enter First." John Rayber Jr., precursor of Sheppard, is the story's protagonist who has replaced Bishop, the "idiot" son of the novel. Similarly, the manuscript Tarwater is more closely modeled on Rufus Johnson, the juvenile delinquent of "The Lame Shall Enter First," than on the Tarwater who appears in the published version of the book. At the same time, two important episodes, a cross-burning and a long passage satirizing the Ku Klux Klan and fraternal organizations in general, distinguish the manuscript from both "The Lame Shall Enter First" and *The Violent Bear It Away*.

The manuscript story opens with John Rayber's discovery that a cross has been burned on his front lawn. Viewing the episode as testimony to his importance and to the strength of his moral convictions, he proudly explains to his son, John Rayber Jr., and to his nephew, Tarwater, just "what a cross means." An odd fusion of the juvenile delinquent Sheppard and the reluctant prophet who finally emerges in the published novel, Tarwater defiantly answers that he knows exactly what a cross means. "It means Jesus Christ was crucified," he explains with some impatience. "What you take me for? A ass?" His cousin tries to convince him that it was instead Rayber's courageous moral stance that provoked the cross burning. Disgusted with this apparent misreading of the symbolism behind the cross, Tarwater argues that organizations like the Klan burn crosses for no logical reason. "I know a woman that the Klan beat up one time. She didn't think no different from nobody else," he explains. When his cousin protests that she was probably "colored," Tarwater notes with finality, "She was a white woman. . . . Spit out the wrong side of her mouth was all" (File 163a). Here the Klan is depicted as a farcical organization with no coherent system of beliefs and with no understanding of the true meaning of the symbol it has adopted. And though it is a fraternal organization ostensibly founded to protect white women from the aggressions of black men, it cannot even apply that principle consistently and resorts to such contradictory and futile tactics as beating white women and burning crosses on the lawns of ineffectual men like Rayber. Thus early in the manuscripts for *The Violent Bear It Away* the narrator introduces challenges to the racial discourses and gendered hierarchies that would characterize O'Connor's published fiction. Although stories such as "The Artificial Nigger" and "Everything That Rises Must Converge" focus sympathetically on the impact the changing racial landscape has on whites, in these manuscripts the focus shifts to an examination of the crude, undignified, and misdirected behaviors that result from racism.

At the same time, these manuscripts link racism specifically to male vanity and egotism, as Tarwater's interpretation of the cross-burning incident is borne out and it becomes increasingly apparent that Rayber is a ridiculous man possessed of an exaggerated sense of his own importance. "I'm not going to school today," he bravely announces to his family the next morning. "I would not be any kind of a man to leave you unprotected. They may try to burn up the house." His wife, for one, recognizes the absurdity of such bravado and attempts to bring him down to size by patiently explaining that it was only "some prankster" who put the cross on the lawn. "For heaven's sake!" she concludes in exasperation, hoping to bring the incident to a close and feeling "provoked" that her husband "should make such an idiot of himself." She sees, however, that his ego has been bruised and that he will stubbornly persist in his insistence that he is being punished for his convictions. "She knew from the expression on his face," the narrator explains, "that it would take a bomb now to justify him." Nevertheless, she continues to take him to task for his false pride. "Have you done anything at all?" she asks him pointedly, "anything at all to make it possible that anybody would want you out of the way? You're nothing but a teacher in a two-by-four girl's school. You don't write editorials, you don't preach, you don't run for offices. My God" (File 163a). This episode, while similar to the satire that O'Connor directs at Rayber in the published novel, is distinguished by the gendered terms in which her critique is couched. Rayber does not suffer simply from intellectual pride but, more specifically, from male pride, a fact that O'Connor chose to bring to light not through the narrator but, significantly, through the eyes of a female character. As Rayber's wife so shrewdly observes, he suffers from the delusion that although he is "nothing but a teacher in a two-by-four girl's school," he has somehow assumed a position of moral authority in his community and that he must now "protect" his family from the consequences of his brave stance. In reality, he has simply been randomly targeted by a ridiculous organization, one whose true convictions are no more coherent than his own. Rayber's desire to assume a manly stance in defense of his family is equated with the Klan's overzealous "protection" of white women. By characterizing both impulses as ridiculous and misdirected the manuscripts pose a challenge to traditional southern justifications of lynching and other practices aimed at maintaining the "purity" of the white South, as well as to the notion that men are the natural protectors of women.

O'Connor continued to pursue this two-pronged attack throughout the remaining manuscript chapters of *The Violent Bear It Away*. Developing her critique both of the Klan and of the foolish sense of male pride and fraternity such organizations foster, the manuscript story follows Tarwater, now called B.K., as he pursues his various delinquent activities. Determined to defy his uncle and prove mistaken his objections to the cross-burning incident, B.K. joins a local Klan-inspired organization called the Master Scout's Secret Order of Hooded Police—a name that aptly captures the odd mix of hierarchy and egalitarianism, vigilantism and cowardice, that characterizes such groups. Though clearly modeled after the Klan in their mission, the Hooded Police are, as the narrator notes with wry sarcasm, far more advanced in their methods. Instead of burning crosses the old-fashioned way, for instance, the Hooded Police use Sterno cans to keep the flames burning longer. Yet despite its modernity, the narrator suggests, the group is nevertheless somewhat lacking in sophistication. With a membership composed exclusively of the Master Scout and young boys from the neighborhood junior high school, the Hooded Police meet in a warehouse on South Deeper Street, a name that obviously alludes to what the manuscripts identify as the peculiarly southern nature of racially motivated fraternal organizations. On one level, the Hooded Police function as a satirical comment on the racist purpose of such organizations. Like the local Klan, they have largely abandoned their original mission and, instead of maintaining racial order, spend their time performing meaningless rituals that serve only to reflect on the members' own lack of dignity and purpose. In addition to burning crosses, for example, the group cuts crosses into each others' arms and deposits drops of blood into a ritual bottle of old Nu-Grape. B.K., for his part, is somewhat embarrassed by the use of such an inglorious icon, but the other members are generally in awe of the Master Scout and his rituals. And the Master Scout himself figures as an appropriate monument to the ridiculous nature of his secret order. He wears a black smock that nearly touches the floor, revealing his "big feet" and cheap trousers. The hood he wears is also black, with a white cross and two small slits for the eyes with what appears to be glass or cellophane behind them, pasted there to keep the slits open or "to keep the color of his eyes from showing," thereby maintaining his sense of inscrutable mystery. Suffering from allergies, the Master Scout must "from time to time . . . pull his smock up one leg and get a handkerchief out of his back pocket and thrust it up under his hood and blow his nose . . . as if he meant to drain the entire contents of his head." When this undignified motion is completed, he examines the contents of his handkerchief and places it back in his pocket, only to continue his lecture "in a hollower, higher voice." None of the boys in the organization, the narrator notes, have ever actually seen the Master Scout without his full regalia, nor do any of them know his real name, all of which he apparently hopes will only add to his aura of mystery and authority (File 170a). Yet as the narrator's comic portrait of him reveals, the Master Scout is hardly the fearsome image of vigilante authority he so obviously seeks to create, but is instead merely a clownish figure who has yet to devise a graceful and discreet method of blowing his nose while wearing his ceremonial garb.

Fancying himself a philosopher, the Master Scout hopes to impart to the boys his personal view of the meaning of life, punctuating his speech with loud blows of his nose. Life, he learned, was never to be easy. "Many a month," he recalls with pride, "I et a spud for breakfast and a spud for dinner and just hoped there'd be a spud lef for me to have for supper with a little buttermilk poed over it." Having overcome these hardships, he managed to go on to live a full life. "I been in the Arm Service, both land and sea, at home and abroad. I been hungry and I been full. I been twict married, three times in jail and oncet in goverment service." He's "worked on ever kind of machine," in addition to working as an undertaker, a police officer, a sailor, and a farmer. As a grand finale, he relates his encounters with hurricanes and tornadoes. "To make a long story short, . . ." he concludes, "you name it I done it." Combining the spirit of Horatio Alger with the plot of a country and western song, the Master Scout has arrived at a distinctly inane and hopelessly literal view of life. Though he has, indeed, "done it all," he has arrived at no true understanding of the meaning of existence and has achieved virtually nothing except dubious status as leader of a boys' group. When the boys question him concerning the exact nature of their future "operations" and whether they will involve murder and blasphemy, the Master Scout is, despite his extensive experience, at a loss. "Why don't you boys ast your private preachers them questions? What you got to ast me for, a plain man?" he answers in exasperation (File 171a). In sum, the Master Scout falls far short of the image of power, authority, and knowledge he tries to convey but reveals instead an insecure man whose ego must feed off of the misdirected admiration of naive young boys.

The Master Scout, with his ridiculous uniform and his nonsensical speeches and rituals, serves as a humorous critique not simply of racially motivated organizations like the Klan but of fraternal organizations in general. Indeed, there exists a certain logic to the speeches he recites and the rituals he performs. On the one hand, he reinforces the hierarchical structure of the group by presenting himself as the undisputed authority on all aspects of knowledge and experience. On the other hand, he has devised a series of democratic rituals that offer the boys the opportunity to simultaneously advance within the order and reinforce their common sense of purpose. Unlike the forms of public cross burning that groups like the Klan use as an act of aggression and intimidation, the Hooded Police employ their cross secretly, as a symbol of their common purpose as a group. The Nu-Grape bottle serves a similar purpose. So too does another practice, widespread among fraternal orders—the use of secret handshakes and symbols, which initiates are taught as they pass through the various stages of membership. These symbols represent the "trials" of initiation that each member must endure, and the only way to learn what level of fellowship another member has reached is through the secret handshakes. The first "trial," for instance, simply involves "coming to the meetings every time and having a cross cut in your arm for some blood for the blood Bottle." At each meeting the Master Scout then shakes the bottle and proclaims the members "blood brothers," explaining that this ritual gives "each of them a power over the others if there should be any double crossing" (File 170b).

These various secret symbols and handshakes, along with the mixing of blood, are designed to create a sense of fraternity. Such symbolism is intended to transform the group from a collection of individual boys to an order of "blood brothers" that remains simultaneously democratic (by offering each of the boys the opportunity to advance to the next stage) and hierarchical (by conferring power on both the Master Scout as well as those boys who have advanced to the inner circles). Thus the Hooded Police bear a distinct resemblance both to the Klan and to more benign organizations such as the Freemasons. Like the Masonic order, the Hooded Police function on variety of levels, at once satisfying a number of contradictory impulses—toward hierarchy and democracy. As her portrait of the Hooded Police suggests, O'Connor was not simply poking fun at what she viewed as the peculiarly southern nature of groups like the Klan, nor was she simply offering a critique of the racist impulses that frequently underpinned such organizations. By characterizing the Hooded Police—an order represented in the most generic terms—as a ridiculous organization that employs undignified rituals as a means of reinforcing questionable impulses, she was offering a critique of all organizations founded on the principles of male fellowship and camaraderie.[7]

That the Master Scout's Secret Order of Hooded Police is founded on specifically masculinist values becomes increasingly apparent as the story unfolds. B.K., for instance, begins to recognize some of the other members as fellow classmates at Benjamin Franklin Junior High, noting with surprise that they "were not very tough." By joining an organization with a tough image, the boys are obviously trying to bolster their standing in the local pecking order, which apparently values such masculinist virtues as physical power, intimidation, aggression, and domination. The irony, of course— one apparently lost on the boys—is that the Hooded Police hardly measure up to the image the Master Scout has cultivated. Perhaps even more ironic is the situation in which the organization's toughest member, Johnson, finds himself. Johnson serves as a model for the other boys; besides being tough, he is the only one among them who, B.K. observes, has likely even seen the Master Scout without his hood. Clearly, Johnson enjoys special favor with the group's leader, and the other boys envy his position (File 171a).

Yet the other boys are unaware of the obligations this special position entails. B.K. learns the truth after Johnson, in an uncharacteristic show of cowardice, hurriedly and somewhat awkwardly attempts to force B.K to accompany him to his private meeting with the Master Scout. "Leave Fat [B.K.] where he is," the Master Scout orders, " 'You is all I want.' Johnson's face twisted. He loosened his grip on B.K. but he didn't move his hand. 'Come here I told you,' the voice under the hood snapped. 'How many times I got to tell you?' " B.K. watches as the Master Scout drags Johnson to the back of the warehouse. "Johnson went forward . . . quickly as if he had been hit on the legs from behind and when he was in reach the Master Scout caught him by the shoulder and propelled him, with one push, into the dark far end of the loft." The pair disappears, and B.K. hears muffled voices. Catching a glimpse of them together, he sees "Johnson's hat and his shoulder with the Master Scout's fingers clutched around it. The hand moved back and forth suddenly as if the shoulder was a broken gear thrusting in and out." He vaguely begins to understand the situation as he hears Johnson plead, "Lemme be. I ain't going to do it" (File 171a). This scene makes clear that there exists a dark underside to the sense of camaraderie that the Hooded Police offer members. Not only does the Master Scout take advantage of the boys' naïveté to satisfy his own insecurities, but he abuses them sexually as well. His choice of Johnson is significant; as the toughest of the boys, he represents a particular challenge to the Master Scout. Having so completely dominated Johnson, he has thus established himself as the undisputed "master" of all the boys. The Master Scout's sexual violation of the boys' unofficial leader suggests that the spirit of male camaraderie that serves as the organization's uniting principle is dependent upon the values of domination and submission. Unlike Tarwater's rape in the published version—which functions as a vehicle for God's grace—Johnson's rape is used to expose the hierarchical and exploitive power relations the manuscripts implicitly associate with patriarchy. By characterizing the value system of closed male circles as rooted in domination, submission, and, ultimately, sexual exploitation, the manuscripts raise critical questions about the role of fraternal organizations in defining and reinforcing cultural constructions of masculinity and about the nature of masculinity itself.

O'Connor, however, took her critique a step further and suggested that organizations like the Klan and the Hooded Police perpetuate the most dangerous of masculinist values, as well as pervert for their own ends what she understood as the most exalted of human virtues, the drive for religious understanding. The Hooded Police, as the Master Scout explains with pride, is "no Sunday School outfit." It is "near to religion," he is willing to admit, but with "no crap in it." There are, significantly, only twelve boys in the order, and the group makes conspicuous use of the cross as a symbol. The boys, for their part, see the Master Scout as a leader in all matters, including the moral and the religious. When he finds himself unable to answer their questions concerning murder and blasphemy, he is forced to remind them, somewhat impatiently, that he "ain't no preacher." Yet he manages to offer one piece of religious wisdom to them: "He don't burn" (Files 170b–171a). Though his words are somewhat cryptic, what the Master Scout no doubt means to suggest is that Christ is not the Savior and that Christianity is therefore a meaningless religion. Thus the Hooded Police functions on yet another level, as a means of filling the void created by unfulfilled religious yearnings. That this void is filled through rituals that are undignified at best, blasphemous and dangerous at worst, suggests, finally, that fraternal organizations like the Klan and the Masonic Order are founded on false and empty premises.

O'Connor's portrait of the Master Scout's Secret Order of Hooded Police offers a critique not simply of fraternal organizations but of the masculinist value system on which they are founded. The search for male camaraderie and fellowship, these manuscripts imply, is intimately bound to the need for hierarchy and leadership, while the drive for power that is an integral component of such organizations often ends in a literal drive for physical and, sometimes, sexual domination. O'Connor's satirical portrait of the Hooded Police suggests that using symbols and rituals loosely founded on Christian models for dubious ends—the fostering of what today would be termed "male bonding"—offers a poor substitute for genuine religion and, worse, encourages a blasphemous form of moral confusion. In short, the manuscripts for *The Violent Bear It Away,* like those for *Wise Blood,* paint a grim picture of the social and moral ramifications of institutionalized fraternization among men and of male dominance. Aware, on some level, that her status as a woman complicated her professional relationship to the de facto literary fraternity established by men like the Fugitive/Agrarians, O'Connor used her manuscripts as a forum for generally negating the power of closed male circles. The manuscripts for *Wise Blood* served a similar purpose. The experiences of Ruby and Leora Watts offer graphic testimony to the inequities and violence to which women are frequently subjected in a culture where men hold most of the power. The significance of O'Connor's decision to rob her female characters not only of narrative sympathy but of their power and vitality and to redirect her satirical gaze from the male to the female cannot be underestimated. While Andrew Lytle may have played a role in the former decision, O'Connor was no doubt solely responsible for the latter. Her years of training at Iowa and her longtime association with critics like Ransom, Tate, Lytle, Warren, and Gordon had made it clear that as long as she played according to New Critical rules, she could expect to earn critical praise. By the time she began work on *The Violent Bear It Away,* O'Connor was no longer willing to risk the consequences of straying from a course that had already proven so rewarding. To succeed as a writer, she knew she would have to keep her rebellions private.

The female-oriented material and the female-sexed voice that appear throughout O'Connor's manuscripts are nevertheless important, not simply as evidence of her difficulty in meeting the expectations of a male-dominated literary culture, but as evidence of a female aesthetic that might, despite appearances, inform the published novels themselves. When read outside the context of the manuscripts, both *Wise Blood* and *The Violent Bear It Away* emerge as highly masculinist novels. Reading the novels along with the manuscripts, however, makes it possible to identify the ways in which the published novels also allude to female consciousness and experience. Like the manuscripts, the published versions of *Wise Blood* and *The Violent Bear It Away* testify, albeit indirectly, to the obstacles O'Connor faced as a woman writer, as she struggled to ensure that what she viewed as her most important work would remain utterly free of feminine "impurities." Aware that the novel was generally regarded as the superior form, she worked especially hard to disprove the general view, articulated by critics like Robert Penn Warren, that she was a "natural" short story writer and, by implication, an inferior novelist.[8] The novel became for O'Connor the form through which she worked the hardest to prove herself as a writer and thus to keep in check any literary qualities that might reveal her gender. Employing the male quest narrative and the classic bildungsroman as her structural models, she transformed *Wise Blood* and *The Violent Bear It Away* into novels in which women assume minor roles or from which they are virtually absent.

This transformation, however, was never complete, as O'Connor created a series of male protagonists with unmistakably "feminine" traits. The manuscripts offer evidence of O'Connor's ongoing attempts at "masculinizing" Haze by, for example, suppressing any evidence of his sentimental attachments to women and eliminating scenes where he is sexually propositioned by other men. Yet despite such changes, he remains a "feminized" hero who displays many of the passive qualities traditionally assigned to women. Subject ultimately to the authority of God, Haze, like Tarwater, fails to achieve the sense of independent manhood that traditionally serves as the driving force behind the quest narrative and bildungsroman forms. Both characters testify to the difficulties O'Connor encountered in attempting to define her work according to the dictates of an androcentric literary culture. Unable to suppress entirely her reliance upon female subjectivity, O'Connor, in effect, created a hybrid narrative form. Distinguished in subtle ways from the male quest narrative and from the classic bildungsroman, *Wise Blood* and *The Violent Bear It Away* nevertheless draw on elements from both to create a narrative structure that testifies, finally, to the multiplicity of forms female aesthetics may assume.

A variety of definitions have been offered to explain the qualities that set the quest narrative and bildungsroman apart from other structural models. For the most part, critics have agreed that the quest narrative properly centers on the hero, understood in mythological terms as one with the authority to speak for or represent entire communities and nations. His quest for knowl-edge, power, social unity, or order serves as the organizing theme of the nar-rative. Although it frequently incorporates elements of the quest narrative, the bildungsroman centers on the protagonist's intellectual or moral devel-opment, that is, his "coming of age." Significantly, though the quest narrative and the bildungsroman have generally been defined as transcendent of gen-der, both forms tend, traditionally, to rely on androcentric assumptions and plot conventions. "Competition," argues Dana Heller, "guides the dialectic structure of the quest and defines male heroism as an aggressive destiny achieved through exercise of physical strength. The world provides the nec-essary stage, a place where one may attain the ultimate boon: manhood" (3). To achieve this goal, the hero must first leave his community and battle the forces that have been unleashed as a test of his physical, moral, or intellectual strength. As Nina Baym argues, this narrative structure, in one form or an-other, has served as the foundation upon which the American literary canon was built. "The myth narrates a confrontation of the American individual, the pure American self divorced from specific social circumstances, with the promise offered by the idea of America." Individuation, the achievement of "complete self-definition" outside of or in opposition to the social order, which is defined in feminine terms, serves as the reward (71). Thus in the American literary tradition, the means (achieving individuation, which is un-derstood in purely masculine terms) becomes more important than the end (fostering social unity or restoring the social order). "No matter how futile his gestures for salvation, no matter how demoralizing his initiation," con-cludes Heller, "the [American] male hero remains heroic by dint of the mo-bility and capacity for action granted him by gender." Despite any setbacks, "he remains also in possession of an active, articulate will: he determines a subject position in the world, and he searches of his own volition" (8).

Historically, two obstacles have faced women writers who sought to ap-propriate the quest form. First, they must learn to disassociate themselves from the social order, and second, they must claim the authority to speak not only for themselves but for others as well. According to Heller, the writer who wishes to appropriate the quest narrative form, like the heroine she seeks to create, must transcend the female self that has internalized patriarchal val-ues of submission and dependence. Heller focuses on "revolutionary" texts of the last forty years that incorporate female characters who manage to break free of social restrictions and dictates. However, such texts, as she concludes, have not traditionally been the norm. Instead, an "established feature of many . . . female quests is a thwarted or impossible journey, a rude awakening to limits, and a reconciliation to society's expectations of female passivity and immobility" (14). In the hands of women writers, the quest narrative has generally been used to reflect the limitations inherent in traditional female experience.

The bildungsroman, like the quest narrative, centers for the most part on the process of individual achievement, wherein, argue Elizabeth Abel, Marianne Hirsch, and Elizabeth Langland, the protagonist is led "from ignorance and innocence to wisdom and maturity." And like the quest narrative, the bildungsroman has not, historically, been a particularly accommodating form for women writers or female protagonists. According to Abel, Hirsch, and Langland, the "fully realized and individuated self who caps the journey of the bildungsroman may not represent the developmental goals of women, or of women characters." Heroines, instead, embark on a "developmental course [that] is more conflicted, less direct: separation tugs against the longing for fusion and the heroine encounters the conviction that identity resides in intimate relationships, especially those of early childhood." Among women writers, then, the bildungsroman assumes a different form, often ending not in individuation but in marriage, death, or sexual awakening. "Women's developmental tasks and goals," the authors conclude, "must be realized in a culture pervaded by male norms," which in itself "generate[s] distinctive narrative tensions—between autonomy and relationship, separation and community, loyalty to women and attraction to men." Conflict, in short, becomes "more relentless in women's stories" (11–12). According to Abel, Hirsch, and Langland, though the female bildungsroman shares features with the classic form—the assumption that the self is coherent, that personal growth is possible, and that it most often takes place within a definable time span and a particular social context—a number of other features set apart the female novel of development. For women writers and their characters, the coherent self does not necessarily equate with the autonomous self, nor does development usually take place uninterrupted by the pressures of social constraints. In the hands of women writers, the bildungsroman, like the quest narrative, has assumed a form that more closely reflects the limitations of traditional female experience and development.

Though authored by a woman, neither *Wise Blood* nor *The Violent Bear It Away* makes any explicit references to female experience or development. Pointed examples of the way in which O'Connor's work generally resists straightforward feminist analysis, the novels more closely conform to masculinist models. On the most obvious level, both *Wise Blood* and *The Violent Bear It Away* rely almost exclusively on male characters. Though *Wise Blood* incorporates a number of female characters, Haze's quest for spiritual understanding is largely defined in opposition to them. Similarly, Tarwater's journey of self-discovery takes place entirely within an enclosed male environment. The individuals who provide the most crucial influences on his development—his two uncles, his cousin, and the mysterious stranger who acts as his double—are all male. Haze is the prototypical American hero who rejects the company of women in order to seek a higher knowledge, while Tarwater, in making his journey from youthful ignorance and rebellion to a mature understanding of his relationship to the "children of God," meets all of the characteristics of the typical bildungsroman protagonist. A superficial reading of both novels would offer little indication that they were written by a woman.

A closer reading of *Wise Blood* and *The Violent Bear It Away,* however, reveals a number of incongruities. For example, Haze's quest is, at the most fundamental level, an impossible journey, one that culminates not in the achievement of an independent manhood but in the disturbing realization that he is subject to the will of God. Nor does Tarwater's journey end in the achievement of autonomous selfhood. Though his development takes place entirely apart from women, it culminates in the realization that he must in fact rejoin the social order from which he has isolated himself and that he views with such contempt. Just as Haze's quest for knowledge ends in submission, so too does Tarwater's developmental journey end in the acceptance of a mature selfhood that is far from autonomous. In effect, both Haze and Tarwater assume the role of traditional female protagonists, transforming the two novels into hybrid narrative forms that employ male characters to create what are essentially female stories of submission, dependence, and a "rude awakening to limits."

Upon a first reading, the published version of *Wise Blood* appears to conform quite closely to the classic quest narrative form. Haze at the start of his journey thinks only in terms of unlimited freedom and independence. Boasting of this freedom to fellow train passenger Mrs. Hitchcock, he outlines for her his plans upon arrival in Taulkingham, his final destination. "Don't know nobody there, but I'm going to do some things. I'm going to do some things I never have done before," he explains with barely concealed contempt (*CW* 5). The things he has in mind include engaging in illicit sex, buying a car, committing various acts of blasphemy, and traveling wherever his desire may take him. Haze's plans at this point conform to nearly every literary convention associated with questing male protagonists. Indeed, in many ways Haze appears as a character straight out of Kerouac's *On the Road,* the prototypical American male quest novel. Alone in the world, his father barely a memory, his mother and two brothers recently dead, he has assumed the role of lone existential hero—a man whose search for higher understanding is forged outside the constraints of family and society. His relationship to Enoch Emery perhaps best exemplifies Haze's drive for independence. A grotesque double of Haze, Enoch too is alone in the world, yet unlike Haze, he recognizes the emptiness of his situation and seeks desperately to belong. "This is one more hard place to make friends in," he remarks of Taulkingham. "I been here two months and I don't know nobody. Look like all they want to do is knock you down" (26). Enoch trails after Haze in a pitiful attempt to establish a friendship, but Haze brushes him aside, even after Enoch tearfully explains how his father abandoned him. Intent on pursuing a life of sin unhampered by emotional ties or friendships, Haze coldly tells Enoch to leave him alone and makes his way back to Leora Watts's apartment, where he is free to come and go as he pleases. With manly stoicism, Haze refuses to develop a friendship with Enoch or with anyone who seeks to impede his journey and prefers instead the company of a prostitute, where his status as a paying client gives him a sense of independence from and control over the terms of the relationship.

"Hitting the road" in a car of one's own is, of course, a central convention in American quest novels, and Haze's story is no exception. Without the physical mobility provided by a car, freedom is, as he comes to realize, necessarily limited. Providing a home as well as a means of transportation, the "rat-colored" Essex he buys makes it possible for Haze to begin his journey in earnest. The car allows Haze to pursue Asa and Sabbath Hawkes at will, just as it provides him with a mobile pulpit upon which he can preach his Godless creed. Speaking to the bored and generally uninterested crowds congregated outside the movie theaters where he sets up shop, Haze boasts of the spiritual and physical freedom he has forged for himself, unhampered by moral considerations or by emotional ties. "I'm going to take the truth with me wherever I go. . . . I'm going to preach it to who ever'll listen at whatever place" (59). As he explains in conclusion, "Nobody with a good car needs to be justified. . . . I knew when I first saw it that it was the car for me, and since I've had it, I've had a place to be that I can always get away in" (64–65).

Getting away assumes primary importance for Haze, who continues to view himself as an independent agent whose quest for understanding will lead him to truth. Like the prototypic questing hero, he has pursued his journey not simply outside the bounds of society but in opposition to women. Characters like Mrs. Hitchcock, Leora Watts, Sabbath Hawkes, and Mrs. Flood become symbols for him of the social order to which women adhere and their blind faith in religion. He seeks first to shock the women and then to reject the hypocrisy of their religion. For example, Mrs. Hitchcock, the very embodiment of southern ladyhood, makes pleasant conversation about her family and mouths empty clichés in an attempt to engage Haze in conversation. "I reckon you think you been redeemed," he responds with open contempt, hoping to embarrass her. Blushing, but determined to overlook the insult, Mrs. Hitchcock explains that "yes, life [is] an inspiration" (6). A true lady, she answers his obvious hostility with a polite, neutral, and inane remark that marks her and women like her as guardians of the empty and meaningless value system Haze seeks to reject. To reject that system he must reject women.

Thus begins his relationship with Leora Watts, a woman whose status as a prostitute serves as an affront to the moral system Haze hopes to violate. When that plan quickly loses its appeal, he sets his sights on Sabbath Hawkes. Her youth and, so he presumes, "innocence" conversely hold the same attraction as Leora Watts's worldliness. By seducing Sabbath, Haze hopes to prove the sincerity of his blasphemy and in this way conform to the requirements of the prototypical questing hero and his need to indulge his sexual appetite outside the bounds and in violation of the social order. And though he never directly seeks out a relationship with Mrs. Flood, as witness to the self-inflicted tortures he endures to foster his spiritual awakening, she too comes to symbolize the larger society and its empty values. When Haze matter-of-factly explains to her that he intends to blind himself, she, for instance, responds not with shock but with puzzlement. Not "a woman who felt more violence in one word than in another," she finds herself at a loss in explaining Haze's action, since she would simply have killed herself. She concludes, finally, that he most likely was "only being ugly, for what possible reason could a person have for wanting to destroy their sight?" Blinding oneself is, in her view, completely impractical. Any person who was, like her, "so clear sighted, could never stand to be blind" (119). The embodiment of a value system that privileges the literal over the abstract and the practical over the symbolic, Mrs. Flood, in her spiritual blindness, cannot fathom Haze's reasons for literally blinding himself. Her impeccably ladylike response to his actions—her refusal to acknowledge his behavior as an affront and her insistence that his decision to blind himself is simply the result of bad manners—points to the ways in which ladies and their value system dominate the social order he seeks to reject. In his hostile confrontation with Mrs. Hitchcock, his pursuit of sexual relationships with Leora and Sabbath, and in his complicity in making Mrs. Flood a witness to his blinding and other acts of self-mutilation, Haze is able at once to reject the hypocritical values of the larger society and to couch his quest for spiritual understanding in gendered terms, as a quest not simply for knowledge but for independent manhood.

Interestingly, however, not every female character is willing to cooperate in Haze's plan. His short-lived relationship with Leora Watts, for example, brings him little more than humiliation and offers the first glimpse of Haze's failure to fulfill the role expected of the questing hero. His first sexual encounter with her—his first ever—leaves him somewhat mortified, as she calls attention to the gaps between his image of himself and the reality that image masks. He recalls with embarrassment the obscene remarks she had made in response to his unsuccessful performance and finds himself "uneasy in the thought of going to her again" (33). His growing sense of humiliation is only confirmed when she laughs at the sight of him in her doorway. Fancying himself a man of the world who is not afraid to look sin squarely in the face, Haze is understandably upset when Leora exposes his sexual inexperience and his failure to conform to the image of manliness he hopes to project. Hardly the unwitting vehicle for Haze's exploration of the moral implications of blasphemy, Leora is in fact an independent agent who refuses to support Haze's self-delusion. Surpassing Haze in her blasphemy, Leora defiles his black preacher's hat; the very symbol both of his religiously inspired pursuit of sin and of his inability to escape his true calling as a man of God. Thus she has assaulted Haze's sense of male pride and autonomous selfhood on numerous levels, unmasking his sexual inadequacy, revealing the false bravado that lies at the heart of his blasphemy, and exposing the vulnerability of his true self—the preacher who needs desperately to have his faith confirmed. In short, Haze's relationship with Mrs. Watts serves as the first indication that he may not be the prototypical questing hero. Since his original motivation for sleeping with her had been "to prove that he didn't believe in sin since he practice what was called it," he must eventually conclude that he has "had enough of her" (62).

Embarrassed by Leora Watts's assault on his masculine pride and aware that she has, for all intents, beaten him at his own game, Haze decides to seduce Sabbath Hawkes, who is, apparently, somewhat less worldly. Here, too, he hopes to use an illicit sexual relationship with a woman as a means of violating the moral standards of the larger society that, in his eyes, she represents. "He wanted someone he could teach something to," explains the narrator, "and he took it for granted that the blind man's child, since she was so homely, would also be innocent" (62). What Haze hopes to reveal to Sabbath, of course, is the naïveté of her sexual and spiritual "innocence." That is, he hopes to establish with her the intellectual and physical dominance he had failed to achieve in his relationship with Leora Watts. Once again, however, his pursuit of sin is thwarted by a power even more blasphemous than his own. Far from innocent, Sabbath is, much to Haze's surprise, the "bastard" child of Asa and an anonymous woman who died shortly after her birth. Moreover, Sabbath seems precociously aware of the moral implications of her illegitimacy. As she had explained in a letter to a local advice columnist, "I am a bastard and a bastard shall not enter the kingdom of heaven as we all know." Should she, then, simply accept her fate and go "the whole hog?" (67) Initially distracted by the apparent contradiction of her situation as a "bastard" and as the daughter of a preacher who is so pious he blinded himself, Haze remains oblivious to the hints Sabbath persistently drops concerning her sexual availability. Still convinced *he* is going to seduce *her,* he can register only shock and disbelief when she attempts to kiss him, explaining that "it don't make any difference . . . how much you like me" (70). Haze flees to the shelter of his car, but Sabbath continues her pursuit. Again, the tables have been turned on him, as he discovers when he arrives home to find Sabbath waiting for him in bed. Talking more like a man of the world than an "innocent" young girl, she tells him that "from the minute I set eyes on you I said to myself, that's what I got to have, just giving me some of him! . . . That innocent look don't hide a thing, he's just pure filthy right down to the guts, like me." She insightfully recognizes that the only difference between them is "I like being that way," and now, she tells Haze, she intends to "teach you how to like it" (95). His attempts at corrupting Sabbath's "innocence" and using her as an instrument of blasphemy have been confounded. Sabbath, like Leora, refuses to become a pawn in Haze's quest. In fact, her assaults on his manhood only serve to undermine his efforts.

The episodes with Leora and Sabbath fit a general pattern that, in fact, emerges quite early in the novel and remains a persistent obstacle in Haze's quest for knowledge and autonomy. His first realization that the journey he has undertaken might not unfold so smoothly comes on the train, when he attempts to shock his female dining car companion with the tactics that had worked so well with Mrs. Hitchcock. "If you've been redeemed," he tells her, "I wouldn't want to be." Surprised to hear only laughter in response, he tries again, explaining that he would not believe in Jesus even "if He was on this train." Much to his surprise, she replies in a "poisonous Eastern voice" whose cynicism physically repels him, "Who said you had to?" (7). Like Sabbath and Leora, his dining car companion does not simply surpass Haze in her blasphemy; she refuses altogether to support his quest for sin. In this way she becomes the first of many obstacles in his path toward becoming the prototypical questing hero. Nor are women the only agents who serve as impediments to his progress; Haze's car presents more obstacles than all of the female characters combined. Indeed, his failure to achieve control over his car—the very symbol of male sexuality and independent American manhood—parallels his failure to dominate the female characters in the novel.

From the moment Haze sets foot in the Essex, it becomes apparent that the car is no more cooperative than Sabbath or Leora and that it is hardly equipped to provide him with the mobility and independence he seeks. When he takes the brake off, for example, the car shoots backward, and it is quite a struggle for Haze to force it to move in the right direction. Driving somewhat "crookedly," he remains unable to hold the car on the road. Finally, he manages to slow the car down, only to find himself stalled (41). Haze's inaugural trip in the Essex thus becomes symbolic of his entire journey: traveling a crooked path, he has difficulty maintaining his commitment to the pursuit of sin and blasphemy as his women and his car—the objects through which he should be able to define his identity as a man—continue to thwart his efforts. The car "would go forward about six inches," the narrator explains, "and then back about four. . . . He had to grip the steering wheel with both hands to keep from being thrown either out the windshield or into the back" (87–88). Haze's journey, like his car, follows a path over which he has little control. When the police officer who pushes the Essex over an embankment asks him where he was planning to go, Haze realizes, finally, that he was not really "going anywhere" (118). As much as he would like to believe otherwise, the Essex is simply not equipped to take him where he wants to go, and as much as he tries to avoid his calling, his quest will eventually lead him toward a preordained destiny. The car, like the women he encounters, conspires to reveal to Haze the many ways in which he fails to meet the requirements of independent manhood and is instead the passive victim of other forces.

Haze's utter lack of control over his situation, little though he realizes, has been evident from the beginning of his journey, when he finds himself inexplicably drawn to Asa and Sabbath Hawkes after he first sees them on the street. Led by a will not entirely his own, he is nearly hit by a car as he blindly follows the pair. When he catches up to them, he cannot even recall what he had wanted to say. "I come a long way," he finally tells them, "since I would believe in anything." Fraud that he is, Asa nevertheless recognizes the urges in Haze that compel him to prove himself a sinner. "You ain't come so far," Asa shrewdly observes, "that you could keep from following me. . . . Some preacher has left his mark on you. . . . Did you follow for me to take it off or give you another one?" (28). Shaken by the accuracy of Asa's remarks,

Haze impulsively undertakes the very mission he had set out to avoid: he becomes a preacher. Having suddenly embarked on his career as a preacher, Haze is next possessed by his inexplicable urge to buy a car. "The thought," as the narrator notes, "was full grown in his head when he woke up," despite the fact that he "had never before thought of buying a car" and that he barely knows how to drive, has no license, and has only fifty dollars to his name (37). The same force that compels him to buy the Essex despite his total lack of driving experience soon urges him to seek out Enoch, despite the fact that Haze feels nothing but contempt for the boy. When Enoch first sees Haze he realizes, like Asa, that Haze is possessed of a will over which he has little control. "He had," Enoch thinks to himself, "the look of being held there, as if by an invisible hand, as if, if the hand lifted up, the figure would spring across the pool in one leap without the expression on his face changing once" (47). It is this same force, finally, that leads Haze to the epiphanic moment when he realizes he must accept his calling. Still unaware of the destiny that inevitably awaits him, Haze tries first to flee. "He had one thought in mind," the narrator explains, "and it had come to him, like his decision to buy a car, out of his sleep and without any indication of it beforehand: he was going to move immediately to some other city and preach the Church Without Christ where they had never heard of it." There he would meet a new woman and "make a new start with nothing in his mind." The only reason this plan was even possible, he realizes, is because he owns a car, "something that moved fast, in privacy, to the place you wanted to be" (105). The irony of his situation lost on him, Haze finds himself lured to his fateful encounter with the police officer by the false hope that the Essex, which has consistently impeded him every step of the way, can offer him escape. Once again, his will has proven weaker than the mysterious force that has, from the beginning of the novel, determined his destiny.

"Freedom," O'Connor wrote in the preface to the second edition of *Wise Blood,* "cannot be conceived simply." For her, as she explained, Haze's integrity lies not in his unsuccessful attempts to escape his destiny but in his inability to escape his calling as a man of God and rid himself of "the ragged figure who moves from tree to tree in the back of his mind" (*CW* 1265). The novel relies on a number of conventions that would belie this intent and suggest a different reading, wherein Haze's quest for "truth" and independent manhood emerges as the central theme of the novel. His journey is, after all, figured in specifically male terms as a drive for physical and spiritual independence outside the constraints of a social and moral order represented by women. Yet Haze's journey is, as O'Connor's introduction implies, a thwarted one. Impeded along the way by the very women he hopes to use as vehicles to further his blasphemous ends, by a car that seems to have a mind of its own, and by an inexplicable force that controls his actions, Haze discovers, finally, that he no longer desires to escape his calling. Nor is he even *capable* of escaping it. He is, despite all efforts to the contrary, subject to the will of God. His sense of manhood already undermined by the aggressive sexuality of Leora and Sabbath, Haze emerges at the end of the novel as a decidedly feminized hero who must answer to a higher male authority, God himself. O'Connor viewed Haze's final submission in purely religious terms, as the natural and appropriate end for a reluctant prophet. If the published novel is read along with the manuscripts, however, a different meaning emerges, one wherein Haze's journey serves, instead, as a female version of the quest narrative; the story of a search for knowledge that leads not to power and autonomy but to subjugation and dependence.

A similar journey serves as the organizing theme of O'Connor's second novel, *The Violent Bear It Away.* Based more closely on the bildungsroman than on the quest narrative, the novel tells the story of a young boy's struggle to achieve a mature sense of self and of the mentors who attempt to offer him guidance and instruction on his path to adulthood. His primary mentor is, of course, his uncle and namesake, the backwoods prophet who raised him. The central question around which the novel is organized has to do with whether Tarwater will follow his uncle's teachings and assume responsibility as his successor, or whether he will move to the city and discover for himself if everything the old man "learnt" him is true (380). Tarwater encounters a number of other teachers along the way—from his pious neighbor, Buford, to his diabolical "friend" in the panama hat, from Meeks, the traveling salesman, to Rayber, his schoolteacher uncle—each of whom represents a conflicting course. Whether Tarwater will choose the way proposed by Rayber, Meeks, his friend, and the Devil, or the way proposed by Buford, the old prophet, and God, is, presumably, the boy's choice, and it is through positioning Tarwater's development this way that the novel draws on the conventions associated with the bildungsroman.

Just as *Wise Blood* draws on the classic quest narrative, in which the protagonist's struggle is linked to the achievement of manhood, so too does *The Violent Bear It Away* incorporate classic elements of the bildungsroman. Tarwater's central conflict hinges on the competing definitions of manhood proposed by each of his mentors. On the one hand is the path suggested by Rayber and the man in the panama hat, which is based on the notion that maturity lies in rejecting the old man's ways and taking action. On the other hand is the conception of manhood proposed by the old prophet himself. Based in Old Testament Christianity, this state of masculinity may be attained, paradoxically, only through passively accepting the will of God. Rayber's path is, initially, the more enticing one. He preys on Tarwater's lingering doubts about the validity of his childhood education, reminding him that, "You could have had everything and you've had nothing. All that can be changed now. Now you belong to someone who can help you and understand you." Rayber's help centers on teaching the boy to develop a healthy skepticism for the Old Testament Christianity of his uncle, which he links ultimately to the achievement of manhood. "It's not too late," Rayber promises the boy, "for me to make a man of you!" (388). In teaching Tarwater to develop a healthy skepticism of the old prophet's religion, Rayber seeks to guide the boy toward intellectual maturity, independence, and the attainment of a masculinity that favors action over passivity. Tarwater's friend in the panama hat similarly lures the boy with the hope that in rejecting the old man's teachings he can become a man. He chides Tarwater for "going to that fancy-house of God, sitting there like an ape letting that girl-child bend your ear" and points out to him the passive fate that will be his destiny should he embrace the old man's teachings (430). "You have to take hold and put temptation behind you," his friend reminds Tarwater. "If you baptize once, you'll be doing it the rest of your life. If it's an idiot this time, the next time it's liable to be a nigger" (433). The only solution is to take action. The only sensible action to take is to drown Bishop. "Be a man," his friend offers in conclusion. "It's only one dimwit you have to drown" (462). Here, then, the novel establishes a dichotomy wherein the worldly value system of Rayber is equated with manhood and the outmoded value system proposed by the old man is equated with passivity and thereby with femininity.

Yet at the same time, the novel struggles to overturn this dichotomy and propose the old man's backwoods religion as the authentic model of manly adulthood. Born, as he so proudly claims, at the scene of a "wreck" in which his mother died, Tarwater has been raised exclusively in the company of men, on a farm known appropriately enough as "Powderhead," a name that suggests the phallic, explosive nature of male sexuality. Taught by his uncle that his mother, grandmother, aunt, and virtually every woman he has ever known are "whores," Tarwater is both frightened and repulsed by women.[9] As he increasingly resists the temptation to equate secularism with manhood, he begins to characterize Rayber's schoolteacher intellectualism as effeminate. Annoyed by his uncle's own passivity, Tarwater employs the authority of the old prophet to question *Rayber's* manhood. "He [the old man] always told me you couldn't do nothing, couldn't act," Tarwater chides. "I ain't like you. All you can do is think what you would have done if you had done it. Not me. I can do it. I can act" (435, 451). Thus Tarwater increasingly defines himself in opposition to what he perceives as Rayber's effeminacy. His uncle has imparted to him an Old Testament version of Christianity that is thoroughly masculinist in orientation, privileging—at least in theory—action over thought, vengeance over mercy, and wrathful indignation over compassion. Having been raised in the company of men, taught to fear women, and schooled in traditional male values, Tarwater equates maturity with the attainment of an independent, active manhood rooted in an Old Testament religious paradigm.

In many ways, the novel works to leave Tarwater with no option *but* to reject Rayber and the value system he represents. Unlike *Wise Blood, The Violent Bear It Away* does not easily lend itself to a reading that would view his Godlessness as appropriate. Somewhat surprised by the number of critics who read her first novel as a tract against religion, O'Connor worked to assure that her second novel could be read only within the context of orthodox Christianity (*HB* 358). She therefore created in Rayber an extreme parody of intellectual humanism; a man who, in a hollow imitation of *The Brothers Karamazov*'s Ivan, can make empty speeches concerning the injustices perpetuated against "exploited children" and then attempt to drown his own son because he is an "idiot" (*CW* 412). Rayber's irrational rejection of his son Bishop, his mouthing of intellectual clichés regarding independence and rationality, and his ridiculous belief that he can "stretch [Tarwater's] mind by introducing him to his ancestor, the fish," make it difficult to support a reading of the novel in which his path emerges as the correct one (417). Moreover, Tarwater's struggle, as he tells Rayber, to remain "outside your head" emerges as a heroic effort that exerts a liberating effect on the boy (400). By this reading, only in rejecting the path proposed by Rayber does Tarwater finally attain the freedom he seeks.[10] The narrator, for example, offers a revealing portrait of the boy as he finally realizes his destiny. "His scorched eyes no longer looked hollow or as if they were meant only to guide him forward. They looked as if, touched with a coal like the lips of the prophet, they would never be used for ordinary sights again" (473). Tarwater's rejection of Rayber and subsequent acceptance of his calling is thus tied implicitly to his attainment of mature adulthood. By the end of the novel, he has arrived at a full understanding of the responsibilities he must assume and has forged an identity for himself independent of the schoolteacher intellectualism represented by Rayber. More importantly, Tarwater has attained selfhood outside the bounds of society and entirely beyond the influence of women. His emergence at the end of the novel as an individual ready to accept the responsibilities of his calling is thus offered as the genuine model for the achievement of independent manhood. In this way, Tarwater's path, unlike Haze's, follows an apparently straightforward course from youth and ignorance to maturity and understanding and in so doing conforms quite rigidly to the classic, androcentric bildungsroman form.

Without doubt Tarwater, like the classic bildungsroman protagonist, achieves mature selfhood by the end of the novel. In O'Connor's own view, *The Violent Bear It Away* was the story of "free will in action." Yet as her defense of this view suggests, she found it difficult, despite her efforts to the contrary, to figure her protagonist's journey entirely within the constraints of the bildungsroman form. "An absence of free will in these characters," she explained, "would mean an absence of conflict in them, whereas they spend all their time fighting within themselves, drive against drive." Free will, she concluded, "has to be understood within its limits; possibly we all have some hindrances to free action but not enough to be able to call the world determined" (*CW* 1173). Herein lies the root of O'Connor's difficulties in conforming to masculinist structural models: she could not envision freedom without limitation or action entirely unhampered by fate. Though Tarwater is presented with moral choices, like Haze, he ultimately finds himself subject to influences he had set out to resist, and the model of manhood he adopts becomes problematic as a result. For example, Tarwater initially intends to honor his uncle's request for a proper burial, but after his encounter with the diabolical stranger, he suddenly finds himself drunk and possessed by an irresistible urge to set fire to both the house and the old man. Similarly, as much as he would like to follow the example set by Rayber and purge himself of his uncle's teachings, Tarwater can barely keep himself from obeying the old man's final request and finds himself "engaged in a continual struggle with the silence that confronted him, that demanded he baptize the child and begin at once the life the old man had prepared him for" (429). When Bishop plunges into a fountain during an outing to a local park, Tarwater can barely resist the urge to baptize him then and there. "He seemed," from Rayber's perspective, "to be drawn toward the child in the water but to be pulling back, exerting an almost equal pressure away from what attracted him" (421). Ironically, it is Rayber who prevents the baptism, pulling Bishop out of the water just as Tarwater is about to reach him. Yet the boy continues to find himself swayed by opposing forces—from the old man to Rayber to his elusive friend in the panama hat—none of which he can entirely control or resist.

His drowning of Bishop perhaps best epitomizes the way in which Tarwater becomes the passive pawn of forces outside of his control. "It was an accident. I didn't mean to," he explains to the truck driver who offers him a ride back to Powderhead. "The words just come out of themselves but it don't mean nothing. You can't be born again" (458). From this point in the narrative, Tarwater is virtually powerless in the face of this outside force. Feeling himself "pleasantly deprived of responsibility or of the need for any effort to justify his actions," Tarwater ignores the old man's warnings about the devil and accepts the ride that will culminate in his rape (471). In the context of the narrative, the rape emerges not as a traumatic incident of physical violation but as the catalyst for Tarwater's final acceptance of God's will. "He knew," the narrator explains, "that he could not turn back now.

He knew that his destiny forced him on to a final revelation." Indeed, Tarwater finds himself imbued with the spirit of God "rising in himself" just as it "rose in a line of men whose lives were chosen to sustain it, who would wander in the world, strangers from that violent country where the silence is never broken except to shout the truth." Enraptured, he feels this spirit "building from the blood of Abel to his own, rising and engulfing him." The power of it is so strong that it "seemed in one instant to lift and turn him" (473). Like the heroine of a romance novel, Tarwater experiences rape as an awakening to the pleasures of submission to the power of the phallus, a divine instrument wielded by a rapist who is, in effect, an agent of God.

Thus Tarwater has embraced the path to manhood established by his grandfather but only, paradoxically, through assuming a "female" role and submitting to the power of God expressed as sexual domination. The path to manhood proposed by Rayber and the man in the panama hat is therefore revealed as false, yet the path to manhood proposed by the old man is revealed as deeply problematic, if not impossible. Having accepted the inevitability of his fate, Tarwater has by the end of his journey attained the level of maturity and knowledge and, presumably, manhood required of the traditional bildungsroman hero. But by submitting to the power of his rapist's phallus he has, in effect, achieved his destiny through relinquishing his claim to an autonomous, active masculinity. Like Haze, Tarwater has been feminized, awakened to the realization that he must submit, both literally and figuratively, to a higher authority. Forsaking action, he accepts his role as the passive instrument of forces over which he has little control and learns to find both pleasure and affirmation in the sexual domination of his physical self. In the end, the peculiarly feminized experiences of Tarwater and Haze undermine the masculinist narrative conventions on which both *Wise Blood* and *The Violent Bear It Away* rely. Those conventions—which O'Connor no doubt embraced as a means of marking her fiction as genderless— functioned in reality as veiled representations of the kinds of limitations characteristic of specifically female experiences. Thus despite her professed goal of producing a body of fiction that remained transcendant of gender, O'Connor created veiled but unmistakably female narratives. This odd juxtaposition of forms—and the violation of reader expectations it entails—no doubt accounts for the widespread critical consensus that O'Connor's novels are not as well constructed as her short stories.[11] That critics have failed to recognize these "weaknesses" as the result of her hybridization of form suggests, finally, that it is not possible to arrive at a thorough understanding of O'Connor's novels without referring to the manuscripts and remaining attentive to the gender dynamics at play.

The manuscript versions of *Wise Blood* and *The Violent Bear It Away* similarly offer new insight into such seemingly idiosyncratic stories as "A Circle in the Fire" and "A View of the Woods." In contrast to the dynamics that inform most of O'Connor's published fiction, the female characters of these stories, like the protagonist of "A Temple of the Holy Ghost," are portrayed with sympathy. Not yet bound by the dictates of ladyhood, these young women enjoy a freedom that few of O'Connor's female characters manage. Consider, for example, the differences between Mrs. Cope and her daughter. Mrs. Cope is clearly related to the banal ladies of O'Connor's published fiction, while Sally Virginia more closely resembles characters who appear in the manuscripts. As a lady, for example, Mrs. Cope must remain gracious to the boys who have overrun her farm, offering them food and politely ignoring their rude behavior. Sally Virginia, however, is free to acknowledge them as troublemakers from the start and is not at all shy about expressing her opinion to their faces, exclaiming "'Ugggghhrhh,' in a loud voice, crossing her eyes and hanging her tongue out . . . as if she were going to vomit" (242). When it later becomes obvious even to Mrs. Cope that the boys pose a real danger, she takes little in the way of action, trusting that her threat to call the sheriff will compel them to leave. Sally Virginia, on the other hand, takes matters into her own hands, dressing in overalls and a man's hat and "arming herself with two pistols." She marches menacingly through the woods threatening, "I'm going to get you one by one and beat you black and blue. Line up. LINE UP!" (247–48). Though she is ultimately as helpless as her mother, Sally Virginia is able to respond to the situation in ways that no lady ever could. "'Ladies,'" as Mrs. Cope reminds her, "don't beat the daylight out of people" (242).

Sally Virginia remains an androgynous figure, able to claim the prerogatives that both her masculine attire and her phallic pistols represent. These qualities link her to the female characters of O'Connor's manuscripts, particularly to such women as Mitzabeth Boldtower and Leora Watts. Like

Mitzabeth, Sally Virginia's first response is to match male aggression with aggression. Significantly, her failure to deter the boys and her subsequent victimization are portrayed sympathetically, much in the same way the narrator portrays Leora's and Ruby's victimization by men like Pete Smith and Dr. Fisher. Sally Virginia even manages to diffuse some of the hostility the narrator directs at her mother. For example, the narrator, in hallmark O'Connor fashion, makes the ironic point that Mrs. Cope is not the person she believes herself to be, wryly explaining that she "prided herself on the way she handled the type of mind that Mrs. Pritchard had. When Mrs. Pritchard saw signs and omens, she exposed them calmly for the figments of imagination that they were" (246). Mrs. Pritchard's "signs and omens" are, of course, accurate, but Mrs. Cope remains blinded by the vain and misguided belief that she, despite being merely "another woman," can command any authority over the boys (242). Yet after they have humbled her at the end of the story we see her not through the narrator's perspective but through Sally Virginia's eyes. "The child . . . stared up at her face as if she had never seen it before. It was the face of the new misery she felt, but on her mother it looked as if it might have belonged to anybody." The narrator likens the boys to prophets "dancing . . . in the circle the angel had cleared for them," but Sally Virginia recognizes the pain they have caused (250–51). In contrast to such characters as Mary Grace of "Revelation," who shares many of the same qualities but who conspires with the narrator to humiliate the ladylike Mrs. Turpin, Sally Virginia allies herself with the lady character. And unlike most of the female characters who appear in O'Connor's published fiction, she manages to hold her own with the narrator, defending both herself and her mother against the more extreme forms of punishment that so often befall O'Connor's women.

A similar pattern emerges in "A Temple of the Holy Ghost." Narrated sympathetically through the perspective of the unnamed protagonist, the story concerns the child's epiphanic realization that she, like the intersexual on display at a local fair, must accept God's will. Significantly, this realization is not accompanied by the usual violence that befalls most of O'Connor's adult female protagonists. Instead, her encounter with grace comes quietly, as she sits in church contemplating the words of the "freak." Later, the child's face does get "mashed" against a crucifix worn by a nun who symbolically and somewhat enthusiastically welcomes her into the Church's embrace (209). This momentary discomfort, however, pales in comparison to the beatings, maimings, maulings, shootings, heart attacks, and strokes that O'Connor's ladies so often suffer. Indeed, by contrasting the girl's quiet insight into her situation with the unthinking, inane, and stereotypically feminine antics of the two teenagers visiting her home, the narrator implies that it is in fact the child's own lack of ladylike traits that protects her. More specifically, it is the girl's refusal to occupy an adult female body that ultimately saves her. Her fantasies of adulthood center not on romance and marriage but on a form of religious martyrdom that requires the mutilation and eventually the annihilation of the body. The girl wonders, for example, if she "could stand to be torn to pieces by lions" and imagines her body ripped apart and finally decapitated (204). With her head removed from her body, she will be free to avoid the pain and humiliation that female embodiment brings and will have achieved the disembodied intellectualism that eludes so many of O'Connor's women. In linking the girl's epiphany to the fate of the intersexual, the narrator suggests, finally, that by rejecting the trappings of adult femininity she might actually attain the genderless state of grace that no lady can ever possibly know.

Even Mary Fortune's fate may be reconsidered in light of the gender dynamics that appear in the manuscripts. Like most of the women in O'Connor's published fiction, she suffers punishment at the hands of vengeful masculine forces, and her death is eroticized and equated with rape. Nevertheless, a number of characteristics set her apart, aligning her instead with the manuscript characters. Like Sally Virginia, she is too young to be a lady and thus enjoys a certain degree of freedom, accompanying her grandfather on his daily business rounds to various construction sites. Named after his mother, Mary is the very image of Mr. Fortune, and she more than equals him in spirit. When a bulldozer threatens to get too close to the embankment on which their car is perched, she runs straight to the edge, shaking her fist at the operator. She refuses to heed the old man's warnings, "not hearing what she didn't want to hear" (529). When Mr. Fortune asks about the "bonus" money he has given her, she warns him, "Don't be buttin into my bidnis." And when he threatens to sell the woods across from the family farm, she calls him a "Whore of Babylon." Using "sass" to defend herself and her family from his manipulative dealings, she exhibits a bold sense of determination that few of O'Connor's ladies could match (531). After Mr. Fortune pointedly reminds her that she "lets" Pitts beat her, she responds defiantly, "Nobody's ever put a hand on me and if anybody did, I'd kill him" (532–33). While she may submit to her father's beatings, Mary Fortune repeatedly defies her grandfather, throwing bottles at him and, finally, beating him nearly unconscious. Like Sally Virginia and the female characters of the manuscripts, she does not passively accept male arrogance or aggression.

In reality, however, Mary Fortune is forced to submit to her father's aggression, and the narrator characterizes her acceptance of it as natural. Yet here, too, Mary Fortune is more closely tied to the manuscript characters than to the women who appear in O'Connor's published fiction. When she steps beyond her proscribed role as a female, Mary, like Hulga, Mrs. May, or Mrs. Turpin, is punished. But the narrator never subjects her to the ironic observation that she is not really the person she believes herself to be. *Her* pride, in other words, remains justified. The narrator's description of Mary as she defies Mr. Fortune is revealing. "Her nose and eyes began to run horribly," as she begins to cry, "but she held her face rigid and licked the water off as soon as it was in reach of her tongue," refusing to admit defeat. She maintains her dignity above all else and stoically ignores the "ugly remark" her grandfather launches at her, just as she stoically endures her father's beatings (537). Even when her grandfather succeeds where Pitts failed, stifling her spirit and killing her in the process, Mary Fortune remains undefeated. Her eyes "pay him not the slightest attention," and her image remains impassively "fixed," with "no look of remorse" whatsoever (545–46). Her dignified stoicism and her tenacity warrant sympathy and admiration; her fate is not deserved. In the case of such characters as Hulga, Mrs. May, or Mrs. Turpin, the punishment may fit the crime, but Mary Fortune is clearly the victim of injustice.

The injustices that Mary Fortune suffers result specifically from gender-based inequities. Like Ruby and Leora of the manuscripts, Mary Fortune becomes the victim of male treachery and of a drive for power and domination that is characterized as part of a masculinist value system. Her grandfather, for example, "had never allowed her mother or her brothers and sisters so much as to slap her," but he refuses to defend her against Pitts, allowing cowardice to get the better of him (529). Having betrayed the close bond between himself and his granddaughter, Mr. Fortune retreats into hypocrisy and blames his daughter, Mary Fortune's mother, for the beatings. In fact, he has little real sympathy for Mary. Instead, he becomes "infuriated" with her. "Why didn't you hit him back?" he asks in exasperation. "Do you think I'd a let him beat me?" (530) Without a suitable male heir, Mr. Fortune has invested his identity in his granddaughter, insisting that she alone of the family bears "his unmistakable likeness in every way" (527). So when Pitts beats Mary, to the old man it "was as if it were he . . . submitting to it" (531). Mary has become the unwilling pawn in the battle between her father and grandfather, as they struggle to determine control of the family property. Integral to the struggle over property is the related issue of lineage. "Are you a Fortune," the old man demands of Mary, "or are you a Pitts?" (541). As a female, Mary is unable to carry on his name, and he is forced to accept the humiliating fact that his heir must bear the name of his rival. Having disowned his daughter because she "preferred Pitts to home," Mr. Fortune hopes to claim Mary. But as Pitts reminds him, "[s]he's mine" (526, 531). Women and property thus become interchangeable goods representing the power of men: he who owns and controls the most is the victor. In presenting Mary as the casualty in the war between her father and grandfather and distinguishing her plight from that of characters like Hulga, Mrs. May, or Mrs. Turpin, O'Connor extended the critique of patriarchy found throughout her unpublished fiction. In her defiance and her victimization, Mary Fortune, like Sally Virginia Cope, becomes, in effect, the daughter of the manuscript versions of Ruby and Leora.

Though a number of critics have considered the role gender plays in O'Connor's fiction, no one has yet looked closely at the ways she was influenced by the literary culture in which she worked. O'Connor's ambivalence toward femininity was more than the product of a profound artistic sensibility or of her discomfort with the requirements of her role as a southern lady. Each of these factors was, without doubt, an important influence. Yet the weight of the evidence suggests that O'Connor's identification with the powerful masculine forces in her work resulted in large part from her association with the southern New Critical establishment and her struggle to adopt an aesthetic founded on the opposition between the female body and the male intellect. Much of O'Connor's published fiction, in its figuring of the female body as the site for male domination, succeeds in this endeavor. The manuscripts, however, offer evidence of the complicated gender dynamics at play in O'Connor's fiction generally and make it possible for characters like Mary Fortune, Haze, and Tarwater to be read in new ways. The manuscripts and their privileging of female subjectivity suggest that O'Connor's obliteration of the female-sexed voice that appears in her high school and college work was never complete. The critique of male power and domination that characterizes the manuscripts for *Wise Blood* and *The Violent Bear It Away* survives in characters like Mary Fortune, and the female subjectivity on which those manuscripts rely survives through the feminized experiences of Haze and Tarwater. While the evidence suggests that O'Connor consciously strove to adopt a genderless persona that would earn her the same consideration as the male writers favored by the southern and New Critical establishments, the manuscripts point to her ultimate failure in keeping her rebellions entirely private.

# Conclusion

FLANNERY O'CONNOR'S manuscripts offer perhaps the most visible evidence of the ways in which a female-sexed voice informs much of her fiction. In them, she offered an explicit and incisive critique of the dangers of male power, just as she explored, through female consciousness, the ramifications of such experiences as pregnancy and abortion. O'Connor extended this critique into the manuscripts of her second novel, as she developed a satirical and somewhat embittered portrait of the kinds of closed male circles she herself had encountered in her professional life. The published versions of *Wise Blood* and *The Violent Bear It Away,* however, complicate the questions surrounding O'Connor's status as a woman writer. Read outside the context of the manuscripts, the novels offer little indication that they were written by a woman. O'Connor worked so hard at conforming to masculinist narrative conventions that she all but erased her female identity beneath a layer of androcentric and often misogynistic characters, narrators, and plots.

Her decision to suppress her female identity was the result of specific historical and cultural circumstances. The available evidence suggests, in fact, that O'Connor sought to follow Caroline Gordon's advice and "write like a man." Although she may not have consciously decided to purge her work of its feminine qualities, O'Connor's attempts at conforming to the critical dictates of her day, which defined writing in masculinist terms, constituted, for all intents, a deliberate effort to suppress any indications of her female self. As a graduate student, she had aligned herself intellectually and professionally with the South's foremost writers and critics and was soon confronted with the realization that her artistic endeavor, as they figured it, was incompatible with her female identity. Not only did the Fugitive/Agrarians define writing as a masculine pursuit, but they based their critical orientation on the assumption that writing by women was necessarily inferior. As they had outlined in such essays as "The Profession of Letters in the South" and "The Poet as Woman," John Crowe Ransom, Allen Tate, and their colleagues hoped to maintain the racial and gender-based boundaries on which the Southern Tradition and the literary culture it inspired were based. In the hands of the Fugitive/Agrarians, a woman with serious literary ambitions, O'Connor no doubt understood, risked dismissal as a "lady writer" of the South's popular and genteel tradition. Hoping to avoid this trap, O'Connor appropriated many of the racial narratives that had characterized Fugitive/Agrarian conceptions of white southern identity. At the same time, she followed Gordon's example and distanced herself from other women writers, using her published fiction to develop a literary landscape in which femininity, where it exists at all, is often portrayed with ridicule, suspicion, and outright contempt. While both writers managed to earn critical acclaim as a result of these strategies, they were nevertheless plagued by personal conflicts and anxieties ultimately generated by working in a literary culture in which a "woman of letters" remained an anomaly, if not an impossibility.

O'Connor's strategies for coping with the constraints she faced as a woman writer hardly involved a self-conscious feminist stance. On the contrary, in her attempts at appropriating traditional masculinist forms like the quest narrative and the bildungsroman, O'Connor set out to purge her work of all taints of feminine "impurity" and in so doing created a series of narratives that are unmistakably misogynist in their orientation. Despite the great lengths to which she went in order to conform to the expectations of a male-dominated literary establishment, she nevertheless remained unable to wholly appropriate the masculinist discourses on which her work was based. Reading *Wise Blood* and *The Violent Bear It Away* in the context of her manuscripts and through the lens of feminist theory makes it possible to uncover the ways in which O'Connor's protagonists, despite appearances, are reflective of her identity as a woman. At the same time, the manuscripts offer new insights into O'Connor's published work, revealing the origins of such seemingly idiosyncratic characters as Sally Virginia Cope and Mary Fortune.

Denying her female self, using male characters and masculinist narrative forms to express the limitations and constraints of female experience, O'Connor developed a complicated but unmistakably female aesthetic, one that grew out of her personal and professional situation. That she chose to reject feminism and instead bury her female self beneath layers of masculinist forms and conventions suggests that the aesthetic strategies adopted by women writers are not always overtly oppositional or subversive and may, on the contrary, involve a certain amount of self-hatred. O'Connor's fiction serves as a reminder of the difficulties involved in defining female aesthetics and testifies, in the end, to the variety of strategies women writers have used to cope with the politics of gender.

# Notes

## Introduction

1. See Genovese, *Southern Tradition*.

2. Throughout I use the term *patriarchy* in the broadest sense as referring to cultural practices, institutions, or social patterns that endorse or promote the domination of men over women and encourage or demand adherence to traditional gender roles.

3. For an extended analysis of the role the Fugitive/Agrarians played in the "invention" of the Southern Literary Renaissance, see Michael Kreyling, *Inventing Southern Literature* 3–18.

4. I am focusing here on figures who were members of both groups—Ransom, Tate, Lytle, and Warren. Though Donald Davidson participated in both the Fugitive and Agrarian efforts, he did not share an extended professional relationship with O'Connor. I have therefore generally excluded him from consideration.

5. On O'Connor's sometimes strained relationship to the Fugitive/Agrarians, see Spivey, and Wood, "Flannery O'Connor." Wood also sees a disjunction between O'Connor and the Fugitive/Agrarians, arguing that her religious convictions lead to a "Christological" conception of southern history and culture, as opposed to the "vaguely theistic" view that prevailed among Tate and his associates (11).

6. As Michael Kreyling notes of O'Connor, "we have been taught not to think of her as sexed" (*Inventing Southern Literature* 105).

7. O'Connor was only the second twentieth-century author to appear in the series; Faulkner was the first. According to Margaret O'Connor, she "attracts the critical attention of more scholars each year than any other twentieth-century American woman writer" (642).

8. I intend the term feminist to refer broadly to any analysis that takes gender into consideration. O'Connor was, for example, referred to only in passing in early

and influential feminist analyses of women's writing such as *The Female Imagination* (Spacks) and *Literary Women* (Moers). More telling, perhaps, is her exclusion from texts such as *Men by Women* (Todd) and *The Mother/Daughter Plot* (Hirsch), considering her status as a canonical female author who wrote extensively about male characters and mother-daughter relationships. Most of the gender-based analysis applied to O'Connor's work has come not from mainstream feminist literary critics but from scholars who specialize in southern literary studies. See, for example, Chew, Gentry, Havird, Hendin, Westling, Whitt, and Yaeger. Manning argues that prevailing biases have long excluded white southern writers like O'Connor as well as black writers, southern or not.

9. A long-standing debate among O'Connor critics concerns the issue of whether her work is, as John Hawkes argued as early as 1962, of the "devil's party" or, as she so steadfastly claimed, the result of a highly devout and unwaveringly orthodox Christian vision. A thorough evaluation of the basis and merits to each side of the argument, which is concerned primarily with defining or evaluating O'Connor's religious vision, remains somewhat tangential to this analysis. For an overview of the debate, see Hawkes; Stephens; Kessler; Driskell and Brittain; Walters; Gentry, *Flannery O'Connor's Religion;* Brinkmeyer, *Art and Vision of Flannery O'Connor;* and Baumgaertner.

10. See Yaeger, "Flannery O'Connor and Aesthetics" 200, and Gentry, "Gender Dialogue" 62.

11. Here Showalter draws on the work of cultural anthropologists Shirley Ardener and Edwin Ardener, "Belief and the Problem of Women" and "The Problem Revisited," cited in Showalter 261.

12. For discussions of the relationship among gender, definitions of "true" literature, and canon formation, see Baym; Gilbert and Gubar, *No Man's Land;* Huyssen; Kolodny; Lauter; and Tompkins.

13. Yaeger describes this dynamic as a form of "textual schizophrenia" ("Woman without Any Bones" 95).

14. For an overview of the scholarship on southern women, see Scott; Grantham; Bartlett and Cambor; Hawks and Skemp; Seidel; Fraser, Saunders, and Wakelyn; Atkinson and Boles; Friedman; Mathews; Bleser; and Prenshaw. As much of this scholarship suggests, many white southern women simply rejected "ladyhood" or, like O'Connor, managed to develop strategies for violating codes of behavior while at the same time maintaining a superficial image of conformity.

15. "A" was Elizabeth Hester (1922–98), a reclusive intellectual, writer, and philosopher who enjoyed an extended correspondence with a number of writers, including Iris Murdoch.

16. During periods when she was confined to home, O'Connor also cultivated

a number of intellectual friendships locally and often participated in reading groups. See Cash.

17. O'Connor admitted to interviewer Richard Gilman that one of the first moves she made as a professional writer was to drop the name Mary and assume instead her more ambiguous middle name. After all, she asked, "[W]ho was likely to buy the stories of an Irish washerwoman?" (52).

18. Romagosa declined to offer comments on the O'Connor letters he made available for publication. However, Sura P. Rath, who edited the correspondence and who consulted Romagosa in preparing the letters for publication, describes them as evocative of O'Connor's "self-effacing" nature. The letters do not contradict this impression. See Rath 1–10.

19. James Tate recalls, "We talked about the Fugitives a lot. She liked them. She said all of them had something to contribute. And, of course, she meant the Agrarians, too" (68).

20. See Satterfield, who argues that O'Connor, despite her Writer's Workshop training, was never confident about her work.

## *1. The Dixie Limited*

1. See Michael Kreyling, introduction to *New Essays on Wise Blood* 15.

2. In later years Tate admitted that he had learned from the French poets an "easy lesson in shocking the bourgeoisie" ("*Fugitive*" 30). On the Fugitives' relationship to local lady patrons, see Donaldson, "Reluctant Visionaries."

3. For more on Poe's influence on Tate, see Donaldson, "Gender, Race, and Allen Tate" 508.

4. Tate's "Horatian Epode to the Duchess of Malfi," ostensibly about the "considerations of the Void coming after," is another early poem in which the death of a woman becomes symbolic of nihilism inherent to the "modern sensibility."

5. See, for example, Tate's "Nuptials," an ironic poem that deals with such topics as murder, prostitution, gambling, and the emptiness of urban existence.

6. For detailed analyses of the hierarchies that underpinned Fugitive/Agrarian aesthetics and politics, see Kreyling, *Inventing Southern Literature* 3–18.

7. For more on Ransom's fear of female embodiment and its influence on his critical faculties, see Karl Precoda. Emily Dickinson's canonical status, he argues, emerged in large part as a result of New Critical efforts, though he attributes the New Critical appropriation of Dickinson to the "oppositional stance" assumed by men like Ransom and Tate. The canonization of Dickinson, Precoda argues, "was an anxiety-laden process," particularly for Ransom, who felt compelled to

correct her idiosyncratic punctuation much in the same manner he "corrected" Millay (99).

8. Tate's text was originally presented as the Phi Beta Kappa Address at the University of Minnesota, 1 May 1952, and makes a number of allusions to Emerson's Phi Beta Kappa address, published as "The American Scholar." Both bemoan the disenfranchisement of scholars, who have been wrongfully deprived of their natural role as leaders of men. Though he and his southern colleagues claimed no kinship to Emerson and the Transcendentalists, Tate, as Louis D. Rubin Jr. argues, nevertheless shared with Emerson an acute anxiety regarding the role of intellectuals in a world where commercialism reigned supreme (*Wary Fugitives* 3). And like Emerson, Tate employed gendered terms to describe the disenfranchised, or "emasculated," condition to which "men of letters in the modern world" were subject. On Emerson and the construction of masculinity, see Leverenz.

9. See, for example, Brinkmeyer, "Jesus, Stab Me." He argues that O'Connor's stories "do not so much celebrate a world diffused by the divine as a body penetrated by it, usually manifest in physical wounding" (88). Yaeger, on the other hand, recognizes the gender-based dynamics at work and links them to O'Connor's anxieties regarding female authorship. Yet Yaeger sees O'Connor's aggression toward female characters in a more positive light, as the author's emphatic demonstration of the notion that "when the little girl is asked by her culture to give up her aggression or rebellion, she can, in fact, cut back" ("Woman without Any Bones" 112).

10. The power of the phallus is used to put a number of O'Connor's female characters into their place, including the "Welfare woman" who has custody of Enoch Emery and Sally Poker Sash, both of whom are properly frightened when a penis is displayed before them.

11. D. G. Kehl argues that despite any pleasure they might enjoy, Manley Pointer's "fetishism" and O. E. Parker's satyr-like behavior are meant to reflect negatively on the modern spiritual condition (262–76).

12. Also see Reesman 40.

13. For more on Riding, see Baker; Graves; and Wexler. At the time of her association with the Fugitives, she was known as Laura Gottschalk.

14. According to Graves, Tate's "admiration" culminated in a brief affair. Baker, on the other hand, disputes this claim and maintains that Tate's interest in Riding quickly faded. Whatever the truth, Tate's initial sexual attraction to Riding likely accounts, at least in part, for his enthusiasm for her poetry in the face of his colleagues' general indifference.

15. For an exception to the general critical tendency to accept at face value

the Fugitive account of this episode, see Donaldson, "Gender, Race, and Allen Tate" 506.

16. O'Connor did not receive the fellowship.

17. Ransom characterized the bulk of O'Connor's stories as "just good tries."

18. See Warren, "Katherine Anne Porter" and "Love and Separateness"; Lytle, "Caroline Gordon" and "Forest of the South."

19. See Jones 3–50, and Donaldson, "Gender, Race and Allen Tate" 494.

20. A prominent exception to this rule is William Yandell Elliott's "Black Man," a poem that attempts to use the language of spirituals to express the existential anguish resulting from a man's nightmare about lynching and hell. Typical of most Fugitive poems that resort to traditional southern themes, "Black Man" betrays Elliott's apparent intention of creating a new poem from an old form and reads instead like the dialogue from a nineteenth-century minstrel show: "Yassuh, dat's me in dat Chariot of Fire—*rollin long, rollin long*" (114).

21. See Rubin, *The Edge of the Swamp,* and Phillips 291. For more on Tate's legacy and its influence on subsequent generations of scholars, see Kreyling, *Inventing Southern Literature* 19–57.

22. Proposed subjects included "The Philosophy of Provincialism," "The Southern Way of Life," "Contemporary Southern Literature," "Humanism and the Southern Tradition," "Religion and Aristocracy in the South," "Philosophers of the Old South" (which was to include a "revival" of prominent southern pro-slavery apologists Thomas Dew and William Harper), "Politics," "Economic Issues," "Education," and "Literature of the Old South."

23. This particular battle pitted Tate, Warren, and Lytle, who viewed the line from "Dixie" as unnecessarily confrontational, against Ransom and Davidson, who wanted the book to assume a more militant tone (see *LC* 406–8).

24. According to Conkin, Davidson did, however, exercise his rights as editor to prevent Warren from using the title "Mrs." in reference to a black woman (72). Always the most extreme racist among his colleagues, Davidson would continue to defend segregation until his death in 1968.

25. Kreyling also examines this episode, though he sees Warren's essay as a challenge to "the utopian ideology" of Ransom and Tate (*Inventing Southern Literature* 18).

26. For a detailed account of the role of gender in Agrarian discourse see Donaldson, "Reluctant Visionaries." For analyses of traditional southern racial ideologies and social relationships, see Genovese, *World the Slaveholders Made* and *Roll Jordan Roll;* Faust; Fox-Genovese; and Williamson.

27. A description of preindustrial southern life, the essay attempts to analyze the effects of industrialization on the traditional agrarian family. While Lytle

acknowledges grandmothers, wives, and daughters as important contributors to the agrarian lifestyle, he presents the male head of the household and his sons as the chief indices by which the decline of southern culture in an industrial economy may be measured.

28. One of the organizing themes of the essays concerns the idea that the Old South had in fact remained the last true embodiment of the great Western Tradition as handed down by the Greeks and Romans.

29. Shackelford argues that blacks, as "intruding agents," become "catalysts" for redemption. Yet he ignores the racist implications of figuring blacks as Other and concludes instead that O'Connor's fiction reveals an "identification" with black suffering and the "spiritual advantages" that accompany it (80, 88).

30. The story's ending and its apparently emphatic affirmation of Mr. Head's salvation have elicited considerable debate among critics. The insistent focus in the critical literature on the question of the narrator's endorsement of Mr. Head is related to the broader question of O'Connor's racism. To argue that the story is, as Deanna Ludwin terms it, "a failure in terms of the author's intention," is integral to the ongoing effort to defend O'Connor against charges of racism (35; also see, for example, Shaw).

## 2. To Cultivate the Masculine Virtues

1. Gordon insisted that the situation was for Nancy's own good: "It is fiendishly cold here in the winter. Then too, there are times when we simply don't eat" (*SM* 27).

2. Typical is her comment in an early letter written to Wood from France. Though Tate, Gordon noted, wanted to return to the United States, she matter-of-factly remarked, "I don't. I have a grand little maid for five hundred francs a month who takes complete charge of the house and keeps Nancy out in the gardens at least five hours a day" (*SM* 46).

3. Gordon maintained that Tate's two subsequent marriages had not, at least in the eyes of the church, nullified theirs. There also appears as an epitaph on her gravestone a quotation by Jacques Maritain, "It is for Adam to interpret the voices which Eve hears" (see Waldron, *Close Connections* 354, 369).

4. Gertrude Stein, for one, refused to recognize Gordon as an artist in her own right (*SM* 127).

5. See Sullivan. Makowsky also notes an emerging pattern in Gordon's fiction, wherein female characters work to bring about the conversion of "recalcitrant" men. "The Presence" is a particularly revealing example.

6. I would like to acknowledge Alexandra Pena's contributions to my understanding of Gordon's use of Catholicism as a tool for empowerment.

7. See, for example, Gordon's comments on *At the Moon's Inn,* which she included in a letter to Dorrance shortly following the book's publication ([1941?] WD).

8. Gordon's end of the correspondence suggests that Dorrance was, in fact, offended by her pedagogical methods. She frequently reminded him, for example, that he had after all solicited her opinion. When this reminder failed to get a response, she assumed a less assertive stance and began to apologize for her behavior.

9. In the 1930s, for example, when Tate and his colleagues devoted much of their attention to writing Civil War novels and biographies, Gordon began work on *None Shall Look Back.* She took extreme pride in her intimate knowledge of battles, generals, and strategy, which more than equaled the expertise of men like Tate or Lytle. Similarly, following her conversion, she acquired a knowledge of early Christian theology and Catholic doctrine that would likely have put the average priest to shame.

10. According to Welty's biographer, Ann Waldron, the mentoring relationship between the two women flourished, in part, because Welty never threatened to compete sexually with Porter. If such is the case, then it suggests another level at which the sexual politics of southern literary culture encouraged division, rather than cooperation and mutual support, among women (*Eudora* 104).

11. Basing her argument on Maritain's definition of Christian art, Gordon concluded that the two writers she most admired, Flaubert and James, were, in fact, Christian artists. Though she continued to support her views with structural analysis, her comments suggest that, following her conversion to Catholicism, Gordon began to value art by the extent to which it could be made to conform to her religious vision.

12. The reference is to Ernest Renan (1823–92), a French philosopher, historian, and theologian. Catholic by birth, he argued that Jesus Christ was not the son of God and that the development of Christianity could be attributed not to historical fact but to the popular imagination (see Chadbourne and Gaigalas).

13. Here O'Connor notes that Gordon, in fact, wrote a review of the book for the *New York Times* but never actually sent it. Fitzgerald deleted the remainder of the sentence, so neither O'Connor's reactions to this development nor the reasons behind it can be determined. However, a comparison of the letters appearing in *The Habit of Being* with those republished nearly ten years later in the *Collected Works* suggests that Fitzgerald's editorial policies were governed by her concern that O'Connor's letters would offend a number of writers, including Gordon, who

were then still living. Unfortunately, only a few of the letters pertaining to Gordon have been republished in their entirety. Yet the letters that do reappear in the *Collected Works* support the conclusion that the vast majority of the original deletions were of negative or critical remarks, which suggests the strong possibility that O'Connor was indeed upset with Gordon's failure to publish the review.

14. The letter, which concerns O'Connor's musings on the theological basis of her writing, plainly refers to her "capacity" as a writer and not to her physical health.

15. O'Connor makes no mention of it in her published correspondence, and her references to Gordon's criticism on "Parker's Back" suggest that she received those comments only about a week before her death.

16. I would like to thank Peggy Whitman Prenshaw for bringing this pattern to my attention.

### 3. Flannery O'Connor and the Problem of Female Authorship

1. True to form, however, O'Connor continued to work on the novel through 1952, although the changes she made were not substantial.

2. The material pertaining to each chapter or thematic section of the manuscripts is organized into folders: one hundred and twenty-nine for *Wise Blood* and thirty-three for *The Violent Bear It Away*. The manuscripts for the two novels comprise the bulk of the collection. O'Connor left behind relatively few drafts of her stories.

3. See Gentry, "Flannery O'Connor's Attacks" and "Gender Dialogue" 57.

4. In addition to Tarwater's rape, a number of homosexual scenes appear in the later *Wise Blood* manuscripts as well as in those for *The Violent Bear It Away*. Haze, for example, narrowly escapes rape not once, but twice, while B.K. of the manuscripts for *The Violent Bear It Away* is sexually abused on a regular basis by the leader of a local Klan-like organization.

5. The hayloft scene in "Good Country People," for example, could just as easily have ended in a literal as well as symbolic rape. So, too, is there the potential for sexual violence in "A Circle in the Fire," as the young girl, hiding in the woods, barely escapes detection by the group of marauding boys.

6. Unlike much of O'Connor's published fiction, "A Stroke of Good Fortune" is not radically different on a plot level from the manuscripts on which it was based. Her discomfort with the story was no doubt related to the realization that the published version did not resolve the ambivalence regarding abortion that characterizes the manuscript passages on Ruby.

7. Quasi-religious ritual, argues Mark Carnes, served a crucial purpose as the

medium through which members of fraternal organizations have, historically, conceived of their social role as men. "The masks and disguises, the pervasive secrecy, and especially the mystical symbols were part of a process of concealment and revelation in which middle-class men, and many workers as well, became accommodated to a social order largely of their own making" (36). Such organizations, he concludes, have also played a crucial role in contributing to cultural constructions of masculinity.

8. O'Connor frequently wrote her correspondents about the difficulties she had with the novel as a form, and she likened finishing a book to "escaping from the penitentiary." Her letters regarding *The Violent Bear It Away* are full of complaints about its inadequacies; so uncertain was she of her abilities as a novelist that O'Connor asked her editor to let her know if the book should be published as a series of short stories. She worried that it was too "slight to stand the attention it would get as a novel" (*HB* 127, 322).

9. Even O'Connor herself, rarely one to consider her stories in terms of gender, was forced to admit that Tarwater's distinguishing feature was his lack of "matriarchal conditioning" (*HB* 390).

10. On the ways in which the novel valorizes freedom, see Barcus.

11. This view, argued Frederick Asals as early as 1974, has evolved into "something approaching critical dogma" (23). For a representative assessment of her talents, see Margaret O'Connor.

# Works Cited

Abel, Elizabeth, and Emily K. Abel, eds. *The Signs Reader: Women, Gender and Scholarship.* Chicago: Univ. of Chicago Press, 1983.

Abel, Elizabeth Marianne Hirsch, and Elizabeth Langland, eds. Introduction to *The Voyage In: Fictions of Female Development.* Hanover, NH: Univ. Press of New England, 1983.

"Announcements." *The Fugitive* 3 (1924).

Asals, Frederick. "Flannery O'Connor as Novelist: A Defense." *Flannery O'Connor Bulletin* 3 (1974): 23–29.

Atkinson, Maxine P., and Jacqueline Boles. "The Shaky Pedestal: Southern Ladies Yesterday and Today." *Southern Studies* 24 (1985): 398–406.

Bacon, Jon Lance. *Flannery O'Connor and Cold War Culture.* New York: Cambridge Univ. Press, 1993.

Baker, Deborah. *In Extremis: The Life of Laura Riding.* New York: Grove Press, 1993.

Barcus, Nancy B. "Psychological Determinism and Freedom in Flannery O'Connor." *Cithara* 12 (1972): 26–33.

Bartlett, Irving H, and C. Glenn Cambor. "The History and Psychodynamics of Southern Womanhood." *Women's Studies* 2 (1974): 9–24.

Baumgaertner, Jill P. *Flannery O'Connor: A Proper Scaring.* Wheaton, IL: Harold Shaw, 1988.

Baym, Nina. "Melodramas of Beset Manhood: How Theories of American Fiction Exclude Women Authors." In *The New Feminist Criticism: Essays on Women, Literature and Theory,* ed. Showalter.

Belsey, Catherine. "Constructing the Subject, Deconstructing the Text." In *Feminist Criticism and Social Change: Sex, Class and Race in Literature and Culture,* ed. Newton and Rosenfelt.

Benstock, Shari, ed. *Feminist Issues in Literary Scholarship.* Bloomington: Univ. of Indiana Press, 1987.

Bleser, Carol, ed. *In Joy and Sorrow: Women, Family, and Marriage in the Victorian South, 1830–1900.* New York: Oxford Univ. Press, 1991.

Bradbury, John M. *The Fugitives: A Critical Account.* Chapel Hill: Univ. of North Carolina Press, 1957.

Brinkmeyer, Robert H., Jr. *The Art and Vision of Flannery O'Connor.* Baton Rouge: Louisiana State Univ. Press, 1989.

———. "'Jesus, Stab Me in the Heart!' *Wise Blood,* Wounding, and Sacramental Aesthetics. In *New Essays on Wise Blood,* ed. Kreyling.

Brooks, Cleanth, and Robert Penn Warren, eds. *Understanding Fiction.* 2d ed. New York: Appleton-Century-Crofts, 1959.

Burns, Stuart L. "The Evolution of Wise Blood." *Modern Fiction Studies* 16 (1970): 147–62.

Carnes, Mark C. *Secret Ritual and Manhood in Victorian America.* New Haven: Yale Univ. Press, 1989.

Cash, Jean. "Milledgeville, 1957–1960: O'Connor's 'Pseudo-Literary and Theological Gatherings.'" *Flannery O'Connor Bulletin* 18 (1989): 13–27.

Chadbourne, Richard M. *Ernest Renan.* New York: Twayne, 1968.

Chew, Martha. "Flannery O'Connor's Double-Edged Satire: The Idiot Daughter vs. the Lady Ph.D." *Southern Quarterly* 11 (1981): 17–25.

Cixous, Hélène. "The Laugh of the Medusa." Trans. Keith Cohen and Paula Cohen. In *The Signs Reader: Women, Gender and Scholarship,* ed. Abel and Abel, 279–97.

Conkin, Paul K. *The Southern Agrarians.* Knoxville: Univ. of Tennessee Press, 1988.

Cowan, Louise. *The Fugitive Group: A Literary History.* Baton Rouge: Louisiana State Univ. Press, 1959.

Crews, Frederick. "The Power of Flannery O'Connor." *New York Review of Books* 37, no. 7 (26 April 1990): 49–56.

Davidson, Cathy, and Linda Wagner-Martin, eds. *The Oxford Companion to Women's Writing in the United States.* New York: Oxford Univ. Press, 1994.

De Beauvoir, Simone. "Introduction, *The Second Sex.*" In *New French Feminisms,* ed. Showalter.

Donaldson, Susan V. "Songs with a Difference: Beatrice Ravenel and the Detritus of Southern History." In *The Female Tradition in Southern Literature,* ed. Manning.

———. "Gender, Race, and the Allen Tate's Profession of Letters in the South." In *Haunted Bodies: Gender and Southern Texts.*

———. "Reluctant Visionaries and Southern Others: The Politics of Storytelling in the Modern South." Unpublished manuscript.

Donovan, Josephine. "Toward a Woman's Poetics." In *Feminist Issues in Literary Scholarship,* ed. Benstock.

Dorrance, Ward. Papers. Southern Historical Collection. Univ. of North Carolina at Chapel Hill.

Driggers, Stephen G. Introduction to *The Manuscripts of Flannery O'Connor at Georgia College,* ed. Stephen G. Driggers and Robert Dunn, with Sarah Gordon. Athens: Univ. of Georgia Press, 1989.

Driskell, Leon V., and Joan T. Brittain. *The Eternal Crossroads: The Art of Flannery O'Connor.* Louisville: Univ. Press of Kentucky, 1971.

Du Bois, W. E. B. *The Souls of Black Folk.* New York: Penguin Books, 1969.

Du Plessis, Rachel Blau. "For the Etruscans." In *The New Feminist Criticism: Essays on Women, Literature and Theory,* ed. Showalter.

Elder, Walter. "That Region." *Kenyon Review* 17 (1955): 664–70.

Elliott, William Yandell. "Black Man." *Fugitive* 3 (1924).

Fain, John, and Thomas Daniel Young, eds. *Literary Correspondence of Donald Davidson and Allen Tate.* Athens: Univ. of Georgia Press, 1974.

Faust, Drew Gilpin, ed. *The Ideology of Slavery: Proslavery Thought in the Antebellum South, 1830–1860.* Baton Rouge: Louisiana State Univ. Press, 1981.

———. *A Sacred Circle: The Dilemma of the Intellectual in the Old South, 1840–1860.* Philadelphia: Univ. of Pennsylvania Press, 1977.

Fitzgerald, Sally. "Chronology." In *Flannery O'Connor: Collected Works.*

———, ed. "A Master Class: From the Correspondence of Caroline Gordon and Flannery O'Connor." *Georgia Review* 33 (1979): 827–51.

———. "The Owl and the Nightingale." *Flannery O'Connor Bulletin* 13 (1984): 44–58.

Fox-Genovese, Elizabeth. *Within the Plantation Household: Black and White Women of the Old South.* Chapel Hill: Univ. of North Carolina Press, 1988.

Fraser, Walter J., Jr., R. Frank Saunders Jr., and Jon L. Wakelyn, eds. *The Web of Southern Social Relations: Women, Family, and Education.* Athens: Univ. of Georgia Press, 1985.

Friedman, Jean E. *The Enclosed Garden: Women and Community in the Evangelical South, 1830–1900.* Chapel Hill: Univ. of North Carolina Press, 1985.

*The Fugitive, April 1922–December 1925.* Reprints. Gloucester, MA: Peter Smith, 1967.

Gaigalas, Vytas V. *Ernest Renan and His French Catholic Critics.* North Quincy, MA: Christopher's Publishing House, 1972.

Gallop, Jane. *Thinking through the Body.* New York: Columbia Univ. Press, 1988.

Genovese, Eugene. *Roll Jordan Roll.* New York: Pantheon, 1975.

————. *The Southern Tradition: The Achievement and Limitations of an American Conservatism.* Cambridge: Harvard Univ. Press, 1994.

————. *The World the Slaveholders Made.* New York: Pantheon, 1969.

Gentry, Marshall Bruce. "Flannery O'Connor's Attacks on Omniscience." *Southern Quarterly* 29 (1991): 53–63.

————. *Flannery O'Connor's Religion of the Grotesque.* Jackson: Univ. Press of Mississippi, 1986.

————. "Gender Dialogue in Flannery O'Connor." In *Flannery O'Connor: New Perspectives,* ed. Rath and Shaw.

Gilbert, Sandra M., and Susan Gubar. *The Madwoman in the Attic: The Woman Writer and the Nineteenth-Century Literary Imagination.* New Haven: Yale Univ. Press, 1979.

————. *No Man's Land: The Place of the Woman Writer in the Twentieth Century.* Vol. 1, *The War of the Words.* New Haven: Yale Univ. Press, 1988.

Gilman, Richard. "On Flannery O'Connor." In *Conversations with Flannery O'Connor,* ed. Rosemary M. Magee. Jackson: Univ. Press of Mississippi, 1987.

Gordon, Caroline. "Cock Crow." *Southern Review* 30 (1965): 554–70.

————. "Heresy in Dixie." *Sewanee Review* 76 (1968): 263–98.

————. *How to Read a Novel.* New York: Viking Press, 1957.

————. "Rebels and Revolutionaries: The New American Scene." *Flannery O'Connor Bulletin* 3 (1974): 40–57.

————. Review of *Wise Blood,* by Flannery O'Connor. *Critique* 2 (1958): 3–11.

————. "Some Readings and Misreadings." *Sewanee Review* 61 (1953): 384–407.

————. "With a Glitter of Evil" (Review of *A Good Man Is Hard to Find,* by Flannery O'Connor). *New York Times Book Review,* 12 June 1955.

Gordon, Caroline, and Allen Tate. In *The House of Fiction: An Anthology of the Short Story.* New York: Charles Scribner's Sons, 1950.

Gordon, Sarah. "'The Crop': Limitation, Restraint, and Possibility." In *Flannery O'Connor: New Perspectives,* ed. Rath and Shaw.

————. "Maryat and Juliat and the 'Not So Bloodless Revolution.'" *Flannery O'Connor Bulletin* 21 (1992): 25–36.

Grantham, Dewey W. "History, Mythology, and the Southern Lady." *Southern Literary Journal* 3 (1971): 98–108.

Graves, Richard Perceval. *Robert Graves: The Years with Laura, 1926–1940.* New York: Viking Press, 1990.

Havird, David. "The Saving Rape: Flannery O'Connor and Patriarchal Religion." *Mississippi Quarterly* 47 (1993–94): 15–26.

Hawkes, John. "Flannery O'Connor's Devil." *Sewanee Review* 70 (1962): 395–402.

Hawks, Joanne, and Sheila Skemp, eds. *Sex, Race, and the Role of Women in the South.* Jackson: Univ. Press of Mississippi, 1983.

Heller, Dana A. *The Feminization of Quest Romance.* Austin: Univ. of Texas Press, 1990.

Hendin, Josephine. *The World of Flannery O'Connor.* Bloomington: Indiana Univ. Press, 1970.

Hirsch, Marianne. *The Mother/Daughter Plot: Narrative, Psychoanalysis, Feminism.* Bloomington: Indiana Univ. Press, 1989.

Hutner, Gordon. "Reviewing America: John Crowe Ransom's Kenyon Review." *American Quarterly* 44 (1992).

Huyssen, Andreas. "Mass Culture as Woman: Modernism's Other." In *After the Great Divide: Modernism, Mass Culture, Postmodernism.* Bloomington: Indiana Univ. Press, 1987.

*I'll Take My Stand: The South and the Agrarian Tradition.* Twelve Southerners. Baton Rouge: Louisiana State Univ. Press, 1977.

Jenkins, William Sumner. *Pro-Slavery Thought in the Old South.* Chapel Hill: Univ. of North Carolina Press, 1935.

Johnson, Rob. "'The Topical Is Poison': Flannery O'Connor's Vision of Social Reality in 'The Partridge Festival' and 'Everything That Rises Must Converge.'" *Flannery O'Connor Bulletin* 21 (1992): 1–24.

Jones, Anne Goodwyn. *Tomorrow Is Another Day: The Woman Writer in the South, 1859–1936.* Baton Rouge: Louisiana State Univ. Press, 1981.

Jones, Anne Goodwyn, and Susan V. Donaldson, eds. *Haunted Bodies: Gender and Southern Texts.* Charlottesville: Univ. Press of Virginia, 1997.

Kahane, Claire. "The Artificial Niggers." *Massachusetts Review* 19 (1978): 183–98.

Kahn, Robbie Pfeufer. *Bearing Meaning: The Language of Birth.* Chicago: Univ. of Illinois Press, 1995.

Kaplan, E. Ann. *Women and Film: Both Sides of the Camera.* New York: Methuen, 1983.

Kehl, D. G. "Flannery O'Connor's 'Fourth Dimension': The Role of Sexuality in Her Fiction." *Mississippi Quarterly* 68 (summer 1995): 255–76.

Kessler, Edward. *Flannery O'Connor and the Language of the Apocalypse.* Princeton: Princeton Univ. Press, 1986.

Kreyling, Michael. *Inventing Southern Literature.* Jackson: Univ. Press of Mississippi, 1998.

———, ed. *New Essays on Wise Blood.* Cambridge: Cambridge Univ. Press, 1995.

Kolodny, Annette. "The Integrity of Memory: Creating a New Literary History of the United States." *American Literature* 57 (1985): 435–63.

Lauter, Paul. "Race and Gender in the Shaping of the American Literary Canon: A Case Study from the Twenties." *Feminist Studies* 9 (1983): 453–63.

LeClaire, Thomas. "Flannery O'Connor's *Wise Blood*: The Oedipal Theme." *Mississippi Quarterly* 29 (1976): 197–205.

Lee, Maryat. "Flannery, 1957." *Flannery O'Connor Bulletin* 5 (1976): 39–60.

Leverenz, David. "Emerson's Man-Making Words." In *Speaking of Gender,* ed. Elaine Showalter. New York: Routledge, 1989.

———. *Manhood in the American Renaissance.* Ithaca: Cornell Univ. Press, 1989.

Love, Betty Boyd. "Recollections of Flannery O'Connor." *Flannery O'Connor Bulletin* 14 (1985): 64–71.

Ludwin, Deanna. "O'Connor's Inferno: Return to the Dark Wood." *Flannery O'Connor Bulletin* 17 (1988): 11–37.

Lytle, Andrew. "Caroline Gordon and the Historic Image." *Sewanee Review* 57 (1949): 560–86.

———. "The Forest of the South." *Critique* 1 (1956): 3–9.

———. "The Hind Tit." In *I'll Take My Stand,* by Twelve Southerners.

———. Introduction to *The Southern Mandarins,* ed. Wood.

Makowsky, Veronica. *Caroline Gordon: A Biography.* New York: Oxford Univ. Press, 1989.

Manning, Carol S., ed. *The Female Tradition in Southern Literature.* Urbana: Univ. of Illinois Press, 1993.

———. "Introduction: On Defining Themes and (Mis)placing Women Writers." In *The Female Tradition in Southern Literature,* ed. Manning.

———. "The Real Beginning of the Southern Renaissance." In *The Female Tradition in Southern Literature.*

Marks, Elaine, and Isabelle de Courtivron, eds. *New French Feminisms.* New York: Schocken Books, 1981.

Mathews, Holly F., ed. *Women in the South: An Anthropological Perspective.* Athens: Univ. of Georgia Press, 1989.

McMichael, George, ed. "Flannery O'Connor." *Anthology of American Literature.* Vol. 2, *Realism to the Present.* 4th ed., 1876–77. New York: Macmillan, 1989.

"Merely Prose." *The Fugitive* 2 (1923).

Moers, Ellen. *Literary Women: The Great Writers.* Garden City, NY: Doubleday, 1976.

Mulvey, Laura. "Visual Pleasure and Narrative Cinema." In *Narrative, Apparatus, Ideology: A Film Theory Reader,* ed. Phillip Rosen. New York: Columbia Univ. Press, 1986.

Newton, Judith, and Deborah Rosenfelt. "Toward a Materialist-Feminist Criticism." In *Feminist Criticism and Social Change: Sex, Class and Race in Literature and Culture,* ed. Newton and Rosenfelt.

Newton, Judith, and Deborah Rosenfelt, eds. *Feminist Criticism and Social Change: Sex, Class and Race in Literature and Culture.* New York: Methuen, 1985.

O'Brien, Michael. "The Endeavor of Southern Intellectual History." In *Rethinking the South: Essays in Intellectual History.* Baltimore: Johns Hopkins Univ. Press, 1987.

O'Connor, Flannery. *Flannery O'Connor: Collected Works.* New York: Library of America, 1988.

———. Flannery O'Connor Manuscript Collection. Ina Dillard Russell Library, Georgia College. Milledgeville, Georgia.

———. *The Habit of Being: Letters of Flannery O'Connor.* Ed. Sally Fitzgerald. New York: Random House, 1979.

———. Letter to John Crowe Ransom, 12 January 1955. *Flannery O'Connor Bulletin* 23 (1994–95): 181–82.

———. *Mystery and Manners.* Ed. Sally Fitzgerald and Robert Fitzgerald. New York: Farrar, Straus and Giroux, 1969.

O'Connor, Margaret Anne. "Flannery O'Connor." In *The Oxford Companion to Women's Writing in the United States,* ed. Cathy Davidson and Linda Wagner-Martin. New York: Oxford Univ. Press, 1994.

"The Other Half of Verse." *Fugitive* 2 (1923).

Owsely, Frank. "The Irrepressible Conflict." In *I'll Take My Stand,* by Twelve Southerners. Baton Rouge: Louisiana State Univ. Press, 1977.

———. *Plain Folk of the Old South.* Baton Rouge: Louisiana State Univ. Press, 1949.

Phillips, Ulrich B. *American Negro Slavery: A Survey of the Supply, Employment and Control of Negro Labor as Determined by the Plantation Regime.* Baton Rouge: Louisiana State Univ. Press, 1969.

Poe, Edgar Allan. "The Philosophy of Composition." In *The Unabridged Edgar Allan Poe,* ed. Tam Mossman. Philadelphia: Running Press, 1983.

Porter, Katherine Anne. *The Collected Stories of Katherine Anne Porter.* New York: Harcourt Brace Jovanovich, 1979.

———. Introduction to *A Curtain of Green and Other Stories,* by Eudora Welty. New York: Harcourt Brace Jovanovich, 1979.

Pratt, William, ed. *The Fugitive Poets.* New York: E. P. Dutton, 1965.

Precoda, Karl. "The Poet as Woman." *New Orleans Review* 19 (1992): 98–107.

Prenshaw, Peggy Whitman. "Southern Ladies and the Southern Literary Renaissance." In *The Female Tradition in Southern Literature,* ed. Manning.

Ransom, John Crowe. "Criticism as Pure Speculation." In *Selected Essays of John Crowe Ransom.*

———. "Criticism, Inc." In *Selected Essays of John Crowe Ransom.*

———. "Forms and Citizens." In *Selected Essays of John Crowe Ransom.*

———. "Judith of Bethulia." *Fugitive* 2 (1923).

———. Letter to Flannery O'Connor, 5 February 1955. *Flannery O'Connor Bulletin* 23 (1994–95): 182.

———. "Piazza Piece." *Fugitive* 4 (1925).

———. "The Poet as Woman." *Southern Review* 3 (1937): 783–806.

———. "Reconstructed but Unregenerate." In *I'll Take My Stand,* by Twelve Southerners.

———. *Selected Essays of John Crowe Ransom.* Ed. Thomas Daniel Young and John Hindle. Baton Rouge: Louisiana State Univ. Press, 1984.

———. *Selected Letters of John Crowe Ransom.* Ed. Thomas Daniel Young and John Hindle. Baton Rouge: Louisiana State Univ. Press, 1985.

———. "The South Defends Its Heritage." *Harper's Magazine* 119 (1929): 108–18.

———. "The South—Old or New?" *Sewanee Review* 26 (1928): 139–47.

Rath, Sura P., ed. "An Evolving Friendship: Flannery O'Connor's Correspondence with Father Edward J. Romagosa, S.J." *Flannery O'Connor Bulletin* 17 (1988): 1–10.

Rath, Sura P., and Mary Neff Shaw, eds. *Flannery O'Connor: New Perspectives.* Athens: Univ. of Georgia Press, 1996.

Reesman, Jeanne Campbell. "Women, Language, and the Grotesque in Flannery O'Connor and Eudora Welty." In *Flannery O'Connor: New Perspectives,* ed. Rath and Shaw.

Reuman, Ann E. "Revolting Fictions: Flannery O'Connor's Letter to Her Mother." *Papers on Language and Literature: A Journal for Scholars and Critics of Language and Literature* 29 (1993): 197–214.

Rich, Adrienne. "Compulsory Heterosexuality and Lesbian Existence." In *The Signs Reader: Women, Gender and Scholarship,* ed. Abel and Abel.

Rubin, Louis D., Jr. *The Edge of the Swamp: A Study in the Literature and History of the Old South.* Baton Rouge: Louisiana State Univ. Press, 1989.

———. *The Wary Fugitives: Four Poets and the South.* Baton Rouge: Louisiana State Univ. Press, 1978.

Satterfield, Ben. "*Wise Blood,* Artistic Anemia, and the Hemorrhaging of O'Connor Criticism." *Studies in American Fiction* 17 (1987): 33–51.

Scott, Anne Firor. *The Southern Lady from Pedestal to Politics, 1830–1930.* Chicago: Univ. of Chicago Press, 1970.

Seidel, Kathryn. *The Southern Belle in the American Novel.* Gainesville: Univ. Presses of Florida, 1985.

Shackelford, D. Dean. "The Black Outsider in O'Connor's Fiction." *Flannery O'Connor Bulletin* 18 (1989): 79–90.

Shaw, Mary Neff. "'The Artificial Nigger': A Dialogic Narrative." *Flannery O'Connor Bulletin* 20 (1991): 104–17.

Showalter, Elaine. "Feminist Criticism in the Wilderness." In *The New Feminist Criticism: Essays on Women, Literature and Theory,* ed. Showalter.

——, ed. *The New Feminist Criticism: Essays on Women, Literature and Theory.* New York: Pantheon Books, 1985.

Silverman, Kaja. "Suture (Excerpts)." In *Narrative, Apparatus, Ideology: A Film Theory Reader,* ed. Philip Rosen. New York: Columbia Univ. Press, 1986.

Simpson, Louis P. *The Dispossessed Garden: Pastoral and History in Southern Literature.* Baton Rouge: Louisiana State Univ. Press, 1975.

Spacks, Patricia Meyer. *The Female Imagination.* New York: Alfred A. Knopf, 1975.

Spivey, Ted R. "Flannery O'Connor, the New Criticism, and Deconstruction." *Southern Review* 23 (1987): 271–80.

Stephens, Martha. *The Question of Flannery O'Connor.* Baton Rouge: Louisiana State Univ. Press, 1973.

Stewart, John L. *The Burden of Time: The Fugitives and Agrarians.* Princeton: Princeton Univ. Press, 1965.

Sullivan, Walter. *Allen Tate: A Recollection.* Baton Rouge: Louisiana State Univ. Press, 1988.

Tate, Allen. "Elegy for Eugenesis." *Fugitive* 1 (1922).

——. *Essays of Four Decades.* Chicago: Swallow Press, 1968.

——. *"The Fugitive, 1922–1925:* A Personal Recollection Twenty Years After." In *Memoirs and Opinions, 1926–1974.* Chicago: Swallow Press, 1975.

——. "Horatian Epode to the Duchess of Malfi." *Fugitive* 1 (1922).

——. "The Man of Letters in the Modern World." In *Essays of Four Decades.*

——. "Our Cousin, Mr. Poe." In *Essays of Four Decades.*

——. *The Poetry Reviews of Allen Tate.* Ed. Ashley Brown and Frances Neel Cheyney. Baton Rouge: Louisiana State Univ. Press, 1983.

——. "The Profession of Letters in the South." In *Essays of Four Decades.*

——. "A Southern Mode of the Imagination." In *Essays of Four Decades.*

——. *Stonewall Jackson: The Good Soldier: A Narrative.* New York: Minton, Balch, 1928.

Tate, James. "An O'Connor Remembrance." *Flannery O'Connor Bulletin* 17 (1988): 65–68.

Thorp, William. "The Way Back and the Way Up: The Novels of Caroline Gordon." *Bucknell Review* 7 (1956): 1–16.

Todd, Janet, ed. *Men by Women.* Women and Literature series, vol. 2. New York: Holmes and Meier, 1981.

Tompkins, Jane. *Sensational Designs: The Cultural Work of American Fiction, 1790–1860.* New York: Oxford Univ. Press, 1985.

Waldron, Ann. *Close Connections: Caroline Gordon and the Southern Renaissance.* New York: G. P. Putnam's Sons, 1987.

———. *Eudora: A Writer's Life.* New York: Anchor Books, 1999.

Walters, Dorothy. *Flannery O'Connor.* New York: Twayne, 1973.

Warren, Robert Penn. "An Interview in New Haven with Robert Penn Warren." In *Robert Penn Warren Talking: Interviews, 1950–1978.* Ed. Floyd Watkins and John T. Hiers. New York: Random House, 1980.

———. "Katherine Anne Porter (Irony with a Center)." *Kenyon Review* 4 (1942): 29–47.

———. "The Briar Patch." In *I'll Take My Stand,* by Twelve Southerners.

———. "The Love and Separateness in Miss Welty." *Kenyon Review* 9 (1947): 249–59.

Welty, Eudora. *The Collected Stories of Eudora Welty.* New York: Harcourt Brace Jovanovich, 1980.

Westling, Louise Hutchings. "Fathers and Daughters in Welty and O'Connor." In *The Female Tradition in Southern Literature,* ed. Manning.

———. "Flannery O'Connor's Revelations to 'A.'" *Southern Humanities Review* 20 (1986): 15–22.

———. *Sacred Groves and Ravaged Gardens: The Fiction of Eudora Welty, Carson McCullers, and Flannery O'Connor.* Athens, GA: Univ. of Georgia Press, 1985.

Wexler, Joyce Piell. *Laura Riding's Pursuit of Truth.* Athens: Ohio Univ. Press, 1979.

Whitt, Margaret. "Flannery O'Connor's Ladies." *Flannery O'Connor Bulletin* 15 (1986): 42–49.

Williams, Melvin G. "Black and White: A Study in Flannery O'Connor's Characters." *Black American Literature Forum* 10 (1976): 130–32.

Williamson, Joel. *A Rage for Order: Black/White Relations in the American South since Emancipation.* Oxford: Oxford Univ. Press, 1986.

Wood, Ralph C. "Flannery O'Connor, H. L. Mencken, and the Southern Agrarians: A Dispute of Religion More than Region." *Flannery O'Connor Bulletin* 20 (1991): 1–21.

———. "Where Is the Voice Coming From? Flannery O'Connor on Race." *Flannery O'Connor Bulletin* 22 (1993–94): 90–118.

Wood, Sally, ed. *The Southern Mandarins: Letters of Caroline Gordon to Sally Wood, 1924–1937.* Baton Rouge: Louisiana State Univ. Press, 1984.

Wyer, Mary. "Mentors." In *The Oxford Companion to Women's Writing in the United States,* ed. Davidson and Wagner-Martin.

Yaeger, Patricia Smith. "Flannery O'Connor and the Aesthetics of Torture." In *Flannery O'Connor: New Perspectives,* ed. Rath and Shaw.

———. "The Woman without Any Bones: Anti-Angel Aggression in *Wise Blood.*" In *New Essays on Wise Blood,* ed. Kreyling, 91–117.

Young, Thomas Daniel. *Gentleman in a Dustcoat: A Biography of John Crowe Ransom.* Baton Rouge: Louisiana State Univ. Press, 1976.

Young, Thomas Daniel, and Elizabeth Sarcone, eds. *The Lytle-Tate Letters: The Correspondence of Andrew Lytle and Allen Tate.* Jackson: Univ. Press of Mississippi, 1987.

# Index

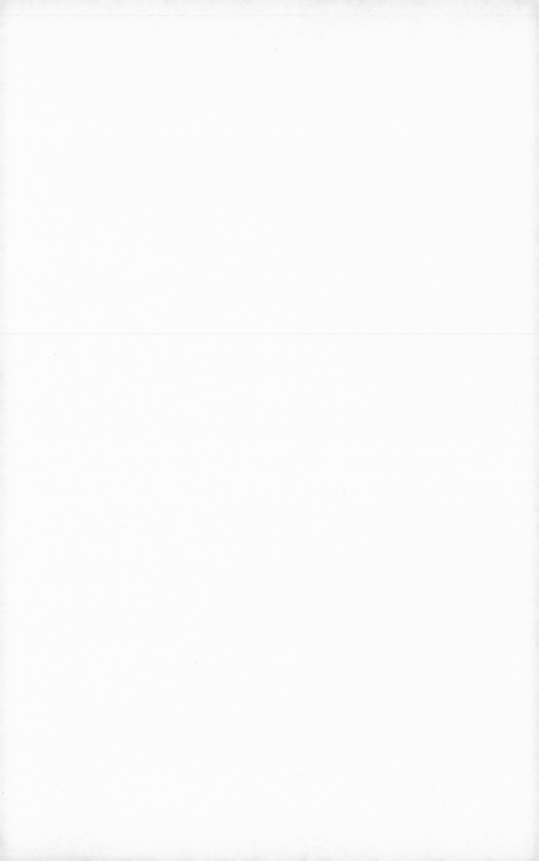

AEC-2734